THE AMERICAN BAR ASSOCIATION

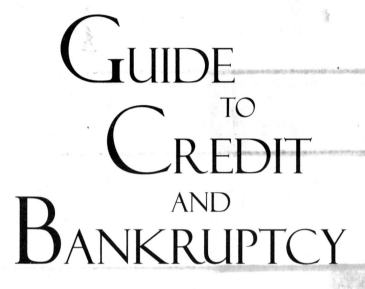

GUIDE TO CREDIT AND BANKRUPTCY

RANDOM HOUSE REFERENCE

NEW YORK   TORONTO   LONDON   SYDNEY   AUCKLAND

Copyright © 2006 by The American Bar Association

Please address inquiries about electronic licensing of any products for use on a network, in software, or on CD-ROM to the Subsidiary Rights Department, Random House Information Group, fax 212-572-6003.

This book is available for special discounts for bulk purchases for sales promotions or premiums. Special editions, including personalized covers, excerpts of existing books, and corporate imprints, can be created in large quantities for special needs. For more information, write to Random House, Inc., Special Markets/ Premium Sales, 1745 Broadway, MD 6-2, New York, NY, 10019 or e-mail specialmarkets@randomhouse.com

Visit the Random House Reference Web site: www.randomwords.com

Library of Congress Cataloging-in-Publication Data is available.

First Edition

Printed in the United States of America

10 9 8 7 6 5 4 3 2 1

ISBN-13: 978-0-375-80926-6
ISBN-10: 0-609-80926-1

AMERICAN BAR ASSOCIATION

Robert A. Stein
Executive Director

Sarina A. Butler
Associate Executive Director, Communications Group

Mabel C. McKinney-Browning
Director, Division for Public Education

Charles White
Katherine Fraser
Series Editors

STANDING COMMITTEE ON PUBLIC EDUCATION

Alan S. Kopit
Chair

PRINCIPAL AUTHOR

David L. Hudson, Jr.
Nashville, Tennessee

REVIEWERS

Barry A. Abbott
Howard Rice Nemeroyski
Canady Falk & Rabkin
San Francisco, California

Sara A. Austin
Austin Law Firm, LLC
York, Pennsylvania

Jean L. Batman
Legal Venture Counsel, Inc.
San Francisco, California

Jan I. Berlage
Ballard, Spahr
Baltimore, Maryland

Thomas J. Buiteweg
GMAC Financial Services
Legal Staff
Detroit, Michigan

Karen Cordry
NAAG Bankruptcy Counsel
National Association of
Attorneys General
Washington, DC

Marc S. Stern
Law Offices of Marc S. Stern
Seattle, Washington

Michael C. Tomkies
Dreher Langer & Tomkies, LLP
Columbus, Ohio

Lorraine E. Waller
National Foundation
for Credit Counseling
Silver Spring, Maryland

Robin K. Warren
Compliance Risk Management
Bank of America
Charlotte, North Carolina

Elizabeth Yen
Hudson Cook, LLP
New Haven, Connecticut

Daniel O'Neal Bernstine
President
Portland State University
Portland, Oregon

David A. Collins
General Motors Legal Staff
Detroit, Michigan

Okianer Christian Dark
Professor of Law
Howard University School of
Law
Washington, DC

James Dimos
Locke Reynolds, LLP
Indianapolis, Indiana

Juanita C. Hernandez
Ogletree Deakins
San Antonio, Texas

Dwight L. Smith
Attorney at Law
Tulsa, Oklahoma

Jeffrey J. Snell
Attorney at Law
Sagamore Hills, Ohio

W. Scott Welch
Butler Snow O'Mara
Stevens, et al.
Jackson, Mississippi

David Williams
Vanderbilt University
Nashville, Tennessee

FOREWORD

Robert Stein, *Executive Director*
American Bar Association

In 2005, bankruptcy law in America experienced its greatest change in almost 30 years. The Bankruptcy Abuse Prevention and Consumer Protection Act of 2005 is a federal law that affects all Americans. With the help of American Bar Association experts from all over the country, in this book we've been able to meet your need for reliable, unbiased information to help you understand the new legal regime and how it affects you.

The American Bar Association is the nation's leading source of legal information. With more than 400,000 members, representing every type of legal practice, the ABA is able to deliver accurate, up to date, unbiased legal information to its members, to the media, and to the general public. The ABA website—www.abanet.org—is an unrivaled database in the legal field.

Credit and bankruptcy are enormously important to Americans. More and more of us have credit card debt, car loans, home equity loans, and other forms of consumer debt—and this debt load is growing dramatically. Not surprisingly, consumer bankruptcies are also surging. The number of personal bankruptcies is approaching two million per year—about six times as many as in 1980, and twice as many as in 1995, just ten years ago.

Obviously, Americans are deeply concerned with their ability to get credit, their credit score, their credit reports, their privacy in credit transactions, and dozens of other credit-related issues. Not surprisingly, laws are rapidly evolving to deal with these concerns, as well as new ones like identity theft. Moreover, bankruptcy law continues to change, as state legislatures and Congress struggle to find the appropriate balance between creditors and debtors.

This book provides you with guidance on a whole range of credit and bankruptcy issues. It gives you the benefit of the ABA's network of hundreds of thousands of lawyers. *The ABA Guide to Credit and Bankruptcy* was written with the aid of ABA members in every part of the country. The contribution of ABA members is especially valuable because they have great experience in dealing every day with credit and bankruptcy.

This book particularly benefited from the careful reading and rewriting offered by the Consumer Finance Committee of the ABA's Business Law Section. Under the leadership of Jeff Langer and Robin K. Warren, this group of experts gave countless hours to making this manuscript accurate, current, and reader-friendly. They reviewed draft chapters, providing clarifications, suggesting additional topics that would be helpful to readers, and polishing the manuscript to make it read even better. A group of bankruptcy experts, including practicing lawyers, law professors, and a bankruptcy court judge, provided similar services for the bankruptcy section of the book.

Finally, the ABA's Standing Committee on Public Education provided oversight for this project. This Committee and its excellent staff contribute the perspective of experts in communicating about the law.

Thanks to all of the lawyers who worked on this book, you can be sure that the information it includes is:

- accurate,
- helpful,
- even-handed,
- current,
- written in a reader-friendly style that you can understand easily, and
- reflects a national picture, since ABA members practice in all jurisdictions.

Public education and public service are two important goals of the American Bar Association. This book shows how the ABA takes an active role in providing the public with information it can use.

The American Bar Association is the largest voluntary asso-

ciation in the world. Besides its commitment to public education, the ABA provides programs to assist lawyers and judges in
their work, and initiatives to improve the legal system for the
public, including promoting fast, affordable alternatives to lawsuits, such as mediation, arbitration, conciliation, and small
claims courts. Through ABA support for lawyer referral programs and pro bono services (where lawyers donate their time),
people like you have been able to find the best lawyer for their
particular case and have received quality legal help within their
budgets.

---

*Robert A. Stein is the Executive Director of the American Bar Associa-
tion. He was formerly dean of the University of Minnesota Law School.*

INTRODUCTION

Alan S. Kopit, *Chair*
ABA Standing Committee on Public Education

"**W**e've never had so many who owed so much," declares an economist with Standard & Poor's. About 150 million Americans have credit cards, including many college students and even high school kids. This is about 80 percent more than had cards just 15 years ago. But in that period the amount they charged grew by a much larger percentage—about 350 percent. Monthly credit card balances are about three times bigger than they were in 1990—and that's not even taking into account mortgage debt, student loans, and automobile loans.

Some people can't handle this debt. Foreclosures and car/truck repossessions are up, as are credit card delinquencies and missed payments. And the number of bankruptcies continues to soar—it's twice as high as it was just ten years ago. Nearly one third of bankruptcy filers owed an entire *year's* salary on their credit cards.

Because of the upsurge in bankruptcies and concerns that the system was too often abused, Congress passed and the President signed the Bankruptcy Abuse Prevention and Consumer Protection Act of 2005. This new law changed the rules for bankruptcy for all Americans.

Whatever your credit status—from unable to get any credit to having maxed-out credit cards—you need this book. It gives you the complete run-down on your rights and responsibilities under the law. It tells you about consumer credit laws designed to help you, and gives you pointers on how to take the maximum advantage of these legal protections. And it also brings you up to date on the new bankruptcy law and how it affects you.

With this book in hand, you'll be prepared to get the benefits of credit with as little expense and hassle as possible. One of the best aspects of this area of the law, from a consumer's perspective, is that the law gives you so many options. For example, legal protections help you:

- Apply for credit;
- Pick the best credit card for your needs;
- Find the best interest rates;
- Check your credit score and credit records—and make corrections if there are errors;
- Avoid identity theft;
- Evaluate home equity loans;
- Learn how to deal with unfair lending;
- Understand auto financing options;
- Deal with debt collectors.

If you're being crushed by a mountain of debt, this book will also help you understand your options, from reliable debt counseling to debt consolidation, or even bankruptcy. And if you have made the decision to declare bankruptcy, we walk you through the process, help you select which form of bankruptcy to choose, and give you suggestions on saving your home and keeping items that are important to you, like your car or boat. We tell you how the new law affects your bankruptcy options and what new steps are required to successfully begin and complete the bankruptcy process.

No matter who you are, no matter what your situation in life, this book will help you save money. It provides background information and suggests the pros and cons of various courses of action. It will help you decide among these options to find what's best in *your* situation, and help you craft a plan that works for *you*.

You won't find legal jargon or technicalities here—just concise, straightforward discussions of your options under the law. This book is easy to read, with examples drawn from real life, short sentences and paragraphs, brief sidebars packed with interesting information, and lots of answers to practical questions from our panel of legal experts.

Our principal author is David Hudson, a lawyer and writer who has written on a wide range of subjects for the public. His manuscript was reviewed and approved by experts on credit and bankruptcy from all over the country, with particular assistance from the Consumer Financial Services Committee of the ABA's Business Law Section. The entire project was under the guidance of the ABA's Standing Committee on Public Education. Together, we've worked to provide you with easy-to-read information that will help you understand and use the law that affects the whole credit and bankruptcy process. Our goal is to help you spot problems before they become major—when they're easiest to handle.

HOW TO USE THIS BOOK

We've structured this book chronologically, from topics that affect all of us like understanding credit and how to apply for it, to important topics that deal with special circumstances such as Internet credit, identity theft, unfair lending, and home equity loans.

Similarly, we begin our consideration of bankruptcy with problem debt and some options for dealing with it. We go on to take a closer look at bankruptcy, including the pros and cons of each type of consumer bankruptcy.

Part One—Consumer Credit begins with an explanation of the various types of credit and the costs of credit, then looks at the many federal laws that protect your rights as a user of credit. We follow that with a discussion of credit scoring and other means of determining creditworthiness. Next up is a chapter on your right to equal credit, with emphasis on the laws that prevent credit discrimination and suggestions on how to use them effectively.

We then look at the process of building a credit record and applying for credit. We also look at the vexing problem of getting credit after a divorce and consider the pros and cons of credit insurance. We give special emphasis to choosing a credit card that's right for you, considering the rate and fees charged. We give some tips on knowing your rights and safeguarding your card once you have it. We also look at your legal protections as a card holder, such as your rights to protest billing mistakes, what happens when you purchase defective goods or services with a credit card, and limitations on the amount of money you are liable for on a lost card.

A poor credit record makes it harder to get a job, rent an apartment, or buy a house. We provide a chapter that tells you about your right to see your report, to protest inaccuracies in it, and even to make a protest to the company that furnished the incorrect information.

Among the specific topics we consider in the rest of this section are Internet credit and other e-commerce issues, including new laws giving consumers protections in electronic transfers and using debit cards. We also look at paying bills online and using electronic checks.

One of the biggest problems of credit in the 21st century is identity theft. We define the basic types of this fraud, discuss how identity thieves work, and give you plenty of practical tips that will help you avoid being the next victim. We also tell you about the new laws dealing with identity theft.

Unfair lending might be defined as loans made to desperate people at a very high rate of interest. Examples can include pay day loans, auto title loans, rent-to-own purchases, and sometimes even home equity lines of credit, where you might fall prey to such ploys as packing, loan flipping, and equity stripping. Our chapters on this topic discuss the legal protections against some of these loans, as well as how to be an informed consumer.

Mortgage loans are almost always the largest loans any of us will take out. We explain what they are, describe your legal protections, and look at the role of mortgage brokers.

Auto financing and leasing is a world of its own, with financing options ranging from the dealer financing, "dealer-assisted" loans, and direct loans. We walk you through the calculations you might have to make to figure out your best option, and also look at leasing and the legal protections you have in lease agreements.

The credit section ends with tips on how to get control of

your finances and figure out how much debt you can handle. We also tell you about your legal rights when a debt collector is after you and some of your options if you're in over your head in debt, including credit counseling.

Part Two—Bankruptcy focuses on the option of declaring bankruptcy. It gives you the pros and cons of consumer bankruptcy—how it can offer you a fresh start but also stays on your credit record for up to ten years, which can make it harder to get credit in the future, rent an apartment, and even get a new job.

We take a long look at each of the two types of consumer bankruptcy—Chapter 7 and Chapter 13—and point out how the requirements for each have changed under the new law. Chapter 7, the more common form of bankruptcy, often involves getting relief from most kinds of debt by surrendering certain assets to a bankruptcy trustee who will sell them and distribute the proceeds to your creditors. We go through the process step by step, beginning with the new "means test" which determines whether this form of bankruptcy applies to you. We help you understand which kinds of debts you can discharge (cancel) in bankruptcy and which you cannot. We point out which kinds of property are out of the reach of your creditors and which are not, and we give you tips on keeping as much as you can lawfully.

Next we look at Chapter 13 bankruptcy, which permits people to keep all their assets but requires them to pay off some or all of their debts from their income. We discuss the effects of the new bankruptcy law on this form of bankruptcy, particularly the rules governing how much of your income you must use to repay debts. We help you understand how to file and how to set up a payment plan, and we discuss what happens in the event that you can't keep up with your payments under the plan.

So what's right for you—a Chapter 7 bankruptcy or a Chapter 13? It depends on what you own and what you owe. We help you understand the pros and cons and weigh the options.

Most people in bankruptcy are very concerned about saving their home. It's bad enough to be bankrupt, worse to have to look for a new place of residence with a bankruptcy hanging over you. We talk about options for saving your home in both forms of bankruptcy, giving you the kind of help that may make it possible to keep that roof over your head.

Our last chapter gives you websites, books, and other sources of useful information—many just a keyboard stroke or telephone call away.

Finally, an appendix wraps up the book by giving options for trying to resolve credit disputes and organizations and agencies that may be helpful to you as you complain about a credit transaction.

WRITTEN WITH YOU IN MIND

We've made a special effort to make this book practical, by using situations and problems you are likely to encounter. Each chapter is clearly laid out and opens with a real-life situation that shows the practical ramifications of the subject.

Within chapters, brief special sidebars alert you to important points. Particular sidebars include:

- sidebars with this icon ▶, which generally give you practical tips that could be of benefit to you;
- sidebars with this icon ⓘ, which provide key additional information;
- sidebars with this icon ⚠, which generally give you a warning about a potential pitfall that you can navigate with the right information and help;
- sidebars with this icon ▤, which provide clear, plain English definitions to legal terms.

Another feature—ask a lawyer—highlights our experts responding to practical questions, giving legal information that may help you as you grapple with similar issues within your own family. This sidebar is denoted by this icon: ❨❩.

At the end of each chapter, in a section entitled, "The "World at Your Fingertips," we direct you where to go for more information if you'd like to explore a topic further—usually to free or inexpensive materials that will fill your mind without emptying your wallet. Our concluding section of each chapter—"Remember This"—highlights the most important points that the chapter has covered.

With this book, you'll be able to make informed decisions about a wide range of credit issues and opportunities. Armed with the knowledge and insights we provide, you can be confident that the decisions you make will be in your best interests.

Alan S. Kopit is a legal-affairs commentator who has appeared on national television for more than fifteen years. He is chair of the ABA's Standing Committee on Public Education and is an attorney in private practice with the firm of Hahn Loeser & Parks, LLP, in Cleveland, Ohio.

CONTENTS

Foreword vii
Introduction xi

PART I

Consumer Credit

CHAPTER 1

Credit—What Is It and What Does It Cost?

How the Law Protects You

You've just finished college and are about to start your first real job. You have a healthy amount of student loan debt, so you don't have much disposable income. You can barely pay your rent. But you believe that you deserve the best, so you decide to purchase a new stereo, a new car, and new furniture. The problem is that you don't have the cash to buy these items. You need to get credit. You apply for several credit cards and—presto!— your problems appear to be solved. Only later do you realize that you've mired yourself even deeper in debt, as the income from your job only allows you to make minimum payments on your credit cards. Now you want to purchase a home and live the American dream. You need more credit. Welcome to what one author years ago called the "credit jungle."

In his 1971 book *The Credit Jungle,* author Al Griffin warned that "[n]ot only is credit grossly oversold to a gullible public, but debt in too many cases has become a commodity in itself." This doesn't mean that credit is a bad thing. In fact, credit is vitally important. Griffin acknowledged the importance of credit to the American economy: "[i]f for any reason consumer credit were shut off at the close of work this afternoon, by tomorrow morning this country would be in a depression that would make the Great Depression of the 1930s look like a minor recession." Indeed, credit remains a critical part of life in the United States in the twenty-first century. If you want to finance your purchase of a new home or car, you need good credit. Only a very wealthy person can afford to buy a home by paying the entire purchase price in cash; when most people purchase homes, they must depend on credit. Similarly, many people who want to attend college can't afford to pay all of their tuition in cash. Most students have to borrow money. They need credit.

Credit, a word once commonly used to mean "credibility," involves trust. It refers to your ability and willingness to make payments when they are due. "Credit" also involves acquiring money for a certain price (known as interest). An individual uses credit to buy goods and services now and pay for them later. For example, credit lets you purchase a car or a washing machine and use it before you have fully paid for it; you pay for it while you use it. Of course, you could save money now to buy the car in the future, but you may want or need the car now—not three years from now. Similarly, you may use your credit card now to buy a pair of shoes or a dinner that you pay for later.

However, there are costs associated with an extension of credit. People do not give you money or sell you products on a deferred payment basis for free. When you obtain credit, you generally owe someone else a debt. A person who extends you credit is called a **creditor.** Creditors include, for example, banks, department stores and other retail sellers, credit card issuers, and finance companies. Sometimes creditors are called **credit grantors.** Recipients of credit are called **debtors** because they owe a debt to their creditors. For example, if you apply for and receive a Visa® credit card from a bank, and then charge $500 on the card, you now owe the credit card issuer $500 plus any related finance charges. You are indebted to the credit card issuer.

Unfortunately, in what *Credit Card Nation* author Robert D. Manning calls our "culture of consumption," many consumers do not realize the dangers of overextending their credit. Consider the following data cited by the Federal Trade Commission: In 1946, outstanding consumer credit in the United States was $55 billion. In 1970, that number had risen to $556 billion. In 2003, consumer credit in the United States had risen to an estimated $7 trillion dollars. As Manning writes, the "ascendance of the consumer credit society" has become "one of the most profound social and cultural revolutions of the post-World War II era."

Too many consumers live by the credo "buy now, pay later" or, even more unfortunately, "buy now and pay much later—if at all." When you obtain credit and then fail to pay your bills on time, you can easily develop a poor credit history and your debts may continue to rise. For many consumers, such a cycle can cause them to become hopelessly mired in debts. Some may even have to seek relief in the form of bankruptcy.

The first part of this book provides an overview of consumer credit, explains certain important federal laws governing consumer credit, and discusses important terms and conditions of common credit extension. The second part of this book discusses the different types of bankruptcy and what the process of filing for bankruptcy entails.

As you read, however, remember that bankruptcy should be a debt management choice of last resort. Many consumers can turn their financial lives around simply by living within a budget and incorporating lifestyle changes that allow them to live within their means.

TYPES OF CREDIT

There are three basic types of consumer credit: (1) noninstallment credit (sometimes called thirty-day or charge account credit); (2) installment credit, or closed-end credit, which is credit that is scheduled to be repaid in multiple installments over a fixed period of time; and (3) revolving, or open-end, credit.

With noninstallment credit, consumers must pay their balances in full within a defined period, commonly thirty days. Payment in multiple installments is not permitted; rather, payment is due in one lump sum. Travel-and-entertainment cards, such as American Express and Diners Club cards, typically operate this way, as do most charge accounts with local businesses, such as service providers like doctors and plumbers.

Installment credit, also known as closed-end credit, requires a consumer to repay the amount owed in multiple installments, typically (but not always) of equal amounts and over a fixed period of time. Automobile credit and personal loans are common examples of this type of credit.

Finally, revolving (or open-end) credit is an arrangement in which the consumer has the option of drawing upon a preapproved line of credit and paying off the entire balance, paying the minimum monthly payment, or paying any other amount in between. This arrangement is called "revolving" credit because

FORMS OF CREDIT

 Type of Credit

Basic Operation

Type of Credit	Basic Operation
Charge account (thirty-day) credit	Balances owed on such accounts usually require payment in full within thirty days. Such arrangements are not considered installment credit, since the debt is not scheduled to be repaid in two or more installments.
Installment (closed-end) credit	A consumer agrees to repay the amount owed in two or more installments (not necessarily equal in amount) over a definite period of time.
Revolving (open-end) credit	The consumer may draw on an open-end credit line from time to time, and then pay off the entire outstanding balance, pay only a specified minimum payment, or pay some amount in between each month. This type of credit is replenishable. The consumer may use the credit, make a payment, and then use the credit again.

the consumer uses the credit, makes a payment, and then uses the credit again. Most common credit cards, such as MasterCard®, Visa®, and Discover®, as well as store credit cards, are examples of revolving credit. So are equity lines secured by a second mortgage on the house.

COSTS OF CREDIT

The first thing to understand about credit is that it is far from free and often costs consumers dearly. Simple common sense tells us that a creditor will not make money if it lends a debtor $500 and then, six months later, simply asks for its $500 back. The only way a creditor can make money is if it charges the debtor a fee for extending credit. That fee is a **finance charge,** sometimes called **interest.** Finance charges can sometimes be very high, since the creditor generally has more bargaining power than the borrower. As Proverbs 22:7 reminds us: "The rich rule over the poor, and the borrower is servant to the lender." Consumers should think carefully before obtaining credit with very high finance charges.

Finance charges are commonly stated in annual percentage rates (APRs). For a given transaction, the finance charge is the total dollar amount that credit costs. The APR is the percentage cost of credit expressed as an annual rate. The amount of the APR will directly affect the finance charge. Generally, the higher an APR, the higher the finance charge.

To buy now and pay later, you generally must pay finance charges. Creditors assess finance charges because they need to make money to stay in business. Instead of lending money to a borrower, a creditor could invest that money and earn interest on the investment; finance charges compensate the creditor for that lost interest, and cover the costs and risks of extending credit. Only you can decide whether it is worth the cost of the applicable finance charge to have a car or other goods and services now, rather than later.

Many states regulate by law the maximum amount you may

be required to pay in finance charges, and provide penalties if a creditor charges more than the maximums allowed by law. However, some states allow unregulated competition among creditors to determine how much you pay. In other words, credit costs vary. You should shop for credit as carefully as you shop for the best deal on a car or television set. The federal Truth in Lending Act and similar state laws allow you to do that.

LEGAL PROTECTIONS

The federal **Truth in Lending Act (TILA),** which is part of the **Consumer Credit Protection Act of 1968,** requires creditors to disclose to consumers the important costs and conditions of credit, and certain additional information, up front. In other words, creditors in consumer transactions must tell consumers the applicable APR and how much will be due in finance charges. For purposes of TILA, creditors include banks, department stores, credit card issuers, finance companies, and so-called pay day lenders, check cashers, and pawn shops.

As TILA states, its purposes are "to assure a meaningful disclosure of credit terms so that the consumer will be able to compare more readily the various credit terms available to him and avoid the uninformed use of credit, and to protect the consumer against inaccurate and unfair credit card practices." TILA is also a **remedial statute** (a law designed to remedy a perceived problem that courts often interpret to the benefit of consumers).

Under TILA, before you sign an installment contract, a creditor must disclose several facts to you in writing (electronic disclosure may also be permitted), including the amount being financed, the applicable monthly payment, the number of monthly payments to be made, the dollar amount of the applicable finance charge, and—most importantly—the APR. The APR is an annual rate that relates the total finance charge to (1) the amount of credit that you receive; and (2) the length of time you have to repay it. Think of the APR as a price per pound—say, 20 cents per pound for potatoes. Whether you buy five pounds of potatoes for $1 or ten pounds for $2, in either case the rate is 20 cents per pound. However, the total cost of the potatoes in dollars will depend on the amount of potatoes you buy. When you buy credit instead of potatoes, you buy a certain amount of credit for a given number of months. The total dollar amount of your finance charge will depend upon how many dollars worth of credit you obtain initially, and for how many months you use those dollars.

TILA also regulates credit advertising. For example, if an automobile ad advertises a low monthly payment (giving a specific dollar figure), it must also disclose other pertinent information, such as the APR. This required disclosure under TILA is useful, since knowing the APR can also help you in shopping for credit cards and other forms of open-end credit.

In 1988, the United States Congress added to the Consumer Credit Protection Act of 1968 by passing the **Fair Credit and Charge Card Disclosure Act of 1988.** This law requires credit card applications and solicitations to disclose the annual percentage rates, annual fees, finance charge grace periods (if any) for purchase transactions, and how purchase balances are figured for finance charge computation purposes. Like TILA, this law provides important protections for consumers. Take the example of *Rossman v. Fleet National Bank Association.* In that case, a credit card company sent a solicitation to a prospective consumer promising "no annual fee." The consumer relied on this information to obtain the card but, less than a year later, the credit card company imposed an annual fee anyway. The consumer sued, alleging a violation of the Truth in Lending Act. The credit card company defended itself, arguing that it had truthfully stated in its solicitation that there was no annual fee, but that it had reserved the right to make future changes to the agreement. A federal trial court ruled in favor of the credit card company. However, a federal appeals court reinstated the consumer's lawsuit on appeal because the solicitation may have been false and misleading. Whether it actually was false and misleading will depend on whether the trial court ultimately determines (based on the evidence presented at trial) that the credit card company had reserved the right in its credit card customer agreement to add new charges (including an annual fee) to the credit card account within one year of account opening.

PROTECTIONS FOR CONSUMERS WHO LEASE PRODUCTS

The federal **Consumer Leasing Act,** which is part of the Consumer Credit Protection Act, applies to any lease of consumer goods lasting more than four months in which the total contractual obligation does not exceed $25,000. (It does not apply to leases of real estate, nor does it apply to consumer goods used primarily for commercial purposes, such as a car or truck leased by a business.) This law requires the **lessor**—the owner of the auto you lease, for example—to disclose certain information before you sign the lease. Among the most important required disclosures are:

 • capitalized cost—that is, the cost of the goods being leased (the capitalized cost is negotiable, to the same extent that the price of goods would be negotiable if you were buying them instead of leasing them);

 • the total amount of any initial payment you are required to make;

 • the number, amounts, and due dates of monthly payments;

 • the total amount for fees, such as license fees and taxes;

 • any penalty for default or late payments;

 • the annual mileage allowance, if applicable, and the extra charges involved if you exceed that allowance;

 • whether you can end the lease early, and the method of computing the charge if you do so;

 • whether you can purchase the goods at the end of the lease and for what price;

 • any liability that you may have for the difference between

(i) DETERMINING CREDITWORTHINESS

Creditors may use any one or more of the following factors to decide whether to extend you credit. If your credit history is bad, they usually will not give you credit, or will charge you a high finance charge to compensate for the added risk they assume in giving you credit.

Factor	Explanation
Ability to repay	This depends on the stability of your current job, other income sources, how much you earn, and the length of time you have worked or will receive your current income. Creditors may also consider your basic expenses, such as payments on rent, mortgage loans or other debts, utilities, college expenses, and taxes.
Credit history	This tells grantors how much money you owe and whether you have large, unused lines of open-end credit. Some very important considerations are whether you have consistently paid your bills on time, and whether you have filed for bankruptcy within the past ten years or had judgments issued against you.
Stability	Your stability is based on how long you have lived at your current or former address and the length of time you have been with your current or former employer. Another consideration is whether you own or rent your home.
Assets	Assets such as a car or home may be useful as collateral for an extension of credit. When used as collateral, the creditor may sell the property and use the money to pay itself if you fail to pay it. Creditors may also look at what else you may use for collateral, such as savings accounts or securities (stocks and bonds).

Creditors obtain information about these indicators of creditworthiness from your application and from your **credit score** (see below). A recent study released by Fair Isaac Corporation—a company that computes consumers' credit scores by analyzing the relationships between their credit records and their performance in paying their debts—revealed that 35 percent of a consumer's overall credit score is typically based on payment history. In other words, if your credit report shows that you consistently repay your debts on time, you are more likely be able to continue obtaining credit. Other important factors, and their respective weights in terms of determining your total credit score, are: amount and types of debt, 30 percent; length of credit history, 15 percent; and amount of new credit sought or gained, 10 percent.

the estimated value of the goods and their market value at the time you end the lease; and

• any extra payment that you must make at the end of the lease.

You can report apparent violations of the Consumer Leasing Act to the same agencies that enforce TILA. The FTC or your state or local consumer protection office may be able to help you find the proper agencies; please consult the appendix at the back of this book for the appropriate addresses and phone numbers.

CREDIT SCORING

A **credit-scoring system** attempts to determine how likely it is that a consumer will pay his or her debts. Creditors may use credit scores to determine whether you are creditworthy. Credit scores range from approximately 300–400 to 800–900; a good credit score is one that is higher than 700. Your credit score may determine whether you are able to obtain a home mortgage loan, an extension of credit to buy an auto, or other credit. As mentioned in the "Determining Creditworthiness" sidebar above, a number of factors are considered when determining your credit score. These factors include: your payment history, the amount of your outstanding debt, the length of your credit history, the number of recent credit applications you have filed, and the number of credit accounts you currently have.

(i) FEDERAL LAWS IMPACTING CONSUMER CREDIT

There are many federal laws that provide certain protections and rights to consumers. Here is a brief description of some of the major consumer credit protection statutes:

CONSUMER CREDIT PROTECTION ACT OF 1968 (CCPA)

This law is the major federal consumer protection statute. Many other well-known consumer credit laws are actually parts, or titles, of this law. For instance, the Truth in Lending Act is Title I of the CCPA, while the Fair Credit Reporting Act is Title VI of the CCPA.

TRUTH IN LENDING ACT (TILA)

This is the popular name for Title I of the CCPA. TILA requires creditors to disclose important costs and conditions of credit to consumers.

FAIR CREDIT REPORTING ACT (FCRA)

This law amended the Consumer Credit Protection Act and became Title VI of the CCPA. This law regulates the furnishing and use of information in relation to credit and requires credit bureaus to maintain accurate information about consumers in so-called consumer reports (credit reports). In 1996, the law was amended to impose some requirements on businesses that furnish information to the credit reporting bureaus. The law was also amended in 2003 by the Fair and Accurate Credit Transactions Act (FACTA) (see below).

FAIR AND ACCURATE CREDIT TRANSACTION ACT OF 2003 (FACTA)

This law amends the Fair Credit Reporting Act to give consumers more rights, including rights to one free credit report, disclosure of credit scores, and the ability to dispute credit information with furnishers.

CONSUMER LEASING ACT (CLA)

This requires disclosure of information that helps you compare the cost and other important terms of one long-term (longer than 4 months) personal property lease (such as a 3-year car lease) with another. It also requires firms that offer such personal property leases to disclose certain important facts to help you weigh the cost and terms of leasing against the cost and terms of buying on credit or with cash.

FAIR CREDIT AND CHARGE CARD DISCLOSURE ACT

This law amended the Truth in Lending Act. It requires a creditor to disclose certain important costs of credit in credit card applications and solicitations.

ELECTRONIC FUNDS TRANSFER ACT

This law provides protection to consumers with respect to the electronic transfer of monies to and from checking and savings accounts, including electronic transfers of funds from such accounts to pay creditors.

EQUAL CREDIT OPPORTUNITY ACT

This law prohibits creditors from discriminating against consumers with respect to credit on the basis of race, color, religion, national origin, sex, marital status, age, welfare assistance status, or the fact that an applicant has in good faith exercised any right under the Consumer Credit Protection Act.

FAIR CREDIT BILLING ACT (FCBA)

This law explains how a credit card holder can resolve billing disputes with credit card issuers.

FAIR DEBT COLLECTION PRACTICES ACT (FDCPA)

This law regulates the conduct of third party debt collectors working on behalf of creditors during the collection of consumer debt.

HOME OWNERSHIP AND EQUITY PROTECTION ACT OF 1994 (HOEPA)

This law, which amended the Truth in Lending Act, provides certain additional protections for consumers from certain high-interest and high fee home mortgage loans.

IDENTITY THEFT AND ASSUMPTION DETERRENCE ACT OF 1998 (IDENTITY THEFT ACT)

This law criminalizes the use of another person's identity or personal identifiable information to commit fraud or theft.

REAL ESTATE SETTLEMENT PROCEDURES ACT (RESPA)

This law requires that borrowers receive disclosures during the real estate settlement or closing process. RESPA requires mortgage brokers and/or lenders to provide borrowers applying for a loan with information on real estate settlement services, a good faith estimate of settlement costs (listing the actual charges the borrower is likely to pay) and a mortgage servicing disclosure statement.

Links to the text of many of these laws can be obtained from the Federal Trade Commission's website at *www.ftc.gov/bcp/conline/*edcams/ *credit/rules_*.

A California corporation known as Fair Isaac (*www.fairisaac .com*) developed credit scoring in the 1950s. Fair Isaac's version of the credit score is called the FICO score. Fair Isaac makes credit scores available for a fee ($12.95 for one credit score and one credit report from one national credit reporting agency, or $38.85 for three credit scores and three credit reports, from each of the three national credit reporting agencies). In addition, as of December 1, 2004, the federal Fair Credit Reporting Act requires consumer credit reporting agencies (such as Equifax, Experian and TransUnion) to give a consumer upon request and payment of a "fair and reasonable fee," the consumer's current credit score and certain related information about the credit score. The Federal Trade Commission (FTC) has indicated that the national consumer credit reporting agencies appear to be charging consumers between $4 and $8 for a current credit score (depending on the consumer's state of residence) and approximately $9 for a current credit report.

The FTC has an online publication about credit scoring at *www.ftc.gov/bcp/conline/pubs/credit/scoring.htm*. You might also want to check out "Don't Let Your Credit Score Strike You Out," an article that appeared in *USA Today*, at *www.usatoday.com/money/perfi/credit/2002-03-29-credit-scoring.htm*. See chapter 6 of this book for more on credit reports.

SELECTING THE BEST WAY TO FINANCE

Let's see how you can use the information made available to you by TILA to get the best deal when financing a used car that costs $5,000 cash. You have $1,000 in savings to make a down payment on the car, and need to borrow the remaining $4,000. Suppose that, by shopping around, you find the four possible credit arrangements shown below:

	APR	Length of Loan	Monthly Payment	Total Finance Charge
Creditor A	11%	3 years	$131	$714
Creditor B	11%	4 years	$103	$962
Creditor C	12%	4 years	$105	$1,056
Creditor D	12%	2 years	$188	$519

Let's begin with an easy decision. Notice that the four-year loan offered by Creditor B is a better deal than the four-year loan offered by Creditor C—that is, Creditor B's total finance charge is less than that of Creditor C. Since the lengths of these loans are equal, we know that an 11 percent loan is cheaper than a 12 percent loan for the same amount of money. Forget about Creditor C.

However, look what happens when the lengths of the loans vary. Even though Creditors A and B both charge an APR of 11 percent, Creditor B's total finance charge on the four-year loan is higher than Creditor A's total finance charge on the three-year loan. Of course, the difference makes sense, since with Creditor B you would have another year to use the creditor's money. In making a decision like this, you have to decide whether you would like to have the lower monthly payment that accompanies the longer loan. Note that it doesn't help to look just at the total finance charge, which is lowest on the loan from Creditor D. Creditor D charges a higher APR than both Creditor A and Creditor B—12 percent rather than 11 percent—so the only reason Creditor D's finance charge is the lowest of the four is that the length of its loan is also the shortest; you would have use of Creditor D's money for only two years. Therefore, you might choose Creditor D only if you wanted to be indebted for a shorter amount of time.

On the other hand, if your chief concern was the best deal in purely financial terms, without regard to length, your choice would narrow to either Creditor A or Creditor B. Your choice would depend on how easy it would be for you to meet the applicable monthly payments. Ultimately, the biggest decision would be whether having a car today, rather than later, was worth the monthly payments at the 11 percent financing rate.

Look at More Than Just the APR

You will not be shopping wisely if you merely compare APRs. For example, in the scenario presented above, you have to decide for how long you want to owe money to a creditor. If you want to minimize that time period, Creditor D might be a good choice. On the other hand, if a shorter period of indebtedness is your main objective, you might consider asking Creditor A if it would make an 11 percent loan for two years. Or you might consider asking both Creditor A and Creditor B whether they would allow

( ) TALKING TO A LAWYER

Q. I understand that the Truth in Lending Act requires creditors to tell me the APR in advance, but when I applied for a mortgage the actual APR turned out to be more than I was quoted. How does this happen? Is this permitted under the law?

A. For certain types of mortgage loans, the Truth in Lending Act (TILA) requires lenders to give you an estimated Truth in Lending (TIL) disclosure statement within three business days of your application. This is just an estimated disclosure statement, and does not necessarily reflect the actual terms of the mortgage loan you may eventually be approved for. You should generally receive a final TIL disclosure statement at or before your loan closing that more accurately reflects the actual terms of the mortgage loan you have been approved for and have agreed to accept. There are several reasons why the initial estimated TIL disclosure may have had a lower APR than your final TIL disclosure, including, for instance, the following: If you did not lock in your interest rate at the time of loan application, and the lender's interest rate for the loan program increased after you applied but before your loan closing, the interest rate (and therefore the APR) for your loan may have increased after you applied. If you applied for a refinancing loan believing that you were applying for a loan of less than 80 percent of the appraised value of the property, but the lender received an appraisal later on indicating that the property was worth less than you had originally thought, the lender might have increased the interest rate on the loan (to reflect the fact that your loan amount was for more than 80 percent of the appraised value of the property), or the lender may have decided to charge you for private mortgage insurance (a type of finance charge that increases the APR on the loan). The initial estimated TIL disclosure also may have assumed that you would pay a certain number of "points" or loan origination fees at loan closing. If you ultimately agreed with the lender to pay a lesser number of "points" (or no "points") at closing, the lender may have increased the interest rate on the loan in exchange for receiving fewer "points" or loan origination fees at closing.

—Answer by Elizabeth C. Yen, Hudson Cook, LLP, New Haven, Connecticut

Q. *Things are tough here, and we're thinking of taking out a loan from a finance company. Are there any laws that we should know about that might protect us? What can we do to assure that we're not paying too much to get the money we need now?*

A. In many states, a law will regulate what the finance company can charge you. Federal law requires that the cost and other important terms of the loan be disclosed to you before you sign. You should read these to make sure you want to go through with the loan. Before you sign, you also should check the ads for several sources of credit or ask about terms to get the best deal, just like you would shop for the best price on a car or other expensive products.

—Answer by Frederick H. Miller, George L. Cross Research Professor, Kenneth McAfee Centennial Professor, McAfee Chair in Law, University of Oklahoma College of Law

Q. *My son is just out of college. He asked me to co-sign a loan so he'd have money to furnish his apartment. What does co-signing mean?*

A. A co-signer on a loan is personally liable to repay the entire loan, even though the co-signer may not have directly benefited from the loan. The creditor may try to collect the full amount of the loan from the co-signer without first trying to collect from the primary borrower on the loan. The co-signer may owe late charges and collection costs on the loan if the primary borrower does not make all payments on time, as required by the terms of the loan. If the loan goes into default, the fact may become a part of the co-signer's credit record as well as the primary borrower's credit record.

—Answer by Elizabeth C. Yen, Hudson Cook, LLP, New Haven, Connecticut you to prepay some or all of the amounts due on their loans early, ahead of schedule, without penalty.

FACTORS TO CONSIDER WHEN USING INSTALLMENT CREDIT

There are several other factors to consider when using installment credit. First, consider whether the interest that you pay for the credit may be deductible when you calculate your federal income taxes. Almost all homeowners may deduct for tax purposes the entire amount of the interest paid on their mortgages. However, the interest that you pay on credit card debt, student loans, auto loans, and other debts is no longer deductible.

If you itemize deductions in preparing your federal income taxes, you might also consider financing major credit purchases through a mortgage or home equity loan. These types of loan are discussed in chapter 10, which explains how they can have both benefits and dangers for consumers. Remember that if you use a mortgage or home equity loan, you are placing your home at risk. And if the total value of the items you are permitted to deduct for federal income tax purposes is less than the amount of your standard deduction, the interest you pay on mortgage or home equity credit will not help to reduce your federal income tax bill.

A final factor to consider is the possibility that you will pay off the loan or extension of credit early. If this is likely, you will need to figure out how your creditor calculates the rebate of any unearned finance charges and whether there is a charge (prepayment penalty) for paying early. In the case of a loan, for example, if the loan allows you to prepay amounts due, in whole or in part, without penalty, you may be able to periodically pay a larger amount than the amount due, which would result in the loan paying off ahead of schedule, and would also reduce the total finance charges accruing on the unpaid principal balance of the loan.

▶ **CAREFULLY EVALUATE YOUR OPTIONS**

The examples on these pages illustrate the importance of checking all financing options before making a decision regarding credit. Fortunately, the law allows you to obtain the information that you need to shop comparatively. You should use this information, and apply it to your own situation and needs to determine which loan or credit arrangement is best for you.

THE WORLD AT YOUR FINGERTIPS

General Information

• You can find the addresses and telephone numbers for consumer protection offices in your local telephone directory. You also can find them online at *consumeraction.gov/state.shtml*, the website of the Federal Citizen Information Center. For a printed list of the offices, ask for the *Consumer Action Handbook,* available free by writing to Handbook, Pueblo, CO 81009; telephoning toll-free 1 (888) 878-3256 (1 (888) 8 PUEBLO), weekdays 8 a.m. to 8 p.m. Eastern Time; or accessing *www.Consumer Action.gov.*

• The Federal Reserve has many publications related to credit available on its website at *www.federalreserve.gov/consumers.htm.* These can also be obtained without charge by writing to Board of Governors of the Federal Reserve System, Publications Fulfillment, Mail Stop 127, Washington, DC 20551. Publications include:

> *Consumer Handbook on Adjustable Rate Mortgages*
>
> *Consumer Handbook to Credit Protection Laws*
>
> *Home Mortgages: Understanding the Process and Your Right to Fair Lending*

How to File a Consumer Complaint About a Bank

Budgeting and Saving

Choosing a Credit Card

When Your Home is on the Line: What You Should Know About Home Equity Lines of Credit

Keys to Vehicle Leasing

Looking for the Best Mortgage

- The Federal Trade Commission has a Consumer Protection website on credit with a long list of publications available online, from "Avoiding Credit and Charge Card Fraud" to "Understanding Vehicle Financing." This site also has links to important federal laws: *www.ftc.gov/bcp/conline/edcams/credit/index.htm*. All FTC publications are available by writing to Public Reference, Federal Trade Commission, 6th and Pennsylvania Avenue, NW, Washington, DC 20580.

- The Legal Information Institute gives a brief overview of consumer credit, and provides links to relevant legislation and to other consumer credit sites: *www.law.cornell.edu/topics/consumer_credit.html*.

- MsMoney.com has a section on credit, which provides some good practical information: *www.msmoney.com/mm/banking/credit/crupdown_intro.htm*.

- The National Consumer Law Center has online information and a variety of publications dealing with consumer credit: *www.consumerlaw.org/publications/*.

REMEMBER THIS

- Credit is an important part of our consumer culture. Credit is obtaining money for a price. It is also defined as the ability to borrow money and defer payment of the resulting debt until later.

- Credit has its costs. A finance charge is a fee that represents the cost of consumer credit in terms of dollars. The annual percentage rate (APR) is a measure of certain credit costs over the course of a year in terms of a percentage. (Some costs of credit, such as optional credit insurance charges, and certain mortgage-related closing costs, are not required to be included in the finance charge or the APR.)

• There are three basic forms of consumer credit: (1) noninstallment credit (sometimes called thirty-day or charge account credit); (2) installment credit or closed-end credit, which is credit that is scheduled to be repaid in multiple installments over a fixed period of time; and (3) revolving, or open-end, credit.

• Creditors analyze several factors when determining whether to grant consumers credit. These factors include a consumer's ability to repay the debt, credit history, stability, and debts and assets.

• There are many laws that impact consumer credit. Make sure to look at the Federal Trade Commission's website, which contains links to many of these laws as well as to publications that describe them in simple English.

CHAPTER 2

Your Right to Equal Credit

What to Do About Credit Discrimination

Betsy recently separated from her husband. Unfortunately, her estranged husband, Al, had been the primary breadwinner for their family. Now, Betsy seeks to establish some credit of her own. But when she attempts to apply for a loan, the loan officer asks her about her marital status, presses her for details about her future child-rearing plans, and then tells her it would be best if her husband co-signed with her on the credit application.

In the scenario presented above, Betsy may have grounds for viable federal lawsuits. Why? Because a federal law known as the **Equal Credit Opportunity Act (ECOA)** prohibits discrimination against credit applicants on the basis of race, color, religion, national origin, sex, marital status, age, receipt of public assistance, or the fact that the applicant has exercised a right under the Consumer Protection Act in good faith. Had Betsy felt that she was discriminated against in getting a mortgage, she might seek the protections of the federal **Fair Housing Act** and possibly also the **Community Reinvestment Act**.

Creditors can deny you credit because you are a credit risk. They can also deny you credit because of your poor financial history or low credit score (provided that the creditor uses a valid credit scoring system). This is common sense—why would anyone want to extend credit to someone who probably won't be able to repay it? However, it is also common sense that people should not be denied credit for reasons that have nothing to do with their ability to repay the loan. Thus, the law provides that creditors may deny credit based only on a person's creditworthiness, and not because of social biases.

THE ECOA

The Equal Credit Opportunity Act says that creditors may not discriminate against credit applicants "with respect to any aspect of a credit transaction." This means that it is unlawful for a creditor to discriminate against an applicant at any stage of the credit process—from the initial solicitation of credit to the actual granting of credit to the refinancing or collection of credit.

The ECOA says that creditors may not discriminate against you in credit deals based on certain factors. For example, a creditor may not use age (provided that you are old enough to enter into a legally binding contract), race, color, national origin, sex, marital status, religion, receipt of public aid, or the exercise of rights under the Consumer Credit Protection Act as a basis for:

• discouraging or preventing you from applying for credit;
• refusing you credit if you otherwise qualify;
• extending you credit on terms different from those granted to someone with similar risk (as determined by such factors as your ability to repay, credit history, stability, and assets); or
• giving you less credit than you asked for, if someone with similar risk would have received the amount you asked for or more.

The Equal Credit Opportunity Act does not, however, *guarantee* that you will receive credit; in order to qualify for credit, you must still meet the creditor's standards of creditworthiness.

The ECOA was passed in 1974 as an amendment to the Consumer Credit Protection Act. Initially, the ECOA only prohibited credit discrimination on the basis of sex or marital status. Many married women were unable to obtain credit unless they had the signature of their husband. Similarly, many single women were unable to obtain credit, including many women who had been recently divorced. Congress recognized this problem.

Congress expanded the scope of the ECOA by also prohibiting credit discrimination based on the other above-mentioned factors such as race, color, religion, national origin, receipt of

ⓘ TYPES OF DISCRIMINATION

There are two major types of discrimination under federal law: disparate-treatment discrimination and disparate-impact discrimination.

Disparate-treatment discrimination occurs when a creditor intentionally treats someone differently than similarly situated individuals who are not members of the same protected category (i.e., who are not members of the same race or sex). For example, let's say that Mr. Smith (a Caucasian) and Mr. Jones (an African-American) both apply for credit and have virtually the same income and credit history, as well as the same down payment or loan-to-value ratio. The creditor offers Mr. Smith a better finance rate than Mr. Jones, and generally makes the credit application process easier for Mr. Smith than for Mr. Jones. This is disparate treatment. Mr. Jones has been treated worse than Mr. Smith.

Disparate-impact discrimination occurs when a practice that seems neutral on its face has a negative impact on a certain category of people. For example, suppose a creditor refuses to grant credit to any person residing in a certain area code, because the creditor deems people living in that area code to be at high risk for default. The creditor applies this rule equally to all persons residing in the area code—both white and black. However, because of housing patterns in the area, the *result* of this policy is that far more African-Americans than Caucasians are being denied credit. This may constitute disparate impact.

If a lending practice has a disparate impact on one of the groups protected under ECOA, the lender must show that the practice has a legitimate business purpose. (Even then, if another practice would work just as well with a lesser disparate impact, a violation may still be found.) An example of a legitimate business purpose is the practice of charging a lower interest rate on mortgage loans to borrowers who make larger down payments. This might have a disparate impact on younger borrowers. However, the apparent disparate impact based on age is justified and legal because the loan-to-value ratio is a legitimate factor affecting the credit risk assumed by the creditor.

public assistance benefits and exercise of rights under consumer protection laws. These amendments went into effect in 1976.

Today, some state laws may be even more protective than the ECOA; for example, they may preclude discrimination on the basis of sexual orientation, or on the basis that a couple has children.

GENDER DISCRIMINATION

The original impetus for the ECOA was to prohibit credit discrimination against women. Today, the law protects both men and women from discrimination that is based on gender or marital status. In general, a creditor may not deny you credit or take any adverse action, such as lowering your credit limit or raising your APR, just because of your gender or because you are married, single, widowed, divorced, or separated. More specifically, the ECOA sets forth the following prohibitions:

- A creditor may not ask your gender when you apply for credit. One exception exists if you are applying for a loan to buy or build a home, or to repair, rehabilitate, or remodel a home, when the federal government requires creditors to ask for information about gender, race, and ethnicity in order to help the government monitor compliance with fair lending laws. However, if asked for your gender in these circumstances, you may still refuse to answer this question. When a credit application is taken in person (rather than online or over the phone), the government requires creditors to provide the information based on visual observation or name;

- Normally, you do not have to use a gender title (Mr., Miss, Mrs., or Ms.) when applying for credit. Sometimes creditors may ask whether you are married, unmarried, or separated, if your marital status relates to their right to obtain repayment. For example, such a request may be made in a state with community property laws, where spouses have more rights to their partner's assets and income than in noncommunity property states. There are eight states that are considered community property states:

Arizona, California, Idaho, Louisiana, Nevada, New Mexico, Texas, and Washington—and an additional two states, Wisconsin and Alaska, that have community property features in their laws. For more information about community property states, visit the Nolo Press website—*www.nolo.com*—and search for "community property."

A creditor might also inquire about a consumer's marital status if the consumer plans to pledge collateral to secure the credit. Because many state laws afford spouses certain rights in property owned by their partners, the creditor must determine whether the spouse must also agree to pledge the property to secure the loan.

• A creditor may not ask women if they use birth control or whether they plan to have children.

• You do not have to discuss child support or alimony payments with a creditor unless you wish the creditor to consider such payments as income. Note, however, that if you are required to *pay* alimony or child support, then the creditor will require you to disclose that information so that the creditor will know how much income you have available to repay a new debt.

The ECOA does not provide protection to those denied credit because of sexual orientation. However, courts can take a broad look at sex discrimination. Consider the federal case of *Rosa v. Park West Bank & Trust Co.*, a case that arose in Massachusetts.

A cross-dressing bank customer alleged that the bank had refused to provide him with a loan application because he dressed in feminine clothes. He alleged that the loan officer had told him to go home and change clothes. He sued, claiming gender discrimination under the ECOA. The bank argued that it had not violated the ECOA because its employee had been legitimately unable to identify the cross-dresser, since his forms of identification showed him in traditional male attire.

A federal trial court dismissed the lawsuit, finding that the ECOA does not prohibit discrimination based on the way a person dresses. A federal appeals court, however, reinstated the lawsuit. According to the appeals court, the bank might have violated the ECOA if it treated women who dress like men differently than men who dressed like women: "Whatever facts emerge, and they may turn out to have nothing to do with sex-based discrimination, we cannot say at this point that the plaintiff has no viable theory of sex discrimination consistent with the facts alleged." (214 F.3d 213, 215 (1st Cir. 2000).)

How do you enforce your rights? A very good place to start is the federal, state, and local agencies that accept and investigate fair lending claims. We provide a list of such agencies in the Appendix to this book.

Another alternative is to file suit. There are some problems with this approach. Discrimination lawsuits are very difficult and costly to pursue and they are rarely successful. Talk to a lawyer if you are considering filing suit.

ⓘ QUOTABLE FROM THE BENCH

Consider the language of the Ninth Circuit in an early ECOA case, in which the court invoked the ECOA to issue a strong condemnation of gender discrimination against women:

> The purpose of the ECOA is to eradicate credit discrimination waged against women, especially married women whom creditors traditionally refused to consider for individual credit. . . . If the spouse were required to sign the credit instrument, the credit offered would be joint, not individual credit, and this would be discrimination on the basis of marital status. (*Anderson v. United Finance Co.*, 666 F.2d 1274, 1277 (9th Cir. 1982).)

However, remember that it is sometimes appropriate for a creditor to require a spouse to sign documents in connection with credit extensions. For example, a spouse may be required to sign security instruments to pledge collateral or to agree that community property assets or income may be used to repay the debt. But a spouse cannot be required to become personally liable on the debt, i.e., the spouse can't be required to sign the note or loan agreement.

Marital Status and Separate Credit Accounts

Married people may open credit accounts that are not also in their spouses' names; they are not obliged to open joint accounts or take out loans with their spouses. Moreover, even if you have a joint account with your spouse, when a creditor sends information about your joint account to a credit bureau, it must report the information in each of your names, so you will not lose your separate identity for credit purposes. The credit bureau will maintain a separate file on you, so that a creditor may be able to access your personal credit history and rely on it when making a credit decision.

Specifically, a creditor may not

- refuse to open a separate credit account just because of your gender or marital status;
- require your spouse to co-sign your account, unless you live in a community property state; or
- ask about your spouse or ex-spouse when you apply for credit based on your own income. However, a creditor may seek this information in a community property state, or if you are relying in part on your income from alimony, child support, or maintenance payments from your ex-spouse for the purpose of obtaining credit.

Change in Marital Status

A creditor may not require you to reapply for credit just because you marry or divorce, or because your spouse has died. In addition, a creditor may not close your account or change its terms for these reasons alone. In order for a creditor to take such actions, there must be a change in your creditworthiness, such as a decrease in your income. For example, if your spouse dies or you get a divorce, and you had used your spouse's income to get credit, a creditor may require you to reapply for credit. However, the creditor must allow you to use the existing account while considering your new application.

RACIAL DISCRIMINATION

The ECOA also prohibits discrimination based on race. Some ECOA lawsuits have alleged that persons of a particular race are treated worse than Caucasian credit applicants. For example, in the 1984 case *United States v. American Future Systems,* the United States Court of Appeals for the Third Circuit rejected a chinaware company's policy of extending special credit to single white females aged eighteen to twenty-one who lived in their parents' homes. Under the policy at issue, such females would receive their merchandise immediately upon ordering it and applying for credit. The plaintiffs showed that similarly situated nonwhite women in the same age bracket were treated much differently: they had to make three payments before being deemed creditworthy and receiving their merchandise. The Third Circuit agreed that this disparate treatment violated the ECOA, determining that the company "perpetuates the past disparities between white and minority women . . . rather than helping all women it aids only white women and slams the door of equal credit opportunity in the faces of minority women." In accordance with the ECOA, courts have thus expressed their unwillingness to tolerate race-based discrimination against applicants for credit.

AGE DISCRIMINATION

A creditor may ask you your age. However, if you have achieved the age of majority and you apply for credit, a creditor may not

• refuse to give you credit or decrease the amount of credit it grants you solely because of your age;

• refuse to consider your retirement income in rating your credit application, if the creditor considers income when it evaluates creditworthiness;

• cancel your credit account or require you to reapply for credit just because you are a certain age or have retired; or

- refuse you credit or cancel your account because you cannot get credit life insurance (or a related type of insurance) due to your age.

However, the law does allow a creditor to consider certain age-related facts. For example, a creditor may consider how long your income will continue, or how long it will be until you reach retirement age. Consider, for example, a loan that will take a long time to pay back. If an older applicant does not provide adequate security, he or she may constitute a high credit risk. In addition, the ECOA does not prohibit creditors from inquiring about the age of an elderly person if the applicant's age is to be used in his or her favor. This provision is known as the "senior preference." For example, a creditor could give favorable consideration to an older credit applicant because of his lengthy payment history. Thus, the ECOA allows preference to be given to older applicants who have much more substantial credit histories than younger persons.

PUBLIC ASSISTANCE

A creditor may not deny an applicant credit solely because he or she receives Social Security or public-assistance payments such as Temporary Assistance for Needy Families. However, a creditor may ask you the age of your dependents, since you may lose federal benefits when they reach a certain age. A creditor may also consider whether you will continue to meet residency requirements for receiving benefits, and whether it can reach those benefits through legal channels if you fail to make payments on your account.

BURDEN OF PROOF IN ECOA CASES

As is the case with most other types of suits in which a plaintiff is trying to show that he or she is the victim of disparate treatment, such as employment discrimination suits, the plaintiff in an ECOA case bears the initial burden of proof. In other words, if you want to proceed with an ECOA case, you must set forth enough facts to establish a prima facie (legally sufficient) claim of discrimination. For example, in a racial discrimination claim under the ECOA, the plaintiff would have to show that: (1) he or she belonged to a specific race; (2) he or she was creditworthy; (3) he or she was denied credit; and (4) other similarly situated persons of another race were treated better.

Once a plaintiff establishes a prima facie claim, the burden shifts to the creditor-defendant to establish a legitimate, nondiscriminatory reason for the denial of credit. In other words, the creditor must show that there was a legitimate business justification for the denial of credit. The final burden then shifts back to the plaintiff to prove that the creditor's stated justification is **pretextual,** or bogus.

DENIAL OF A CREDIT APPLICATION

Under the ECOA, a creditor must notify you whether it has approved or denied your credit application within thirty days of your completion of the application. If the creditor denies you credit, the notice of such denial must be written (it can be electronic under certain circumstances), and must list the reasons for the denial of credit, or instruct you how to request an explanation of those reasons.

Another law, the **Fair Credit Reporting Act,** affects credit denials as well. It requires that a notice of credit denial tell you whether the creditor relied upon a credit report to deny you credit and, if so, the name and address of the credit bureau that provided the report. You are then entitled to ask for a free copy of your report. These rights also apply if a creditor takes any adverse action against you, such as closing an existing credit account or reducing an open line of credit.

If a creditor will not reveal why it has taken an adverse credit action against you, ask the creditor to supply a written explanation as required by the ECOA. If you think the creditor's written notice does not disclose the reasons it has taken an adverse credit action, ask for a written statement of the primary reasons credit was denied. If you think the creditor has discriminated against you, tell the creditor why you think this, and try to resolve the issue through negotiation. If the creditor continues the adverse action and has not given a satisfactory explanation, you may complain to the creditor's federal regulatory agency, the Federal Trade Commission, or the United States Attorney General's Office. See the Appendix of this book for contact information for all of these. In addition, the adverse action letter sent to an applicant who is denied credit will identify the creditor's primary regulator and provide the address where the regulator may be contacted with inquiries or to lodge a complaint.

DAMAGES

The ECOA provides individuals with the right to sue if they have been discriminated against while applying for credit. Creditors who violate the ECOA can be held liable for **compensatory** or **actual damages,** which compensate people for any actual damages they sustain as a result of the violation. If the plaintiff can show the requisite causal injury, such damages could include compensation for injury to reputation, mental anguish, costs associated with finding other credit sources and out-of-pocket expenses.

The law also allows individuals to recover up to $10,000 in punitive damages under appropriate circumstances. **Punitive damages** are not designed to compensate the plaintiff for actual harm suffered as a result of the violation; rather, they are designed to punish the wrongdoer and deter such unlawful conduct in the future. Punitive damages are intended to penalize creditors for violating the law.

The amount of punitive damages awarded will depend on whether the creditor should have known it was violating the law, and on other factors such as the number of violations. In the case of a **class action lawsuit**—a lawsuit filed on behalf of a class of people all harmed by the same illegal conduct—the law allows punitive damages of up to $500,000, or one percent of the creditor's net worth. In all cases, the law also allows individuals to recover court costs and reasonable attorney's fees expended in the litigation process.

The ECOA also allows aggrieved individuals to sue for more than just monetary damages: they can sue for injunctive and declaratory relief, and attorney's fees. **Injunctive relief** refers to an injunction, or court order, prohibiting a party from engaging in certain unlawful conduct. **Declaratory relief** refers to a court's declaration, or pronouncement, that a certain practice violates the law. In many discrimination cases, a plaintiff wishes to have the court declare, on the record, that a certain practice is unlawful, and to get an injunction against the company preventing it from ever engaging in similar conduct again.

Many courts have determined that ECOA plaintiffs are also entitled to have their cases tried before a jury.

ⓘ OTHER LAWS PROHIBITING CREDIT DISCRIMINATION

The Equal Credit Opportunity Act is the broadest of the existing credit discrimination laws, but it is not the only law that provides protection from credit discrimination. The **Fair Housing Act** also prohibits discrimination, specifically in the renting, leasing, and buying of residences. In some ways, the Fair Housing Act provides even greater coverage than the ECOA. For instance, the Fair Housing Act prohibits discrimination based on familial status and handicap. Furthermore, there is no cap (limit) on punitive damages under the Fair Housing Act.

Victims of credit discrimination may also pursue remedies under the more general federal civil-rights statutes. For example, victims of intentional racial discrimination have broad remedies under a statute known as **Section 1981** (42 U.S.C. Section 1981). State laws, including state fair-housing laws and state unfair-and-deceptive-trade-practices laws, may provide additional remedies for discrimination victims.

A CASE STUDY

Credit discrimination claims are often very complicated. A case study is a good way to understand the factors at work. We are indebted to Robin K. Warren of the Bank of America of Charlotte, North Carolina, for this example.

Let's say you and your husband applied for a mortgage loan to refinance your house after a co-worker told you he'd refinanced his loan with the same creditor for a very attractive interest rate. The mortgage rate information in the newspaper the weekend before you applied for your loan showed rates for 30 year fixed rate mortgages at about the same rate as the rate your co-worker obtained. The creditor's loan application asked you to provide information about our race, sex, and ethnicity. Then, while the loan application was being processed, you were asked to provide copies of recent income tax returns in order to prove the amount of your husband's income from the business he owns. Your application was finally approved six weeks after you submitted your application, but the approved loan amount was less than you'd asked for, and the interest rate was .50 percent higher than the rate your (white) co-worker got. You and your husband are African-American. You think the creditor used the information you provided about your race to discriminate against you by dragging the application process out, making the process more difficult, and by offering you a higher interest rate. What can you do about it?

It's possible that you were the victims of discrimination. It does, indeed, constitute illegal discrimination if, based on your race, the creditor discouraged you from pursuing your credit application, made the application process more difficult for you, or offered you less favorable credit terms than other credit applicants. However, it is also possible that your financial circumstances differed just enough from your co-worker's to cause the difference in your experience with your loan application and with the interest rate offered to you.

The creditor was required by federal law to ask you to pro-

◖◗ TALKING TO A LAWYER

Q. I just got turned down for credit, and I think it's because of my race. They gave other reasons for turning me down, but they don't seem like the real reasons to me. What can I do?

A. First, contact the creditor to ask for a more complete explanation. Write or ask to speak to a manager or senior executive of the company who can review the actions taken by subordinates and may have greater discretion to approve your credit application. If you still are not satisfied with the creditor's actions, you can submit a complaint to the creditor's primary regulator (as noted in the Appendix of this book, these are the Office of the Comptroller of the Currency, the Federal Reserve, the FDIC, the Office of Thrift Supervision, the National Credit Union Association, or the Federal Trade Association), or to the U.S. Department of Justice, to your state's office of consumer affairs, or the state attorney general. Keep in mind that there are a number of factors a creditor will consider when evaluating a request for credit: your income; your existing obligations, including housing costs, other debt, any obligation to pay alimony or child support; your financial stability (how long you have been employed), how consistent your income level has been; how long you have lived at your current and former residences); your history of making timely payments on other debt; whether the loan will be secured by collateral (a car or a home, for example); and your equity in the collateral (in other words, the value, of the collateral over and above any other loan amounts that are secured by the collateral). If your credit bureau report discloses many recent inquiries by other creditors, that might also negatively impact the creditor's evaluation of your credit.

You have the right to request a free copy of the credit bureau report upon which the creditor relied when turning you down for credit. Order a copy of the report. If you believe information on the report is incorrect, notify the credit bureau to dispute the incorrect information. If you have a good explanation for negative information that appears on the report, tell the creditor about it. The creditor is not required to accept your explanation, but it might make a difference in how the creditor views your creditworthiness.

—Answer by Robin K. Warren, Bank of America, Charlotte, North Carolina

vide information about your race, sex, and ethnicity. The government gathers this information pursuant to the Home Mortgage Disclosure Act so that it can monitor mortgage lending practices and detect violations of fair lending laws. You are not required to provide that information to the creditor, but if you fail to provide the information voluntarily, the government requires that the creditor provide that information based on visual observation and surnames.

One of the key pieces of information a creditor uses to evaluate a credit application is the borrower's income. Typically, the creditor can contact the credit applicant's employer to verify the income amount shown on the credit application. However, it is common for creditors to request copies of income tax returns to verify income when a credit applicant is self-employed. Since tax returns are signed "under penalty of perjury," creditors can be reasonably confident that the information reported to the IRS is accurate.

The ECOA requires that the creditor notify you of its decision within 30 days after receipt of a completed application. An application is not considered to be "complete" until the creditor has received all the information it normally needs to render a decision, including income verifications (such as wage confirmation from your employer or a tax return for a self-employed person), property appraisals, and credit reports. For mortgage applications, the application might not be "complete" until several weeks after the initial written application form is submitted.

As for the higher interest rate you were quoted, there might be legitimate reasons for it. If you did not lock in an interest rate at the time you submitted your application, it is possible that mortgage interest rates rose during the six weeks that the creditor was reviewing (underwriting) your application. It is also possible that there were factors in your credit history (some late payments on other loans, for example) that caused the creditor to determine that you were a riskier borrower and, therefore, should pay a higher interest rate to compensate for the greater credit risk.

The reduction in the loan amount might have been due to the appraisal on your house. If it reflected a value lower than the amount you stated on your application, that could have reduced the amount of credit the creditor could offer. Creditors set maximum loan amounts based on the loan-to-value ratio on the property being mortgaged. The loan-to-value ratio is the loan amount divided by the value of the property. So, for example, if a homeowner seeks to borrow $80,000 and secure it with a mortgage on a $100,000 house, the loan-to-value ratio would be 80 percent. However, if the house was appraised at a value of only $90,000, then the loan-to-value ratio would climb to 89 percent. Many creditors will not make loans with loan-to-value ratios over 90 percent or 95 percent. If an appraisal shows that a house is worth less than the amount on the mortgage application, the creditor might offer to reduce the loan amount so that the loan can be made within the creditor's loan-to-value guidelines. Keep in mind, also, that the higher the loan-to-value ratio, the riskier the loan for the creditor and therefore the higher the interest rate you'll be charged. You have the right to request and obtain a copy of the appraisal used by the creditor.

You should ask the creditor to explain why you were offered a lower loan amount and a higher interest rate than you originally applied for. If, after considering the lender's explanation and all the above factors, you still think you may have been a victim of discrimination, write a letter of complaint to the creditor and ask that your loan amount and interest rate be reconsidered. If you still are not satisfied, you can contact the creditor's primary regulator or the Department of Housing and Urban Development or your state Attorney General to lodge a discrimination complaint.

THE WORLD AT YOUR FINGERTIPS

• The Federal Trade Commission has an FTC Facts for Consumers publication entitled "Equal Credit Opportunity" available at *www.ftc.gov/bcp/conline/pubs/credit/ecoa.htm.*

• The National Consumer Law Center has information about credit discrimination on its website, taking a rather controversial view of an unsettled area of law. Included are links providing a general overview and a way to order in-depth written publications, at *www.consumerlaw.org/initiatives/credit_discrimination/index.shtml.*

REMEMBER THIS

• The Equal Credit Opportunity Act prohibits discrimination against credit applicants on the basis of race, color, religion, national origin, sex, marital status, age, welfare assistance, or the fact that an applicant has in good faith exercised any right under the Consumer Credit Protection Act.

• The ECOA does not provide a cause of action simply because someone is denied credit. Creditors can deny credit to those that are deemed non-creditworthy based on legitimate factors. However, denying persons credit because of any of the above-mentioned criteria may well run afoul of federal, and possibly state, law.

• The ECOA is not the only law that may benefit someone victimized by credit discrimination. Other laws that may help include the Fair Housing Act, the federal civil-rights statutes (42 U.S.C. 1981 and 1982), and various state laws.

• A creditor must provide you with an answer to your application for credit within 30 days. If you are denied credit, it must also provide you with specific reasons for the denial.

CHAPTER 3

Applying for Credit

Information About Legal Protections in the Credit Application Process

You have just entered the job market. For years you have not had to apply for credit because you have always lived with your parents. Unfortunately, when you go to apply for credit now, you struggle to find someone willing to offer you credit, because you have never had a credit record and cannot show a history of repaying debts.

HOW TO ESTABLISH A CREDIT RECORD

First-time borrowers will quickly realize that in order to get credit, they must have a credit history. There are several ways to start building a good, solid credit history. For example, you may

• open a checking or savings account. When creditors see such accounts, they can judge whether you have adequate money and know how to manage it;

• apply for limited credit from a large, local department store, and use it. If you want to build a credit history, remember that some small local retailers, travel-and-entertainment cards, credit unions, and gasoline card companies may not report your credit performance to credit bureaus;

• obtain a secured credit card (a credit card secured by a bank deposit that can be applied to the debt if you do not pay) or deposit money in a bank, savings and loan, or savings bank, and then borrow against it; or

• have someone co-sign a loan with you; that person must have a favorable credit record, and will be liable for the debt if you cannot pay. Having a cosigner will make it easier for you to get a first loan, and you will also find it easier to get credit on your own after you pay back the loan. If you are asked to co-sign for another person's loan, be very careful—if that person fails to pay, the debt will be your responsibility.

The Federal Trade Commission has an online publication that helps explain ways to establish credit, at *www.ftc.gov/bcp/conline/pubs/credit/gettingcredit.htm*.

Getting Credit In Your Own Name, Even If You Are Married

If you are married and you have your own sources of income, you should establish a credit history in your own name in case you become divorced or your spouse dies. This is also important if your spouse has a poor credit record, and you do not want your credit record tarnished by his or her payment performance.

Unfortunately, many divorced or widowed persons who did not earn a separate income do not have credit histories separate from those of their former spouse. In these cases, creditors will look at the credit histories of any accounts held jointly with the former spouse. A non-earning spouse may also be able to obtain credit by showing with checks, receipts, or other records that he or she is worthy of credit. For example, the spouse can provide checks and receipts simply to show that he or she has a purchasing history and has paid off debts before. If a former spouse had a poor credit record, a non-earning spouse may show that this record does not reflect whether he or she deserves credit by producing the following: previous explanatory letters sent to creditors, copies of contracts signed only by the former spouse, receipts, or other evidence demonstrating that the bad credit was generated only by the former spouse.

CREDIT INSURANCE

Credit insurance is insurance that consumers buy to pay their loan if they are or become disabled or involuntarily unemployed.

ⓘ CREDIT AND DIVORCE

Divorce can negatively impact people's credit for many reasons. It is important for people getting divorced to know whether their various accounts are individual or joint accounts. If an account is an individual account, then only the individual is responsible for the debts of that account, except in community property states (see below). However, if the account is joint, then both persons listed on the account are responsible for its debts. This can prove costly when a spouse or ex-spouse refuses to act responsibly or does not pay his or her bills.

If you are getting separated or divorced, make sure you send a certified letter to all of the credit card companies telling them that you are leaving the relationship and directing them to take you off the joint account for any obligations incurred after the date of the letter.

In some states known as community property states (Arizona, California, Idaho, Louisiana, Nevada, New Mexico, Texas, and Washington, though Alaska and Wisconsin also have community property features in their law), creditors may seek repayment from both spouses for debts incurred during their marriage, even in the case of individual accounts.

Just as couples getting divorced usually negotiate settlements in which they agree to divide their property, couples dividing responsibility for debts usually negotiate as well. If a couple can't agree on a settlement, a court will divide its assets and debts. However, this will not prohibit the creditor from going against either party to collect joint debts.

The Federal Trade Commission has a short publication entitled "Credit and Divorce" that is available online at *www.ftc.gov/bcp/conline/pubs/ credit/divorce.htm*.

There are many different types of credit insurance. **Credit life insurance** will pay off the balance owed on covered debt in the event of your death. **Credit accident and health insurance** will make minimum monthly payments on the covered debt for the period of time that you cannot work as a result of accident or illness. However, such coverage may not become available until after you have been disabled for a specified number of days. Occasionally, you may be offered **unemployment insurance,** which would provide for payments on covered debt during a period in which you were involuntarily unemployed. Again, such coverage may require a waiting period.

There are certain basic rules that creditors must observe in offering you any of these forms of credit insurance:

• Whether or not you accept credit insurance should not be a factor in the creditor's decision to approve your application for credit, and that fact should be disclosed to you in writing, although electronic disclosure is permitted under some circumstances.

• The cost of any credit insurance offered must be disclosed to you in writing (in some circumstances, electronic disclosure is allowed). If a lender requires credit insurance, the cost must be disclosed and included as part of the finance charge. However, if the lender does not require credit insurance, a lender does not have to disclose the cost of the insurance as part of the finance charge if certain other conditions and disclosures are met. The bottom line is that generally the lender must reveal the cost of the credit insurance.

• You must provide an affirmative, written indication of your desire to purchase such insurance. Usually this means that you must check the "yes" box on the credit agreement and sign a form or a section of a form indicating that you want the insurance.

Do You Have to Get Credit Insurance? Should You?

Consumers do not have to purchase credit insurance. If you do not have other insurance that will cover you in case of death, disability or involuntary job loss, buying credit insurance could be a wise choice. If nothing else, it might provide peace of mind.

Whether or not you should buy credit insurance is a personal decision. Surveys of consumers who have purchased such insurance indicate that they have done so because they did not

( ) **TALKING TO A LAWYER**

Q. *I'm just out of a bad marriage, and my ex screwed up the finances beyond belief. How do I get credit in my own name with this history? What can I do to show that I am responsible?*

A. You can open a checking or savings account and establish a responsible record. You can also open a limited credit account from a department store, or apply for a secured credit card and use it responsibly. If you can find a person to co-sign with you for credit and establish a successful payment history, this can also help rebuild or establish a good credit history.

—Answer by Frederick H. Miller, George L. Cross Research Professor, Kenneth McAfee Centennial Professor, McAfee Chair in Law, University of Oklahoma College of Law

have much other life insurance and did not wish to leave their families with the obligation of paying off their debts. Generally, the cost per $100 of credit insurance will be higher than the cost per $100 of, say, a decreasing term life insurance policy. However, credit insurance may generally be used to cover much smaller amounts than a life insurance policy—a fact that may be useful if you wish to obtain coverage for a $5,000 auto loan. (The minimum amount of life insurance you can purchase is usually $50,000 or $100,000, depending on the insurer.) Thus, although you should expect to pay more per $100 of coverage for credit life insurance than for life insurance, part of that added cost can be chalked up to convenience—just as you would expect to pay more per ounce for a glass of milk in a restaurant than for a gallon of milk at the supermarket.

However, some consumer advocates argue that such insurance is not a good deal for consumers. If possible, you should decide ahead of time whether or not you want to buy credit insurance; otherwise, once you are at the point of sale, you may feel pressured to accept it, just as you may feel pressured in a sales situation to buy a more expensive TV set or more options on a car. Be sure that your decision is respected when it comes to credit insurance. Tell the salesperson whether or not you want the insurance. If you are told to "sign here, here, and here," be sure to study the credit agreement to ensure that your wishes regarding credit insurance have been observed. When you are at the final closing, check again. If you have made arrangements over the phone for a loan, and have specified that you do not wish to purchase credit insurance, check the loan document when you go to the lender's office to collect the loan. If you have stated that you do not want to purchase credit insurance, but find that such insurance is provided by the loan agreement, don't sign the agreement—even if the lender moans that the form will have to be completely redone.

As for credit insurance for credit cards, remember that credit insurance makes only the minimum payment each month, even though you may have been paying a larger amount toward your credit card bills before the disability or unemployment that triggered the benefit.

If you think credit insurance makes sense, you should investigate purchasing decreasing term life insurance instead. Though you may have to purchase a high minimum amount, and pay more upfront, such insurance may protect your family better.

The Federal Trade Commission has a publication on credit insurance that is accessible online at *www.ftc.gov/bcp/conline/ pubs/alerts/credinsalrt.htm.*

THE WORLD AT YOUR FINGERTIPS

• The Federal Trade Commission has a publication entitled "Getting Credit," available online at *www.ftc.gov/bcp/conline/ pubs /credit/gettingcredit.htm.*

• The Federal Trade Commission has a short report entitled "Credit and Divorce" that is available online at *www.ftc.gov/ bcp /conline/pubs/credit/divorce.htm.*

• The Federal Trade Commission has a publication on credit

insurance entitled "Credit Insurance: Is It For You?" available online at *www.ftc.gov/bcp/conline/pubs/alerts/credinsalrt.htm.*

REMEMBER THIS

• In order to obtain credit, you need a credit record. Opening both a checking and savings account with a local bank is a way to establish a credit record.

• Credit insurance is insurance consumers buy to help them pay a creditor for a loan if they die or become disabled or involuntarily employed. There are many different types of credit insurance.

• You do not have to purchase credit insurance in order to obtain a loan. Think carefully before purchasing such insurance—many consumer advocates believe it is not a good deal.

CHAPTER 4

Applying for a Credit Card (and Choosing the Right Card)

Credit Cards, Their Cost, and Their Potential Effect on Your Credit Rating

A credit card company sends you an attractive mailing. It says you are a select customer, preapproved for a gold or platinum card. It offers enticing cash advances, balance transfers with little or no transaction fees, and no annual fee. What could be wrong with this picture?

It sounds nice and easy, but there may be more to such a mailing than meets the eye. With credit card offers, you must look beyond the cover letters and examine all of the relevant information; remember to keep reading after the asterisks at the bottom of the first page. What happens with the balance transfers and cash advances when the introductory period runs out? How are the payments applied? What is the interest rate?

Many cards have high APRs (annual percentage rates), charge high penalties if you miss any payments, and charge even higher rates for cash advances. In addition, card companies offering initial low rates may increase those rates if you miss a payment or fail to pay another creditor.

REVOLVING CREDIT

Revolving (open-end) credit is popular in this country, as more people have credit cards than ever before. Discover®, MasterCard®, Optima®, and Visa® are just a few of the many credit

ⓘ HISTORY OF THE CREDIT CARD

In the 1920s, several businesses began issuing credit cards to their customers for use only at their respective businesses. In 1946, John C. Biggins offered the first third-party credit card, called Charg-It, which was available for use in a two-block neighborhood in New York City. In 1949, the Diners Club offered a credit card called the "Diner's Card" for entertainment expenses. American Express issued a card in 1958 that is still known for its famous advertising slogan, "Don't leave home without it." In 1959, Bank of America in San Francisco issued its first BankAmericard, which became available in other states in 1966. The BankAmericard became known by its present name, Visa, in 1976. Competing banks began offering the card known as MasterCard in 1969.

cards issued by banks, savings banks, and credit unions. When shopping for a credit card, you need to recognize that cards with the Visa® and MasterCard® logos are issued by thousands of different institutions; hence, if you do not like the terms on one Visa® card, you can always check with other issuers to see if their terms are preferable. Major retailers issue their own credit cards (or make special arrangements with banks or other third parties to have their store credit cards issued by third parties), and oil companies also have their own cards, although many oil companies do not offer revolving credit—only thirty-day credit (except on purchases of tires, batteries, and accessories).

CHOOSING A CREDIT CARD

Selecting a credit card is like selecting a suit or dress: you want a good "fit." Because there are many card issuers, you have a wide variety of cards from which to choose. In this section, we will examine terms that are typically offered to consumers by banks and other issuers of credit cards. Excerpts from actual solicitations will help you to understand whether a card offered to you is a good fit for your own credit needs.

First, be aware that it is illegal for a card issuer to send you a credit card unless you have asked for it, or unless it replaces a card for which you previously asked. Second, under the Truth in Lending Law (TILA), every solicitation and application for a credit card must contain a brief disclosure statement (in the form of a table or chart), summarizing some (not all) of the important fees, Annual Percentage Rates, and other terms that apply to the credit card account. More extensive disclosures should be provided (often as part of the credit card customer agreement) before you use a credit card you have applied for, and specific disclosures about finance and other charges and transactions are also required to be included as part of your periodic billing statements, which are usually sent monthly.

Annual Percentage Rate

The law requires a creditor to quote the APR of a credit card, and to tell you the balance calculation method it uses to work out the finance charge you pay on credit card purchases. Since creditors use many different methods to compute the balances to which APRs are applied, grantors who quote identical APRs

▶ **ONLINE HELP IN CHOOSING CARDS**

There are several places online where you can get information that will help you choose credit cards. These include:

CardWeb.com: *www.cardweb.com*

Bankrate.com: *www.bankrate.com*

CreditCardSearchEngine.com: *www.creditcardsearchengine.com*

may charge you very different dollar finance charges each month. Each finance charge will depend on how you use the applicable account, and on how the creditor calculates the unpaid balance for purposes of assessing its finance charge.

Computing the Balance

For purposes of determining the finance charge you must pay for each billing period, credit card issuers can compute your account balance in a number of different ways. In the most common method, card issuers determine your **average daily balance** for the billing period, and then apply the APR to that average figure to determine the amount of interest you owe. Credit card offers typically use the following language to indicate that this method will be used:

> *Method of Computing the Balances for Purchases:* Average Daily Balance (including new purchases)

Occasionally, retailers will use the **adjusted-balance method,** in which they compute your balance by subtracting payments made or credits given during the billing period from the total amount you owed as of the start of the billing period. Other creditors may use the **previous-balance method,** in which any payments you make during the billing period are not subtracted from the total amount that you owed at the start of the billing period. The previous-balance method can cost you more than the other two methods, depending on how you use your account.

Issuers may use other methods to compute your balance and finance charge, but the three methods mentioned above are the most common. Let's look at an example that demonstrates the differences between them. For each method, assume that your credit card has a billing period of one month and an APR of 1.5 percent, you have a previous balance of $500, and you make a payment of $400 on the fifteenth day of your billing cycle:

	Average-Daily-Balance Method	Adjusted-Balance Method	Previous-Balance Method
APR	1.5%	1.5%	1.5%
Previous balance	$500	$500	$500
Payment on 15th day	$400	$400	$400
Calculation of finance charge	$300 × 1.5% equals $4.50. (During the billing period, the daily account balance was $500 for 15 days and $100 for 15 days, assuming no new purchases or other transactions during the billing period,* for an average daily balance of $300, multiplied by the monthly rate of 1.50%.)	$100 × 1.5% equals $1.50. (The amount owed as of the start of the billing period, minus payments made during the billing period, multiplied by the monthly rate of 1.50%.)	$500 × 1.5% equals $7.50. (The amount owed as of the start of the billing adjustment, multiplied by the monthly rate of 1.50%.)

*The average daily balance may be substantially higher than $300 in this example, if there were new purchases or other transactions charged to the account during the billing period, in which case the finance charge for the billing period would also be higher.

⚠ PROTECT YOUR CREDIT CARDS AND KNOW YOUR RIGHTS

1. Sign new credit cards as soon as they arrive. Cut up and throw away expired credit cards. Destroy all unused preapproved credit applications.

2. Keep a list of your credit card numbers, expiration dates, and the toll-free telephone number of each card issuer in a safe place, so that you can report missing or stolen credit cards and possible billing errors (see chapter 8 for information about identity theft).

3. Don't lay your credit card down on a counter or table. Hand it directly to the clerk or waiter. Keep an eye on your card after you give it to a clerk. Make sure that he or she imprints only one charge slip and, if he or she makes an error and has to imprint a second charge slip, make sure he or she tears up the first one. Take your card back promptly after the clerk is finished with it, and make sure that it is yours. If the vendor is still using the old machines that produce carbon copies, tear up any carbons when you take your credit card receipt.

4. Never leave your credit card in the glove compartment of a car. Never leave your credit card in an unlocked desk drawer, grocery cart, or hotel room.

5. Never sign a blank credit card receipt. Draw a line through any blank spaces above the total when you sign receipts.

6. Open credit card bills promptly, and compare them with your receipts to check for unauthorized charges and billing errors. If your monthly statement doesn't arrive on time, call the issuer immediately.

7. Write or telephone the card issuer promptly to report any questionable charges. As a practical matter, most consumers would prefer to call the card issuer's 800 number for billing questions, and most disputes can be settled in this way. (You can find the correct 800 number on your billing statement.) However, written inquiries will leave a paper trail that might be helpful in certain situations. Written inquiries

will better preserve your legal rights because the Fair Credit Billing Act only protects written—not telephone—inquiries. Such inquiries should not be included with your payment. Instead, check the billing statement for the correct address for billing questions. Either a written or telephone inquiry must be made within sixty days of the statement date to guarantee your rights under the federal Fair Credit Billing Act, which is part of the Consumer Credit Protection Act.

8. Never give your credit card or checking account number over the telephone unless you have placed the call yourself. Never put your credit card number on a postcard or on the outside of an envelope.

9. Do not write your credit card number on a check (except for the checks paying your credit card bill), and do not allow any merchant who takes your check to do so either.

10. If any of your credit cards is missing or stolen, report the loss as soon as possible to the card issuer. Follow up your telephone calls with a letter to each card issuer. Send each letter by certified mail and keep a copy. Each letter should contain your credit card number, the date the card went missing, and the date you called to report the loss.

11. If you report the loss of a credit card before it is used by another party, under federal law the issuer cannot hold you responsible for any subsequent unauthorized charges. If a thief uses your card before you report it missing, the most that you will owe for unauthorized charges on each card is $50, though if you lose a number of cards you could be out hundreds of dollars. However, this limitation of liability does not apply to debit cards.

12. This may seem obvious, but it happens—don't lend your credit card to a family member or friend. You're liable for the charges, which may be way more than you expected.

As you can see from these examples, finance charges may vary greatly depending on how the creditor calculates the balance that is subject to its finance charge.

Finance Charges

Many credit cards offer a finance charge grace period for purchases (but typically not for cash advances or balance transfers), which is the time between the end of the billing period and the date that you must pay the entire account balance shown on the bill in full to avoid paying a finance charge on new purchases charged to the account during the billing period. This finance charge grace period for purchases is usually between twenty and twenty-five days. The finance charge grace period for purchases may be shown on a credit card solicitation or application in the following manner.

> *Grace period for repayment of the balance for purchases:* No finance charges are assessed on current purchases if the balance is paid in full each month within twenty-five days after billing.

In this example, note that the grace period starts on the billing date. Thus, by the time you receive the bill, you may have only two weeks left to make your payment before the finance charge grace period ends. You must be careful to ensure that your payment is received (not just postmarked) before the end of the finance charge grace period. Also, be aware that the full account balance must be paid each month to avoid finance charges on purchases, and that the grace period typically applies only to purchases. Thus, if you obtain, say, a cash advance with your credit card, you will almost always have to pay finance charges on the advance from the date you obtain it until the advance is repaid in full, and probably a cash advance transaction fee as well.

Note that the creditor may adjust the grace period using a method of assessing monthly charges called the retroactive or two-cycle average daily balance method. Under this method, if the opening balance on your bill is zero, and then you make purchases but do not pay your entire bill in full, your next monthly bill could include a finance charge for those purchases retroactively from the dates that they were posted to your account.

For example, suppose that you use a credit card on an account with no outstanding balance to buy a $500 item that the creditor posts to your account on March 15, and also assume no other transactions are posted to your account during the month of March (apart from the monthly payment that was posted to the account in March). Suppose the creditor bills you on April 1 for your March account activity, and suppose that you must pay in full by April 20 to avoid a finance charge on your March 15th purchase. However, assume further that you make a payment of only $200, which the creditor credits to your account on April 18. Then your next bill (dated May 1 in this example) could include a finance charge composed of two parts. One portion of the finance charge would be for the use of $500 for the period from March 15 to March 31. The other charge would be for the period from April 1 through April 30. You must read the disclosure statement or cardholder agreement very carefully to determine whether the card issuer uses this retroactive method.

Variable APRs

Often a credit card will have a **variable-rate provision** in which the credit card issuer sets an APR that varies based on some in-

---

▶ HOW MANY CARDS SHOULD YOU HAVE?

Consumers are often deluged with credit card solicitations in the mail and over the Internet. It is easy and often tempting to apply for more credit cards, but you should think carefully before taking on more than one. Having too many credit cards could lower your credit score, because you could be deemed to be at risk of having too many credit repayment obligations and being overextended with respect to your disposable income. Remember that a key aspect of your credit score is the relative ratio of your debts to your assets. It is a mistake to open new credit accounts merely to increase your available credit.

terest rate index, such as the market rate on three-year U.S. Treasury bills (T-bills) or the prime rate charged by banks on short-term business loans. Where such a provision applies, the issuer must disclose in its solicitation to you that the rate may vary and how the rate is determined. This may be done by detailing the applicable index and the **spread** (sometimes also called the **margin**) that is the percentage points added to the index rate to determine the rate you will pay. A typical disclosure for a variable-rate credit card will look something like this:

> *Variable Rate Information:* Your Annual Percentage Rate may vary quarterly. The rate will be the Prime Rate as published in *The Wall Street Journal* plus 9%. The rate will not go below 15.0% or exceed 19.9%.

Issuers of fixed-rate cards can also change their rates from time to time, in accordance with the applicable cardholder agreements and with state and federal law, often simply by sending the cardholder fifteen days' advance written notice of a rate increase.

⚠ IF YOU'VE GOT BAD CREDIT

You'd like to have a credit card, but you've got bad credit. Be careful— you might not like the deal you're offered. Consumers with bad credit may get credit card solicitations promising a card if they pay an up-front fee. These fees can be very high, and the interest rates on the cards can be very high too.

Maybe a better approach is to get your spending under control, improve your credit rating, and then apply for a card—maybe a secured card. Also, if you cannot pay off the entire balance on your credit card, you should pay as much of that balance as you can afford. If you only pay the minimum amount due each month, it may take you more than ten years to pay off your credit card debt, even if you never use your card again.

Annual Fees

A credit card solicitation or application must disclose any annual or other periodic fee that applies to your account, as well as certain other fees such as transaction, cash advance, and late fees, if they are imposed.

Few, if any, credit cards issued by or through retailers have annual fees. However, such fees are common in the case of credit cards issued by financial institutions. Such fees usually range from $15 to $25, and perhaps from $35 to $60 or more for "premium cards" that provide higher lines of credit. Charge cards, such as American Express® or Diners Club®, are different from credit cards in the sense that full payment is due when you are billed. They have annual fees that often exceed annual fees charged for credit cards. If you pay your credit card account balance in full each month and thus do not generally expect to pay finance charges, you should shop for a credit card with no annual fee or an annual fee that is low, without much regard for the card's APR. However, if you often don't pay your balance in full, then a low APR may be more important to you than a low annual fee. Some credit cards have a minimum finance charge even if you pay in full each month.

Other Fees

Assuming that transaction, cash advance, over-the-limit, and late fees are a part of your credit card plan, your disclosure statement will likely include a statement that looks something like this:

> *Transaction fee for cash advances, and fees for paying late or exceeding the credit limit:* Transaction fee for Cash Advances: 2% of the amount of the advance ($1.00 minimum; $10.00 maximum). Late payment fee: $15.00, if the amount due is $2 or more. Over-the-limit fee: $15.00.

Unless you expect to be late with your payments, your choice of a card should not be heavily influenced by the size of its late fees. Note that your plan may provide for other fees as well, such as replacement card fees, copy fees, wire transfer fees, and insufficient-funds fees, that are not required to be disclosed as part of a credit card solicitation or application.

Most credit card issuers set a limit on the amount of credit that they are willing to provide you at any one time. To encourage you not to exceed this limit, some card issuers may charge over-the-limit fees. Unless you keep careful track of your charge slips, it may be difficult for you to know how much you owe in relation to your credit limit. Thus, if you believe that you might be close to your credit limit from time to time, you might want to shop for a credit card that does not have over-the-limit fees, or that has very a low over-the-limit fee.

 CHOOSING THE *RIGHT* CREDIT CARD

A credit card must fit your financial habits. If you often do not pay your account in full each month, you should pay more attention to the annual percentage rate (APR) than someone who pays in full every month and never owes a finance charge. That person will be more concerned with an annual fee that might be levied.

Just knowing the APR is not enough, since there are different ways of calculating the balances against which the APR is applied. If you don't think that your income will rise if interest rates go up, you might prefer a credit card with a fixed APR rather than one with a variable rate. However, it is important to remember that the APR on a fixed rate credit card may still go up if the card issuer gives you fifteen days' advance written notice of the rate increase.

If you expect to use your credit card to obtain cash advances, the card's cash advance fee should be an important consideration. Moreover, if you have a hard time keeping track of charges on your credit cards, cards with high over-the-limit fees may be worth avoiding. Finally, if late fees promise to be a major problem for you, perhaps it is in your best interest to refrain from taking on another credit card at all.

IN CASE OF REJECTION

What if the credit card company turns you down? You may want to consider applying for a **secured credit card.** This is a credit card issued by a bank or other financial institution that is secured by a savings account that you have deposited with that particular institution. You need to shop carefully for the best terms. Try to avoid having to pay an application fee for a secured credit card. Your line of credit will typically be limited to between 90 and 100 percent of the balance in the savings account that is securing the credit card. As you shop around for a secured card, compare the rates paid on savings accounts, the APR charged on the credit card account, and the fees that may be charged on both the savings account and the credit card account. Especially important are the amounts of late fees and any over-the-limit fees, which can sometimes be quite high with secured credit cards.

Secured cards are something like training wheels on a bicycle: once you have shown that you can use them, you should be al-

---

ⓘ THE CYCLE OF DEBT STARTS EARLY

Credit card companies have learned that the key to growth in their industry often lies with young people. According to recent statistics cited by Congress, 55 percent of college students obtain their first credit cards in college and 83 percent of college students have at least one credit card. As of 2002, nearly 50 percent of college students had significant credit card debt, with an average debt of more than $3,000 per student.

Many consumer groups have been formed to teach young people about finances and credit, including Jump$tart Coalition for Personal Financial Literacy, which offers a number of resources online at *www.jump start.org.*

It is important to learn about credit early in life, particularly in an era where credit card marketers target young people as customers.

lowed to move on to the "real thing." Once you have shown that you can handle a secured credit account, you should ask the institution that issued you the secured credit card to offer you the opportunity to switch to an unsecured card with more favorable terms. If your request is declined, even after you have established a good credit record, you should take your business elsewhere and apply for a regular credit card from another financial institution.

PROTECTIONS FOR THE CONSUMER

Truth in Lending Act

As explained in chapter 1, the federal Truth in Lending Act (TILA) helps you to choose credit wisely by requiring creditors to give you plenty of information before you make a choice. However, the law alone cannot protect you fully; you have to do your part by being an informed consumer.

TILA does not set finance charges, nor does it tell you what rates are fair or unfair. In some states, laws do exist to prevent you from paying finance charges that are thought by legislators to be too high, but often these laws are not applicable to out-of-state banks. In any event, in most cases it is simply marketplace competition that serves to keep credit card rates in line. But for competition to continue as an effective mechanism for controlling rates, consumers must reward with their business only those credit card companies that offer the most favorable terms. Thus, you the consumer must use the information provided by creditors to select the credit card that best fits your needs.

Violations of TILA

A creditor violates TILA if it fails to disclose timely information, or if it provides you with inaccurate information. In the event of such a violation, you should inform the proper federal enforcement agency. The consumer protection office of your state or local government should be able to help you find the appropriate agency; you can also use the appendix of this book to find the appropriate agencies to contact. To enforce your rights under TILA, you have the right to bring a lawsuit for actual damages (any money loss you have suffered as a result of the violation). Under TILA, you may also sue for an amount equal to twice your finance charge or $100, whichever is greater. Even if your finance charge is high, however, the most you can recover is $1000 for an account that is neither secured by real estate nor by any type of residential property (such as a manufactured home). Should you win your lawsuit, the law also entitles you to recover your court costs and lawyers' fees.

PROPOSED AMENDMENTS TO TILA

Congress continues to remain active in proposing amendments to the Truth in Lending Act that would provide more protection to consumers from credit card companies. However, the law has not been changed for nine years, and there is no guarantee that any of the proposed changes will become law.

In 2003, Representative Bill Pascrell introduced H.R. 1573, the Credit Card Consumer Protection Act of 2003, which would require credit card issuers to mail monthly statements to consumers at least thirty days before the due date of their next payment. The bill would also require credit card issuers to include on their statements the following prominently displayed disclosure: "If payment is not received by [payment due date], a late fee of $ [amount of late fee] will be charged to your account."

That same year, Representative Jim McGovern introduced H.R. 1747, the Consumer Credit Disclosure Act of 2003. This bill would require credit card issuers to provide "enhanced information regarding credit card balance payment terms and conditions." For example, credit card issuers would have to disclose "the number of months (rounded to the nearest month) that it would take to pay the entire amount of that balance, if the consumer pays only the required minimum monthly payments and if no further advances are made."

Regulation Z is the rule, issued by the Federal Reserve Board, which implements the federal Truth in Lending Act. In the American system of law, Congress—as the legislative branch of our federal government—passes laws that generally affect a set of actions or a particular aspect of society. However, these laws often grant the power to implement and expound them through additional rules or regulations to different administrative agencies of the executive branch of our federal government. Regulation Z is one such regulation. Regulation Z governs how creditors must disclose terms of credit, compute credit costs, and resolve credit disputes. Its stated purpose is "to promote the informed use of consumer credit by requiring disclosures about its terms and costs." For example, TILA and Regulation Z generally prohibit creditors from issuing credit cards unless consumers request the cards. Regulation Z also provides that creditors must disclose finance charges, and other important terms. It also provides remedies for billing errors and limits liability, as described in the next chapter.

Under some state laws, a violation of TILA is considered an unfair or deceptive act or practice or a violation of other state law, in which case other remedies may be available. For instance, some state laws impose greater penalties, such as treble (triple) damages, upon violators. You should contact your state attorney general's office for more information on relevant state laws, since deciding whether to proceed under federal or state remedies is often a complex issue that requires learned guidance.

Limiting Finance Charges

Shopping carefully for credit plays a key role in minimizing the finance charges that you will eventually have to pay, regardless of whether you are looking for closed-end credit (installment credit) or open-end credit (revolving credit). And even though many states impose rate ceilings on various creditors or types of credit—for example, state law usually limits the rates that finance companies may charge—careful shopping can still save you money.

( ) TALKING TO A LAWYER

Q. My card issuer just raised my rate—which I thought was locked in— with no explanation. When I called them they said it was because I had become a worse credit risk (even though I'm paying off my balance with them regularly). How did this happen, and how can I prevent it from happening again on another account?

A. Your credit card agreement may have included a provision allowing the card issuer to increase your Annual Percentage Rate (APR) if you have become past due on any account you have with any other creditor (not just your credit card account with the card issuer), or allowing the card issuer to increase your APR if the card issuer has good reason to believe that you now pose a higher risk of nonpayment than before (for instance, because your credit report might show a larger number of accounts past due now than before, or because your credit report might show a larger dollar amount of total debt outstanding now than before). In addition, your credit card agreement may allow the card issuer to increase your APR by giving you fifteen days' advance written notice of the increase. You should review your credit card agreements carefully to determine the circumstances in which your card issuers may have reserved the right to increase your APR. You may also wish to consider transferring the balance you presently owe on a higher APR credit card account over to a lower APR credit card account, and discontinue using the higher APR account.

—Answer by Elizabeth C. Yen, Hudson Cook, LLP,
New Haven, Connecticut

Q. Credit card applications are full of small print and stuff I don't understand. What should I look for? What can I do if I find something I don't agree with?

A. Look for universal default clauses, arbitration clauses, grace periods, how payments are applied, the method of computing the finance charge and the manner in which the terms of the agreement can be changed. If you find terms you do not like, don't accept the card and let the credit card company know why.

—Answer by Marc S. Stern, Law Offices of Marc S. Stern, Seattle, Washington

Q. Is it worthwhile to sue under TILA? It doesn't seem like you can recover much money.

A. As a general rule, suing is never a good idea unless you feel strongly that you have been harmed. As for TILA, it depends upon the circumstances. If it involves a $50 credit card charge, maybe not. If it is your house involved, probably yes.

—Answer by Marc S. Stern, Law Offices of Marc S. Stern, Seattle, Washington

When shopping for the best terms for you, check the *Wall Street Journal* and other newspapers that frequently publish shopping guides to credit cards from financial institutions. Such guides typically cover all of the relevant terms discussed in this chapter. In addition, you can easily shop for credit cards and compare terms by logging on to *www.cardweb.com/cardtrak/* and other sites that provide information on credit cards. The Federal Reserve Board also gathers credit card rates for publication.

High Credit Card Rates

Many states impose rate ceilings on store or bank credit cards. However, these limits do not always apply across the board. For example, under federal law national banks may **export** their finance charge rates and related fees on credit cards. State-chartered, federally insured banks generally have the same rate and fee exportation rights. Thus, a national bank or a state-chartered FDIC-insured bank may issue cards from headquarters located in (for example) South Dakota, enabling it to charge its cardholders in Iowa any rate the credit card agreement specifies, since South Dakota does not have a rate ceiling on bank

( ) TALKING TO A LAWYER

Q. When I checked in at a hotel I gave them one card, but when I paid I gave them another—and now I'm having a problem with the first card company. They've earmarked an amount to pay the bill, so I'm blocked from using that money till they're satisfied that the bill has been paid. What can I do?

A. Hotels and car rental companies often estimate the amount they will eventually be charging to your credit card, and ask the credit card company to place a "hold" on your account for that estimated amount. This is done to ensure that you will have enough available credit on your account to cover the total amount owed to the hotel or car rental company when you check out or when you return the rental car. If you make your payment with a different credit card from the card you used when you first checked in, the first card company (the company that issued the card you used when you checked in) may still be waiting for the hotel or car rental company to post the final charge to your account, and may not agree to release the "hold" on your account until the hotel or car rental company authorizes them to release the "hold" (by telling them that you have paid your bill with a different credit card). Ask the hotel or car rental company to contact your credit card company about releasing the "hold" on your account, or give your credit card company a copy of your final hotel or car rental bill and a copy of your credit card charge receipt showing that you used a different credit card to pay that bill.

—**Answer by Elizabeth C. Yen, Hudson Cook, LLP, New Haven, Connecticut**

cards. While most retailers selling to Iowa consumers may not charge rates on their store credit cards higher than Iowa law permits, some major retailers have made arrangements with banks headquartered in South Dakota (or other states with no rate ceiling on bank cards) to have those banks issue credit cards for use only at the retailers' store locations. In such instances, the bank-issued store credit cards are generally subject to the laws of the state where the bank is headquartered. Of course, competition forces banks and retailers to keep their rates in line with those charged by other financial institutions and retailers. In this particular South Dakota example the pressures of the marketplace—the choices made by informed consumers—set the rates. The law does not set them.

Nonetheless, if you believe that you are being charged a rate that violates state law, you should report your case to the Office of Consumer Protection (or a similar office), your state's attorney general, or the federal authorities for national banks or federal credit unions (depending on whether the credit card is issued by a national bank, a federal credit union, or some other type of financial institution). Consult the appendix of this book for information about where to go in the event of such problems. As explained above, competition and enforcement activities usually prevent such violations on the part of credit card issuers, but if there is a violation, you may be able to recover some or all of your finance charges plus a penalty, depending upon the applicable state's law.

THE WORLD AT YOUR FINGERTIPS

- The Federal Reserve Board website contains useful information about choosing a credit card at *www.federalreserve.gov/pubs/SHOP/default.htm.*
- The Federal Trade Commission provides a useful fact sheet for consumers, "Choosing and Using Credit Cards," at *www.ftc.gov/bcp /conline/pubs/credit/choose.htm.*
- Cardtrak is a resource that provides information—APRs, annual fees, and so on—about different credit cards, and is a useful tool when shopping for a credit card, at *www.cardweb.com/cardtrak/.* Other websites like *www.kiplinger.com* provide similar information. In addition, many large banks offer information on their websites about the cards they offer.
- For a detailed overview of credit cards, from their history to the meaning of all types of charges, see *money.howstuffworks.com/credit-card1.htm.*
- For an excellent resource from Fair Isaac explaining credit

scoring, see *www.myfico.com/Offers/myFICO_UYCS%20booklet.
pdf.*
• The Federal Trade Commission has a publication entitled
"Privacy: Tips for Protecting Your Personal Information," available
online at *www.ftc.gov/bcp/conline/pubs/alerts/privtipsalrt.htm.*

REMEMBER THIS

• All credit cards are different. Selecting one is a decision that
should be made carefully. You want and need a good fit.
• Remember that federal law requires credit card companies
to disclose the costs of credit to you, the consumer. They must
tell you the APR, finance charges, how finance charges are com-
puted, and a host of other financial information.
• However, bear in mind that the Truth in Lending Act (TILA)
is primarily a disclosure statute. It does not set limits on the interest rates that credit card companies may charge.
• Some cards do not offer fixed APRs. Many cards have variable rates, usually tied to an interest rate index. If you plan to
use your card for cash advances, carefully consider the cash advance fee. Credit card companies use different methods to calculate the balance upon which you pay finance charges. Pay
attention to this methodology when you receive a credit card ad-
vertisement.
• The APR, fees, finance charge grace periods, and other
terms and conditions of a credit card may change after the account is opened, in many cases after the credit card company
gives you fifteen days' advance written notice of the change.
• Identity thieves would love to get their hands on your credit
cards. Guard your cards and know where they are at all times.
• If you have too many credit cards, you could increase the
chance that your total credit repayment obligations might exceed your disposable income, and you could lower your credit
score and overall credit rating.

CHAPTER 5

How to Correct Billing
Mistakes

*Your Rights Under the Fair Credit Billing Act
and Other Consumer Protection Laws*

You receive your credit card bill and are surprised to find it contains a charge for an item you bought and returned the next day. There was plenty of time to reverse the charge before the bill was sent out, but it didn't happen. What can you do? Does the law offer any help?

After you have established credit, the best way to remain in good standing is to repay your debts on time. If you fail to pay a bill, the relevant creditor can hurt your credit record by reporting your delinquent account to credit bureaus.

However, what happens if the creditor makes an error on your bill? What if you are billed for an item that you did not buy or for a product that you returned as defective? This section discusses what you can do to correct creditors' mistakes on your credit card or other revolving (open-end) account.

BILLING ERRORS

Fair Credit Billing Act

Your credit rating will not suffer if there is an error on your account and you bring the error to the attention of the creditor. However, if you don't pay, and you don't bring the error to the attention of the creditor, your rating could suffer.

The Fair Credit Billing Act requires revolving (open-end) account creditors, such as credit card issuers, to correct billing errors promptly. It defines a billing error as a charge on your credit card or other revolving account:

- for something that you didn't buy, or for a purchase made by someone not authorized to use your account;
- that is not properly identified on your monthly account statement, or that is for an amount different from the actual purchase price; or
- for something that you refused to accept on delivery because it was unsatisfactory, or that the supplier did not deliver according to your agreement.

Billing errors may also include

- errors in arithmetic;
- failure to reflect a payment that you made or other credit to your revolving account; or
- failure to mail an account billing statement to your current address (if the creditor received notice of that address at least twenty days before the end of the billing period).

For a summary of mistakes that constitute billing errors in revolving (open-end) accounts, see the Federal Trade Commission's short publication available online at *www.ftc.gov/bcp/conline/pubs/credit/fcb.htm*.

In Case of Billing Errors

If you think your revolving (open-end) bill is incorrect, or if you simply want more details about it, you should take the following steps:

1. In order to preserve your legal rights, notify your creditor in writing of the potential billing error. Many creditors readily handle billing complaints over the phone, and calling is a lot faster and easier than writing a letter—be prepared to provide your name, address, account number, and a description of the error. However, it is safer to send a letter as well, because sending a letter will trigger the protections of the Fair Credit Billing Act.

2. If you aren't satisfied with the results of your phone call, note the name of the person that you talked to and send a letter to the address your creditor has supplied for this purpose so that the creditor receives the notice within sixty days after the bill

was mailed. The sixty-day period is very important. Use the address for billing error inquiries on your account statement—do not send your letter to the address for account payments. If you don't do this, you may lose your rights under the Fair Credit Billing Act. The letter should contain your name, address, and account number. State that you believe your bill contains an error, describe the error and explain why you believe your bill is wrong, and include the date and the suspected amount of the error.

For an example of what may happen if a consumer does not provide sufficient written notice of a billing error to a credit card issuer, see *Conn-Burstein v. Saks Fifth Avenue & Company*. In that case, the federal appeals court upheld a lower court ruling in favor of a store credit card issuer, where the jury had found that a customer's letter did not provide the credit card issuer with enough information to enable the card issuer to identify and investigate the customer's alleged billing error. The court noted that, although the consumer claimed her account had been double-billed for certain purchases, her "letter failed to identify any specific instances of double-billing and failed to specify the amount of any alleged billing error."

▶ KEEP SALES RECEIPTS

One reason to keep sales receipts is so that you may return an item in the event that it is defective, damaged, or the wrong size or color. Another reason to keep sales slips is to protect against billing errors. Most credit and charge card companies do not provide sales slips with your monthly statement; rather, your statement usually gives only the date and amount of purchases and the store where you bought each item. Therefore, you need to keep all sales slips, at least until you have checked them against your monthly credit and charge card billing statements. Keeping your receipts will also enable you to determine whether some unauthorized person is charging purchases to your account.

Duties of the Creditor After Notice

The law requires a revolving (open-end) account creditor to acknowledge your billing error letter within 30 days. (This does not apply if the creditor fixes the billing error within thirty days.) The creditor must investigate and correct your revolving (open-end) account within two billing periods. Fixing the error should never take more than ninety days from the time the creditor receives written notice of your billing dispute. If the creditor does not correct the error, it must tell you in writing why it believes the bill is not wrong.

If the creditor reviews your bill and does not find an error, it must promptly send you a statement showing what you owe. On this statement, the creditor may include any finance charges that accumulated and any minimum payments you missed while you were disputing the bill.

In some cases, consumers may not have to pay finance charges on the contested amounts owed on their revolving accounts under the Fair Credit Billing Act, provided they have sent a written billing error notice. There are two possible outcomes. If the bill is not correct, you do not have to pay the finance charges on the amount that was improperly billed to your account. If you have already paid these amounts, the creditor should refund them. If the bill is correct, you must pay the amounts owed, including finance charges.

Effect on Credit Rating

A creditor may not threaten your credit rating because you fail to pay a disputed amount, a related finance charge, or other charges owed on a revolving account while you're trying to resolve a billing dispute. Once you have taken the required steps described above by writing down your question and sending it to the creditor, the law prohibits your creditor from reporting the account as delinquent because you have not paid the disputed amount or related charges. Until the creditor answers your written billing error notice, the law forbids it from taking any action to collect the amount in dispute. You must, however, continue to pay any undisputed amounts.

However, if the creditor finds that the disputed bill is correct, then you must pay the bill. If you fail to remit payment, then the creditor may take action to collect the amount, and may report you to credit bureaus as overdue for the amount in question.

If the creditor finds that the disputed bill is correct, but you still disagree with this finding, notify the creditor of your views in writing within ten days of receiving the creditor's written explanation to you of why the creditor believes your bill is correct. Then, if the creditor reports your account as past due because of the billing dispute, it must also report that you have challenged the bill, and must give you written notice of the name and address of each person who has been told by the creditor that your account is past due because of the billing error dispute. When you settle the dispute, that outcome must be reported by the creditor to each person who was previously told by the creditor that your account was past due because of the billing error dispute. If you are unable to settle the dispute to your satisfaction, you may want to consult a lawyer.

If the creditor does not follow each of these rules within the time limits required by the Fair Credit Billing Act, then the creditor cannot collect the disputed amount (including finance charges on the disputed amount), even if the disputed bill turns out to be correct and the amount is thus money you truly owed. In addition, the creditor is subject to any remedies available for violations of the Truth in Lending Act.

DEFECTIVE GOODS OR SERVICES

The Fair Credit Billing Act also provides some assistance to certain consumers who purchase certain defective goods or services with a credit card. If you use a credit card to purchase shoddy or

damaged goods or poor-quality services, the Fair Credit Billing
Act might help. If you have not already paid off your credit balance, the FCBA allows you to withhold payment that is still due
for the disputed transaction, provided that you first notify the
card issuer or merchant of your claim or defense, and have made
a real attempt to solve the problem with the merchant. You can
demonstrate such an attempt by providing the card issuer with,
for example, a copy of a letter you have sent to the merchant's
complaint department, or with notes you took at the time you
made a phone call to the complaint department, including the
name of the person with whom you spoke.

You have the right to withhold payment if you bought the
goods or services with a bank card such as Visa® or
MasterCard®, or with a travel or entertainment card, or a store
credit card. For example, if you purchase a tour or air travel
ticket using your credit card, and the tour or airline goes bankrupt before your trip, you may be able to withhold payment on
that charge. However, when you use your credit card, the law
generally limits your right to withhold payment to credit card
charges greater than $50, which took place either in your home
state or within 100 miles of your home address. (The $50 limit
and the home state/100 mile rule do not apply to a purchase

◖◗ TALKING TO A LAWYER

*Q. This chapter has a lot of information on legal protections regarding
credit cards, but in practical terms, how can someone best protect
himself in disputes with a credit card issuer?*

A. Write a letter, send it certified mail, and keep a copy.

—Answer by Marc S. Stern, Law Offices of Marc S. Stern,
Seattle, Washington

charged to a credit card that was issued by the retailer or by a company related to the retailer, and also do not apply to goods or services charged to a credit card as the result of a direct mail solicitation made or participated in by the card issuer.)

If you refuse to pay for a charge on your credit card statement because goods or services are defective, the credit card issuer might sue you for payment. If a court finds the goods or services to be truly defective, you probably won't have to pay for the credit card charge, provided that you tried in good faith to resolve your dispute about the defective goods or services directly with the retailer. Moreover, during the dispute period, the card issuer cannot report the disputed amount to a credit bureau as delinquent.

LOST OR STOLEN CREDIT CARDS

The Truth in Lending Act limits your liability in the event that your credit cards are lost or stolen. It is very important that you notify the credit card company as soon as you notice the loss or theft of one or more of your cards, since you are not responsible for any unauthorized charges made after such notification. Moreover, under TILA, the most you will have to pay for any unauthorized charges made before you notify the credit card company is $50 on each card. However, this limitation of liability does not apply to debit cards.

Being Prepared for Lost or Stolen Credit Cards

As noted in chapter 4, it is a good idea to keep a list of all your credit cards, their account numbers, and the information needed to notify the credit card issuers of theft or loss. Since you may lose credit cards when traveling, always take a copy of this list with you and keep it separate from your credit cards. And be sure to keep the list itself in a safe place, since someone with your account numbers may be able to make purchases on your account, even if he or she does not have the actual cards. Also, it is advisable to keep your Social Security number separate from your credit cards, since some issuers of credit cards use Social Security numbers to check the identities of card users.

THE WORLD AT YOUR FINGERTIPS

- The Federal Trade Commission provides information on the Fair Credit Billing Act, and a sample letter that could be copied and sent to a creditor, at *www.ftc.gov/bcp/conline/pubs/credit/fcb. htm.*
- The Federal Trade Commission also has a helpful publication for consumers that discusses the Fair Credit Billing Act, entitled "Billed for Merchandise You Never Received? Here's What To Do," at *www.ftc.gov/bcp/conline/pubs/credit/billed.htm.*
- The Colorado State University Cooperative Extension published a paper on credit cards that explains consumers' rights under the Fair Credit Billing Act, including when defective goods are purchased on credit cards. It is available at *www.ext. colostate.edu/pubs/consumer/09144.pdf.*
- 'Lectric Law Library provides a concise overview for consumers confronted with billing errors, available online at *www.lectlaw.com/files/cos73.htm.*

REMEMBER THIS

- The Fair Credit Billing Act is the federal law that governs billing errors and the rights of consumers when disputing errors on credit card or other revolving (open-end) accounts. The law establishes time limits for consumers and creditors that are designed to establish a framework for resolving such disputes.
- Make sure that you give written notice of a billing error to the creditor within sixty days after you receive an erroneous bill. This is an important time limitation for consumers. Generally, creditors have thirty days to acknowledge a consumer's written dispute of a credit card charge.

- The Fair Credit Billing Act also provides a degree of protection to consumers who purchase defective goods or services with a credit card, requiring the prompt crediting of payments and providing rights with respect to credit balances on your account.
- The Truth in Lending Act limits your liability for lost or stolen credit cards.

CHAPTER 6

Credit Records

Your Rights Under the Fair Credit Reporting Act

You receive an invitation in the mail for a credit card with an excellent APR, no annual fee, and other favorable terms. You believe this is a good deal and apply for the card. Unfortunately, a short while later you receive a letter from the credit card company denying you credit. You are shocked, because you know that you have excellent credit, have always paid your bills on time, and do not carry large balances. You are mystified as to this development and recognize that your credit report must be flawed. You are not alone. Many people have mistakes on their credit reports.

In 1990, former Illinois Congressman Frank Annunzio said in the House of Representatives, "a poor credit history is the 'Scarlet Letter' of twentieth-century America." The same is true in the twenty-first century. Bad credit can harm many aspects of your life.

Imagine that you are denied credit based on a bad credit history. In denying you credit, the creditor relies on a negative consumer report from a major credit bureau or credit-reporting agency. You request a copy of the credit report from the credit bureau and, much to your dismay, find that the report contains items relating to another individual with the same name, information more than ten years old, and other inaccuracies. What can you do to correct these mistakes on your credit report?

Fortunately, a federal law known as the **Fair Credit Reporting Act** (**FCRA**) is designed to protect consumers from inaccurate information in consumer reports, as well as to protect the privacy of that information. The law, passed in 1970, provides that "whenever a consumer reporting agency prepares a consumer report it shall follow reasonable procedures to assure maximum possible accuracy of the information concerning the individual about whom the report relates." The FCRA regulates

(i) PRIVACY PROTECTION UNDER THE FCRA

The FCRA regulates consumer-reporting agencies to protect the accuracy and privacy of credit information. Chapters 5 and 6 have discussed the accuracy requirements at length. But privacy of credit information is also a very important topic, particularly in this age of identity theft (discussed in chapter 8). In 1996, Congress added a series of amendments to the FCRA that provided additional privacy protection for consumers. As a result, the FCRA now protects consumers' privacy in a number of ways. For example, it prohibits any person from obtaining a credit report without a permissible purpose. The law also limits the release of credit reports to those with a "legitimate business need" for such reports. A "legitimate business need" might arise, for example, if you applied for life insurance, a job, or an apartment, in which case a person might legitimately need to examine your credit report.

The FCRA also generally prohibits so-called target marketing, which occurs when credit issuers make unsolicited contacts with consumers. In a long-running battle between the Federal Trade Commission and TransUnion (one of the three main credit-reporting bureaus), a federal appeals court has ruled that the FTC can prohibit credit bureaus from selling target-marketing lists. The court determined that the ban on target-marketing lists serves the substantial state interest of protecting privacy.

Even though the FCRA prohibits target marketing, it does allow prescreening—the process of selecting individuals for firm (that is, guaranteed) offers of credit or insurance.

The FCRA does, however, recognize the need for consumer privacy with respect to prescreening. To this end, the law provides that any prescreening must allow consumers a way to opt out of future prescreenings. This means that if you receive a prescreened offer, the credit solicitation must include some information in the offer telling you how to avoid receiving such offers in the future.

For additional information, the FTC has a publication entitled "Privacy Choices for Your Personal Financial Information" available online at *www.ftc.gov/bcp/conline/pubs/credit/privchoices.htm#whatstop.*

the behavior not only of credit-reporting agencies, but also of "users" of credit reports prepared by such agencies.

CREDIT BUREAUS

Credit bureaus (sometimes called **credit-reporting agencies** or **consumer-reporting agencies**) maintain records of your financial-payment histories, public-record data, and personal-identifying data. (They do not maintain information about your medical history.) There are three major competing credit-reporting agencies: Experian, Equifax, and TransUnion Credit Information Company. You can find the bureaus serving your area by looking for "credit-reporting companies" in the yellow pages of your phone book. The Fair Credit Reporting Act governs activities of credit bureaus, and several states have enacted similar laws.

Credit bureaus do not make credit decisions. Instead, they provide data to creditors for use in making such decisions. How does this work? Creditors provide information on their customers' debts and payment habits to credit bureaus, usually on a monthly basis. Credit bureaus then make this data available, sometimes online, to other creditors to whom you apply for credit. For this reason, a good credit record is very important to your ability to obtain credit for purchasing goods and services, renting an apartment, or buying a home. Credit reports may also be used when you apply for insurance or for employment.

The availability of credit history information is a key driver in making credit widely available to the American consumer. The information credit bureaus provide to creditors enables the creditors to make credit available to all kinds of consumers quickly, conveniently, and relatively easily. Without credit reports, creditors would be hard pressed to approve credit requests made by telephone or online, where there is no face-to-face opportunity to verify the credit applicant's identity and creditworthiness. We all appreciate the convenient access to credit. However, as with most good things, there are some downsides to this system. Negative information in a credit report (whether accurate or inaccurate) can adversely affect a consumer's ability to obtain credit or it can cause the consumer to pay a higher price for credit. Also, unscrupulous identity thieves can hijack a consumer's credit record, leaving the consumer with a poor credit history that may take many months to correct.

Because credit reports contain highly confidential information, the law permits credit bureaus to disclose credit reports only under very specific circumstances when the requester (such as a creditor) has a legitimate purpose for obtaining the information in connection with a transaction with a consumer. Among the authorized purposes for which credit reports may be furnished are when:

- a consumer applies for credit
- maintenance or collection of a credit account takes place

(i) FURNISHERS OF INFORMATION

The FCRA regulates more than the behavior of credit-reporting agencies or credit bureaus; it also regulates the behavior of those companies that furnish information to credit bureaus. It imposes a duty on furnishers of information to provide accurate information. The law provides that "[a] person shall not furnish any information relating to a consumer to any consumer reporting agency if the person knows or consciously avoids knowing that the information is inaccurate." If a consumer disputes a debt, then the furnisher of information must provide notice of the disputed debt to the credit bureau. Furnishers of information have a further duty to correct and update information.

The **Fair and Accurate Credit Transactions Act of 2003,** better known by the acronym **FACTA,** amended the FCRA. A key change made by the new law is that now consumers may dispute inaccurate information directly with the furnishers of information, as well as with the consumer-reporting agency, as was previously required. Under the new law, consumers can dispute directly with furnishers, who must investigate all disputes and cannot report negative information while an investigation is pending.

- certain credit offers known as prescreened solicitations (like those preapproved credit card offers that sometimes arrive in the mail) occur.

The law punishes unauthorized persons who lie to obtain credit reports, or credit bureau employees who supply credit reports to unauthorized persons. Such persons may receive fines or prison terms, or both, if they are found guilty. In addition, they may also face civil liability, in the form of money damages imposed on them by a court. The law has also been amended to provide protection in relation to identity theft.

Since your credit record is critical to obtaining credit, it is very important that you check to make sure that each item in your credit record accurately reflects your own credit history, and not that of another person. Whenever you apply for credit, you should use the same name. Thus, if you are James R. Jones, Jr., always append the "Jr.," and do not use "J. Randall Jones" sometimes and "J. R. Jones" other times. If you use the same name with every credit application, then your complete credit record will be under one name. You will typically be asked for your Social Security number on a credit application. If you are asked, you should provide it. The request is not made to invade your privacy, but to assure that your credit records do not get mixed in with those of some other person named James Jones. (But remember that you should *only* give out your Social Security number and other confidential information if you have initiated the communication and you are sure about who you are talking to. Never give out your Social Security number or other confidential information to anyone who calls you or sends you an e-mail.)

YOUR CREDIT REPORT

Understanding Your Credit Report

Contrary to popular belief, a credit bureau neither tracks all aspects of your personal life nor explicitly evaluates credit applications. Credit bureaus are simply organizations that collect and transmit four principal types of information: identification and employment data, payment histories, credit-related inquiries, and public-record information.

Though credit bureaus don't evaluate your credit per se, the fact that creditors can request a **risk score summary** from credit bureaus does suggest that such bureaus have a significant effect on your ability to acquire credit.

As required by the Fair and Accurate Credit Transactions Act of 2003, creditors must disclose credit scores to mortgage loan applicants. Later in this chapter, we discuss how to improve a credit score with which you are dissatisfied.

A good credit report is vital to ensuring your access to credit. Therefore, it is important for you to understand and find out what your credit report contains, how to improve your credit report, and how to deal with credit problems.

Checking Your Credit Report

You have the right to know the content of credit files that contain information about you, and many consumer credit experts suggest that you examine these credit files about once a year. A periodic checkup will enable you to find out what information credit bureaus will provide to credit issuers about your credit. Whenever you ask to learn the contents of your file, you will need to provide adequate identification to the credit bureau to ensure that you receive your own report, and not the report of someone with a similar name. These identification procedures also help ensure that others with similar names will not see your credit report inadvertently.

The FCRA allows you to review your file at any time, and it is particularly important for you to do so if you plan to apply for an apartment, a job, a home mortgage loan, or some other major loan or credit purchase. Historically, under the FCRA, a credit bureau was permitted to charge you a reasonable fee for providing this service. However, the Fair and Accurate Credit Transaction Act (FACTA), which was signed into law in December 2003, amended the FCRA in several respects. One of these amendments provides that consumer-reporting agencies must provide consumers with one free credit report per year. Consumers can obtain their free credit report from the nationwide agencies simply by making a phone call. The FCRA and FACTA allow credit bureaus to charge a "reasonable fee" for providing additional credit reports. Recently, the FTC issued a ruling setting the maximum fee, as of January 1, 2005, at $9.50 per report.

Also as required by FACTA, the Federal Trade Commission issued a rule that requires the nationwide consumer-reporting agencies—Equifax, Experian, and TransUnion—to create a "centralized source" for accepting consumer requests for credit reports. This source includes a website, a toll-free telephone number, and a mailing address. The FTC's website has helpful information pertaining to this. Visit the FTC website at *www.ftc.gov*; you'll find the credit information by clicking on "For Consumers," then on "Credit." Free credit reports can be obtained at the credit bureaus' centralized site, which is now up and running: access *www.annualcreditreport.com* or call 877-322-8228.

As noted above, a creditor may turn down your application for credit or take other adverse credit action because of a report from a credit bureau. If you are denied credit or if you are offered less favorable credit terms on the basis of information contained in your credit report, the law requires that the creditor give you the name and address of the bureau from which it obtained your report. You are allowed to request information from the credit bureau by phone, by mail, or in person. If a creditor has denied you credit within the past sixty days because of information supplied by a credit bureau, the bureau must provide your credit report information free of charge (even if you have previously received your one free annual credit report).

Finally, still another provision of FACTA requires that a financial institution that extends you credit must send you a notice before or no later than thirty days after it furnishes negative information about you to a credit bureau. Such negative information includes information about late payments, missed pay-

( ) TALKING TO A LAWYER

Q. It's maddening to find the same mistakes over and over again in a credit report. How can you get rid of information that's just plain wrong?

A. If you have notified the credit bureau and the creditor that the information is being reported incorrectly and the mistake has not been corrected, you can file a complaint with the Federal Trade Commission (which regulates the credit bureaus) and with the creditor's regulator. If you still are unable to get this problem resolved and if the erroneous information has caused you harm or could cause harm in the future, you might consider suing the credit bureau and/or the creditor for failing to fulfill their responsibilities under the Fair Credit Reporting Act to investigate disputed information and make appropriate corrections. FCRA authorizes recovery of your actual damages, plus your attorney's fees and other costs to bring the action and, if the noncompliance with the FCRA is determined to have been willful, punitive damages.

—Answer by Robin K. Warren, Bank of America,
Charlotte, North Carolina

ments, partial payments, or any other form of default. Most creditors provide this notice at the time credit is extended or soon thereafter, informing customers of their practice and what they report to the credit bureaus.

Format of a Credit Report

Credit reports will vary slightly depending on which of the three national credit-reporting bureaus compiles them. Generally, however, the same types of information will be on every credit report, including:

- Identification and employment data: Your name, birth date, Social Security number, addresses (present and former), and employment history.

- Your residential information, including how long you have resided at your current location.

- Public-record information: Events relating to your credit-worthiness that are a matter of public information, such as bankruptcies, foreclosures, tax liens, or court cases, such as a record of a dispute between a consumer and an appliance dealer that was settled in small-claims court.

- Payment history: Your account record with different creditors, showing how much credit has been extended and how you have repaid it.

- Inquiries: Credit bureaus maintain a record of all creditors who have checked your credit record within the past six months, including for prescreening purposes. Prescreening occurs when, for example, credit bureaus enable issuers of credit cards to develop mailing lists to which they can distribute preapproved offers for their cards. Credit bureaus typically do not include credit-prescreening inquiries in credit reports for credit issuers, though they will provide records of prescreening inquiries to consumers as part of their disclosure duties under the law.

- Credit score: Your credit score and a list of the factors that most affected that score. Such factors could include the number of delinquencies with which you are credited, the average balance on your revolving accounts, and the collection amounts you owe.

Correcting Your Credit Record

If you find that information in your credit report is inaccurate, incomplete, or outdated, you may challenge its accuracy or completeness by notifying the credit bureau. You can contact the agencies by phone or online, as follows:

Equifax: 1-800-685-1111, or *www.equifax.com*
Experian: 1-888-397-3742, or *www.experian.com*

TransUnion: 1-800-916-8800, or *www.transunion.com/
                index.jsp*

Unless it believes that your request is "frivolous or irrele-
vant," the credit bureau must reinvestigate and either verify the
disputed information within thirty days or delete the information from its files. (The "frivolous-or-irrelevant" provision is
there in part to deal with certain credit repair clinics, discussed
in chapter 14, that challenge all negative information in a person's credit report, whether there is a basis for such a challenge
or not.) If your complaint is justified, the credit bureau will automatically notify the other bureaus of the change and, if you request it, notify you of any creditor that has checked your file in
the past six months. The bureau will also notify you of anyone
who has made an employment-related check of your credit
within the last two years.

STATING A CLAIM UNDER THE FCRA

The vast majority of courts have determined that the FCRA provides a private right of action for individual consumers. In order to
make a claim under the FCRA, a consumer must establish that:
(1) inaccurate information was included in his or her credit report; (2) the inaccuracy was caused by the consumer-reporting
agency's failure to follow reasonable procedures to assure maximum possible accuracy; (3) he or she suffered an injury; and (4)
the injury was caused by the inaccuracy in his or her credit report.

Credit-reporting agencies are not strictly liable for posting
inaccurate information. In other words, the mere fact that there
is inaccurate information on a person's credit report does not automatically mean that a credit-reporting agency must pay that
person monetary damages. If a credit-reporting agency shows
that it followed reasonable procedures under the circumstances,
it will not be liable. (Note: There is a two-year statute of
limitations for bringing claims for inaccurate information under
the FCRA.)

( ) TALKING TO A LAWYER

Q. *The law says you can put up your version of a dispute on a credit report, but does anyone pay attention to that? What can I do to avoid having a dispute hurt my credit rating—besides paying the disputed amount, of course?*

A. If you dispute an item on your credit report, it is always a good idea to make sure that the report gives your side of the story. Creditors will look at that information and will consider it, but if you are turned down for credit you should contact the creditor to call attention to the dispute and make sure that your side of the story was considered. Keep in mind that a single isolated adverse item on a credit report ordinarily can be overcome if all of the other reported credit accounts show that you have a history of making timely payments.

—Answer by Robin K. Warren, Bank of America,
Charlotte, North Carolina

Q. *I was laid off from my job last year and had trouble keeping up with payments on my loans and credit cards until I was able to land a new job. I'm thinking about buying a home, but I know that my credit history will hurt me. I've gotten solicitations from a company that says it can repair my credit history. Can they really help me clean up my credit record?*

A. There is little that a credit repair clinic can do to alter the payment history reflected on your credit report. Beware of firms that claim that, for a fee, they can clean up your credit record. These firms will sometimes try to get you to "game" the system by repeatedly disputing legitimate information on your credit report so that reporting on the negative items is suspended while your "disputes" are being investigated. If you apply for credit while the negative information is suspended, they contend that what your prospective creditors can't see won't hurt you. Some credit repair companies will charge sizable fees up front and then either will not do anything you can't already do yourself (like disputing erroneous information on your credit report) or will engage in conduct of questionable legality. For more information about how to avoid becoming a victim of a credit repair scam, check out the FTC's brochure "Credit Repair: Self Help May Be Best" at *www.ftc.gov/bcp/conline/pubs/credit/repair.htm.*

Assuming that the information being reported about your payment history is accurate, the best thing you can do to clean up your record is to continue building a current record of paying your bills on time. Pay down or pay off any credit card debt as soon as you are able. The best cure is time (usually a minimum of twelve months) and a current record of prompt payments and paying off credit card debt. Before you make an offer on a house you want to buy, go talk to a mortgage lender to explain your situation and find out what the lender will want you to show in order to overcome the negative credit history while you were unemployed.

—**Answer by Robin K. Warren, Bank of America, Charlotte, North Carolina**

Q. *I am recently divorced. When I went to apply for a car loan recently, I discovered that my credit report shows a delinquent payment history on my mortgage loan. The mortgage loan was a joint account in my name and my ex-spouse's name. Under our divorce agreement, my ex-spouse was responsible for making the mortgage payments. What can I do to delete this negative information from my credit report?*

A. Even though you and your ex-spouse agreed that he or she would be responsible for making payments on the mortgage, the mortgage lender did not agree to release you from responsibility for the loan. Although you might not be able to get the negative history removed from your credit report, there are some things you can do. First, the Federal Reserve's regulations that implement the Equal Credit Opportunity Act require the creditors to consider, at your request, information that indicates that the credit history on the credit report does not accurately reflect your creditworthiness. You should explain your situation to the auto lender. Be prepared to provide a copy of the legal agreement or court order that makes your ex-spouse responsible for paying on the account. The auto lender must take this information into consideration, but that doesn't necessarily mean that the lender must or will disregard the negative information.

—Answer by Robin K. Warren, Bank of America,
Charlotte, North Carolina

Your Right to Sue

Under the Fair Credit Reporting Act, you have the right to bring a lawsuit against any credit bureau or creditor that violates any provisions of the Act. This includes any credit-reporting agency that fails to observe the restrictions about who may access your credit file, and any credit bureau that does not properly investigate and correct

( ) TALKING TO A LAWYER

Q. Is it worthwhile to sue a credit-reporting agency if its incompetence hurts you?

A. Suing is rarely worthwhile, but sometimes it's something that you need to do. You need to decide how much damage the reporting agency's incompetence cost you and, more importantly, what this continued incompetence will cost you in the future. You must then weigh this against the cost of a lawsuit, which will consist of the attorney's fees and costs. They also include the amount of time you will have to spend dealing with the issue, the stress it will cause in your life, and emotional distress that being involved with the lawsuit will bring.

Is it worthwhile, then? This is a subjective decision that incorporates all of the above.

—Answer by Marc S. Stern, Law Offices of Marc S. Stern,
Seattle, Washington

◖◗ TALKING TO A LAWYER

Q. I recently applied for a credit card and was shocked when I was turned down because of loans that were "charged off" or in "collections." I have always paid my accounts on time and I'm not aware of any that were in a collection status. What can I do about this?

A. If you were turned down for credit because of information in a credit report, you have the right to request that the credit bureau send you a free copy of the report. The creditor should have sent you an adverse action letter that shows the name and address of the credit bureau from which the creditor purchased a credit report on you. When you get your report, check to see if all of your accounts accurately report your payment history. If any account histories are incorrect, contact the creditors on those accounts immediately to dispute the information and request that the creditor investigate and correct the information reported. You may initiate this request by phone, but be sure to follow up in writing because the law imposes obligations on the creditors and credit bureaus only when they receive written requests.

When you get your credit report, you may discover that it lists accounts with which you are unfamiliar. Could these be accounts that you co-signed or guaranteed for someone else (for example a relative or a close friend)? If so, then the creditor has correctly included those accounts in your credit history. If the person for whom you co-signed did not pay on time or failed to pay at all on an account, you are legally responsible. Contact the creditor to find out the current status of the account. The creditor might agree to remove the account from your credit history or remove the negative information about the account if you agree to bring the account current or pay it off.

If there are unfamiliar accounts that you know you neither opened nor co-signed or guaranteed, it is possible that you have been the victim of identity theft. Someone may have used your good name and credit history to get credit and then leave you holding the bag. If that's the case, you should notify the credit bureau and the creditor immediately that the account is not yours. For more information on what to do if you are a victim of identity theft, see chapter 8.

—Answer by Robin K. Warren, Bank of America,
Charlotte, North Carolina

inaccurate data in your file that you have disputed. However, if an agency has followed reasonable procedures, it has obeyed the law.

If you win a lawsuit brought under the FCRA, you are entitled to receive actual damages (which might include lost wages for a job you did not get or the amount of additional interest you paid because you could not obtain a loan on the best credit terms). These are subject in some cases to a minimum but also to a maximum amount. You may be entitled to punitive damages if you prove the violation was intentional. If you are successful, you will also receive court costs and a reasonable amount for lawyers' fees.

Effect of Time on Credit Reports

Under the FCRA, most negative information (such as late payments, accounts charged off, and so forth) may only be maintained on your credit record for seven years. There are a few exceptions, which include: criminal convictions (no time limit); bankruptcy information (generally ten years); information provided in response to an application for a salaried job of more than $75,000 per year (no time limit); information provided in response to an application for more than $150,000 worth of credit or life insurance (no time limit); and information about a lawsuit or unpaid judgment (seven years or the length of the applicable statute of limitations—whichever is longer).

THE WORLD AT YOUR FINGERTIPS

• The text of the Fair Credit Reporting Act can be found online at *www.fair-credit-reporting-act.com/index.htm.*
• The Federal Trade Commission publishes a useful summary of your rights under the Fair Credit Reporting Act, which in-

cludes information on whom to contact in the event of a complaint, at *www.ftc.gov/bcp/conline/edcams/fcra/summary. htm*.

• The Federal Reserve Board has a section on credit histories and records in its Consumer Handbook to Credit Protection Laws, at *www.federalreserve.gov/pubs/consumerhdbk/histories. htm*. The same handbook contains other relevant information in the chapter entitled "Other Aspects of Using Credit," at *www. federalreserve.gov/pubs/consumerhdbk/aspects.htm*.

• TransUnion has a sample credit report available online at *www.transunion.com/Documents/samplecreditreport.pdf*.

• The Fair and Accurate Credit Transactions Act of 2003 amended the FCRA in numerous ways. For an overview and summary of these amendments, see the National Consumer Law Center's summary of the new law at *www.nclc.org/initiatives/ facta/contents/nclc_analysis_content.html*.

• The Consumer Data Industry Association provides general information for consumers on credit reporting and the laws governing the credit reporting industry at *www.cdiaonline. org/consumers.cfm*.

• The Federal Trade Commission provides information on how to obtain free credit reports, as well as general information about consumers' rights under the Fair Credit Reporting Act at *www.ftc.gov/bcp/conline/edcams/credit/ycr_free_reports.htm*.

• Two other useful publications about credit bureaus are *The Credit Reporting Dispute Resolution Process* and *Credit Reports, Credit Reporting Agencies and the FCRA*. These publications are also available in Spanish and can be obtained by writing to:

Associated Credit Bureaus

1000 Vermont Ave., NW, Suite 200

Washington, DC 20005-4905

REMEMBER THIS

• The Fair Credit Reporting Act (FCRA) gives consumers the right to sue to ensure that their credit reports contain accurate information.

• Most would-be creditors obtain information about consumers from major credit bureaus or credit-reporting agencies when making credit decisions, as well as in connection with the maintenance and collection of credit accounts. These credit bureaus possess files detailing your financial-payment history, data from public records, and personal-identification data. Your credit history should not contain any medical information.

• Since the passage of the Fair and Accurate Credit Transactions Act of 2003 (FACTA), consumers are entitled to one free annual credit report per year. It is important to review your credit report annually in order to confirm that the information being reported about you is accurate and to make sure that you have not been a victim of identity theft.

• The FCRA imposes duties upon creditors and credit bureaus to submit and maintain accurate information on consumers. If you dispute items in your credit report, the applicable credit bureau must either verify the disputed information within a reasonable period of time or remove the information from its files.

• Negative information does not stay on your credit report for life. Most information must be removed after seven years. However, records of bankruptcies can be reported for ten years.

CHAPTER 7

Internet Credit

Your Rights in Cyberspace

Every month, you balance your checkbook using your bank statements. Much to your chagrin, one month you notice that your bank statement includes two identical withdrawals from an ATM on the same date, but you know that you only made one withdrawal on that day. Obviously, an error was made. You go to the bank to speak to a representative, who assures you that you are in error. What recourse do you have? How can you contest what you believe to be "double-dipping" from your bank account? Fortunately, a law known as the Electronic Funds Transfer Act provides relief to consumers in such situations.

The Electronic Funds Transfer Act focuses on deposit accounts, savings accounts, and other types of consumer "asset" accounts (not consumer "credit" accounts) involved with electronic fund transfers. The world of electronic withdrawals and transfers is new and fluid, and we take the opportunity in this chapter to discuss a wide range of transactions under new technology.

In the past, commerce primarily consisted of transactions conducted using cash, checks, and credit cards at merchants' physical places of business. Today, commerce has changed dramatically, and many consumers now shop for their goods over the Internet, using credit cards to make online purchases. Other consumers use debit cards for their online transactions, simply entering their four-digit PINs (personal identification numbers) and having the money for their purchases immediately debited from their accounts. According to the Federal Reserve, use of electronic payment methods (including credit and debit cards) surpassed the use of checks in 2003. E-commerce creates greater ease and convenience for us as consumers.

But problems can arise in the world of electronic commerce,

just as in the world of physical commerce. Ultimately, even a marketplace that relies heavily on computers is not immune to human error.

ELECTRONIC FUNDS TRANSFER ACT

In 1978, Congress amended the Consumer Credit Protection Act through passage of the **Electronic Funds Transfer Act** (**EFTA**). The stated purpose of the EFTA was "to provide a basic framework establishing the rights, liabilities, and responsibilities of participants in electronic fund transfer systems." Its primary objective, as the law itself states, is "the provision of individual consumer rights."

Recent amendments to the EFTA require automatic teller machines (ATMs) to disclose to you any fees that you must pay to withdraw money from them. Usually, a consumer who does not have an account with a particular bank must pay an extra $1.50 or $2.00 to withdraw money from one of that bank's ATMs.

In addition, the EFTA applies to several kinds of electronic fund transfers to and from consumers' checking and savings accounts, including ATM transactions, point-of-sale purchases, certain pay-by-phone transactions, and automated clearinghouse transactions. There is a Federal Reserve Board proposal to extend coverage to payroll cards, in which your employer directly deposits your pay and you can access the account with a card, and to also apply the law to all electronic conversion services where information from your check is used to initiate an electronic transfer at a store rather than using a debit card. It also applies to direct deposits—transactions in which an employer, insurance company, or pension plan may send a monthly paycheck or monthly or quarterly disability or retirement payments directly to your checking or savings account. The EFTA is an important law, particularly given recent exponential growth in the number of electronic fund transfers. The Electronic Payment Association reports that the use of debit cards has been growing at about a 25 percent rate *per year* in the past several years; the association reports that electronic payments are rising at about a 13 percent rate per year.

Another provision of the EFTA provides that neither creditors nor employers (nor anyone else) may require you to repay loans "by means of preauthorized electronic fund transfers" from a consumer-purpose checking or savings account, nor can they require consumers to set up an account for receipt of electronic fund transfers with a particular financial institution as a condition of employment. Lenders may, however, offer cost-related incentives (such as interest rate or closing cost reductions) to encourage borrowers to agree to repay their loans automatically each month by electronic debiting of their checking or savings account.

Paying Bills Online

Almost all banks now offer a service enabling consumers to pay their bills online. Consumers can usually arrange payments of regular bills—including rent, mortgage payments, and insurance payments—and bills that change every month, like utilities. Many banks offer incentives to consumers who make the change from writing checks to paying bills online. According to banks, online customers tend to be better customers, in that they save administrative costs by receiving online statements instead of paper, and make fewer calls to call centers.

If you pay your bills online, you will not receive a separate receipt for each electronic payment you've pre-authorized. This may mean that you'll need to pay extra careful attention to your bank statement to ensure that the right amount has been paid. You can stop regular payments by giving notice to your bank three days before the scheduled transfer. Your bank may require further written notice within fourteen days.

Consumer Liability

If there is an unauthorized electronic transfer from your checking or savings account, you can limit the amount of your loss to

$50 if you notify the bank of the unauthorized activity within two business days after you discover the loss or theft of your ATM or debit card or your personal identification number (PIN). However, if you fail to provide such notification, you could be liable for up to $500 in unauthorized electronic transfers. If you do not provide notification to the bank of an unauthorized electronic transfer within sixty days after the bank sent you the account statement showing that unauthorized transfer, you could lose an even greater amount of money. For this reason, you must take great pains to make sure that you retain control over your debit and ATM cards and PINs at all times, and you must carefully review your checking and savings account statements for possible unauthorized transfers, immediately after you receive those statements.

The law provides guidelines for identifying and correcting errors in electronic transfers. You have sixty days from the time a periodic statement is sent to dispute an electronic charge. The bank then has ten business days to conduct an investigation, though it can take up to forty-five days more if it provisionally recredits the money to you in the meantime.

If the bank determines there was an error, it must correct it and notify you within one business day after it determines that an error occurred. If the bank determines that there was not an error, it must notify you in writing within three business days of making that determination. (See above sidebar, "The Law in Action," for details about what can happen if a bank fails to provide the required notice.) The bank must also supply an explanation and notify you of your right to receive a copy of the documents that the bank used to make its findings.

Under the EFTA, consumers must first consent to automatic deductions from their account and can order banks to stop making such deductions. If a consumer requests a stop payment of a particular regularly scheduled automatic payment three business days or more before the scheduled date of the automatic deduction, the bank must comply with the request. (To permanently stop future automatic payments to a particular business from your checking or savings account, you should notify the business and make alternative payment arrangements with the business.)

If you notice a discrepancy or error with respect to an automatic-payment deduction, contact your financial institution immediately. Document your discussion; it is usually prudent to follow up telephone requests with written documentation. Specifically, the Federal Trade Commission recommends that you notify the financial institution by certified letter, return receipt requested, so you can prove that the institution received your letter, and that you keep a copy of the letter for your records.

The Federal Trade Commission offers several tips for consumers who make electronic fund transfers (EFTs) with debit or ATM cards. One FTC publication suggests that you should keep your EFT receipts and compare them to your periodic bank statements, just as you compare your credit card receipts with your monthly credit card statements.

ELECTRONIC CHECKS

More and more businesses are converting the paper checks you write into electronic payments made directly from your checking account. These are also known as **e-checks.** When a business uses e-checks, a store clerk processes information from your paper check through an electronic system that records your bank account information and the amount of the check. The store then asks you to sign a receipt, a copy of which you may keep for your records. The store presents information from your check to your bank electronically, and the funds are transferred electronically to the store's account. A store must tell you if it is processing your checks electronically and, in many instances, you may be able to pay for your purchase with a credit card or a debit card if you do not want to have your paper check converted to an electronic check.

It is important for consumers to realize that there is no "float" when they use e-checks—that is, no waiting period before

(i) THE LAW IN ACTION

FACTS

The 1986 case *Bisbey v. D.C. National Bank,* involved a bank customer who set up monthly debits from her account to pay for life insurance premiums. For two consecutive months, her account had insufficient funds to make the required payments, and no transfers were made to cover her insurance premiums. In each case, her bank made the required payment and sent the customer an overdraft notice. The customer, however, having forgotten her nonpayment in the first month, believed that the bank had erroneously made two payments from her account in the second month.

The customer informed a bank employee of what she thought was a double-withdrawal error, and confirmed her complaint in writing. Ten days later, an official of the bank telephoned the customer and orally explained to her that there had been no improper duplication of her premium payments. The customer remained unsatisfied, and eventually filed suit under the EFTA. The bank argued that it had not violated the EFTA, in part because the consumer had not been harmed. In fact, the bank argued, the consumer had benefited because the bank had paid her insurance premiums, which otherwise would have remained unpaid.

DECISION

In finding for the plaintiff, the *Bisbey* court focused on the plain language of the EFTA, which provides in pertinent part:

If [a] financial institution determines after its investigation . . . that an error did not occur, it shall deliver or mail to the consumer an explanation of its findings within three business days after the conclusion of its investigation, and upon request of the consumer, promptly deliver or mail to the consumer reproductions of all documents which the financial institution relied on to conclude that

such error did not occur. The financial institution shall include notice of the right to request reproductions with the explanation of its
findings. (793 F.2d 315 (D.C. Cir. 1986))

Though admitting it seemed "odd" for the consumer to win her case
when the bank's disputed transactions had actually benefited her, the
appeals court nonetheless sided with the consumer on account of the
statute's plain language. Specifically, the appeals court noted that
the bank had not complied with the provision of the EFTA quoted
above, because it had provided the customer only with oral, and not
with written, notice. (Today, under certain conditions, the notice may
be electronic, but that does not include oral notice.) Furthermore, the
bank had failed to give the consumer notice of her right to request reproductions of the documents on which it had relied to reach its con-
clusions. The appeals court remanded the case to a lower court,
ordering the bank to pay attorney's fees and what would likely be only
a nominal damage award to the plaintiff.

The lesson of the *Bisbey* case is that banks and other financial institutions must comply with the statutory language of the EFTA or face
civil liability, including liability for attorneys' fees.

the amount of the check is debited from their account. Checks
processed electronically are processed immediately. This means
that you don't have an extra day or two to deposit funds into your
account to cover the amount of an electronic check. If a paper
check you write is converted to an electronic check, and the
electronic check bounces, both your bank and the store may
charge you fees. And, of course, bounced checks (including
bounced electronic checks) can tarnish your credit record.

Much of this "float" discussion applies equally to "substitute
checks" created as a result of federal Check 21 legislation.
Check 21 is a federal law that is designed to enable banks to
handle more checks by transferring check images electronically
instead of by paper. Because of this law, checks may be processed
faster, meaning less of a float period.

⚠️ AUTOMATIC-DEBIT SCAMS

The Federal Trade Commission has warned consumers about an automatic-debit scam perpetrated by some telemarketers. The scenario works like this: A telemarketer calls to say that you have won a free prize or have qualified for a major credit card. At some point during the call, the telemarketer asks for your checking account number, which he explains the offer or prize requires. Then he or she puts that number on a computer-printed paper "demand draft." This is processed like a check but, unlike a check, does not require your signature. The telemarketer is then able to withdraw funds from your account.

As a precaution, the FTC warns that you should never give out your checking account number over the phone unless you know the company requesting it and the reason they have requested the number. For additional information, see the FTC publication "Automatic Debit Scams," at *www.ftc.gov/bcp/conline/pubs/tmarkg/debit.htm.*

INTERNET LOANS

Obtaining a loan used to require a trip to the bank or other lending office to speak with a bank manager or loan officer. In the past, this process often required several trips. Now, in the twenty-first century, the process is much easier. People can obtain certain types of loans right over the Internet from consumer direct-lender companies and/or loan brokers such as E-loan, which has a website at *www.eloan.com.* On various websites, consumers can apply for a whole range of loans: mortgage loans, home equity loans, personal loans, and much more, including extensions of credit to buy a car.

Internet loans are a part of the growing field of e-commerce, which accounts for billions of dollars in consumer spending each year. Just as the credit card industry revolutionized the way consumers spend money, Internet loan sites have made it that much easier for consumers to acquire more credit. The potential pitfall of this convenience is that consumers now have a heightened ability to overextend themselves financially. Another potential pitfall of e-loans is the problem of identity theft, to be discussed in chapter 8.

THE WORLD AT YOUR FINGERTIPS

• The Electronic Payments Association has a website that provides a great deal of helpful information to consumers, including a variety of tips for avoiding losses from electronic payments, at *www.nacha.org/*.

• The Federal Trade Commission has a host of publications available online to help consumers understand e-commerce. These include:

   • "Credit, ATM and Debit Cards: What to do if They're Lost or Stolen," available at *www.ftc.gov/bcp/conline/pubs/credit/atmcard.htm*.

   • "A Consumer's Guide to E-Payments," available at *www.ftc.gov/bcp/conline/pubs/online/payments.htm*.

   • "FTC Facts for Consumers: E-Checks (Electronic Check Conversion)," available at *www.ftc.gov/bcp/conline/pubs/credit/echeck.pdf*.

REMEMBER THIS

• The Electronic Funds Transfer Act is a consumer protection statute designed to provide a remedy for consumers when monies are wrongfully taken from their checking or savings account through some type of electronic-payment transaction.

• If you report an electronic payment loss within two business days after you discover the loss or theft of your ATM or debit card or your personal identification number (PIN), you will not be responsible for more than $50 of any unauthorized use of your card or PIN (e.g., someone steals your ATM card and withdraws a large amount of money). If you report the loss within sixty days after your bank sent you the account statement showing the unauthorized transfer, your maximum exposure is $500 for unauthorized use of your card or PIN. If you miss the sixty-day deadline, you could lose all the money in your account.

• More and more stores are using electronic checks, in which merchants turn your paper checks into an electronic payment. Remember that you don't have time to "float" checks when the merchant is making electronic payments. You also lose the float period with substitute checks under the new Check 21 legislation.

CHAPTER 8

Identity Theft

What It Is and How to Protect Yourself

You open your mail and suffer a horrible shock. You have received a credit card statement for a card you never applied for and, worse yet, the statement includes a bill for thousands of dollars worth of merchandise that you never purchased. Welcome to the not-so-wonderful world of identity theft.

You should be aware of the growing problem (some have called it an epidemic) of **identify theft,** or **ID theft.** The Identity Theft Resource Center (*www.idtheftcenter.org*) refers to it as the "nation's fastest growing crime." Others have called it "the crime of the new millennium."

There are different types of identity theft, a term that is used to cover a variety of fraudulent activities. The FTC and others label lots of different kinds of fraud "identity theft." The problem is that using this one label for everything blurs important distinctions that have ramifications for consumers. Consumers' rights and liabilities can vary depending upon which of three types of fraud they've been the victims of. Here are three major types of "identity theft" and their legal ramifications:

1. **Basic fraud:** Someone uses your credit card or debit card number to make purchases. This can happen either through loss/theft of the card or by someone using your card number to make telephone or online purchases (or to produce a phony credit card). Though there may be some fraudulent transactions on your account, your identity hasn't been compromised. Your credit report, for example, will not show any accounts that aren't truly your accounts.

If fraudulent (or other unauthorized) credit card or debit card transactions appear on your account, you should notify the card issuer immediately. For unauthorized credit card transactions, The Truth in Lending Act limits your liability to no more than $50 for unauthorized transactions. Many card issuers will waive the $50 liability and not hold the consumer liable for any of the unauthorized transactions.

Unauthorized debit card transactions are covered by the Electronic Funds Transfer Act (EFTA). Under EFTA, you can have unlimited liability for unauthorized transactions if you do not notify the card issuer within sixty days after an unauthorized transaction first appeared on an account statement. Liability for debit card transactions that occur prior to that sixty-day window is generally limited to $50, but can be as much as $500 if you were aware that your card was lost or stolen and failed to report it to the card issuer. As with TILA liabilities, many debit card issuers voluntarily waive their rights and do not hold consumers liable for any unauthorized transactions if the consumer provides prompt notice.

It is important, therefore, to be on the lookout for your monthly account statements and notify the card issuer if a statement fails to arrive when expected or reflects erroneous or unauthorized transactions. Review your account agreements or contact your card issuers to learn whether they offer greater protections than those afforded by TILA or EFTA.

2. **Account Takeover:** Someone, posing as you, contacts your card issuer or bank to notify it of a change of address. The card issuer begins mailing your credit card or checking account statement to a new address. Some time after changing the address on your account, the fraudster, again posing as you, requests a new credit or debit card to be mailed to him or her at "your" new address. The fraudster is betting that it may be several months before you notice that you haven't received a credit card bill or a checking account statement. Meanwhile, the fraudster is racking up hundreds or thousands of dollars worth of purchases and they're being billed to your account.

As with basic fraudulent transactions, your liability for these transactions is limited by TILA and EFTA. If you want to avoid potentially unlimited liability for debit card transactions, be sure that you maintain an awareness of when your checking account statement should arrive each month and notify your bank if the statement doesn't arrive when you expect it.

There's another risk with account takeover, though. Because you aren't receiving your account statement each month, you might not be aware that you are incurring other charges, like late payment fees or overlimit fees on your credit card or overdraft charges on your checking account. Your card issuer should reverse those fees after you notify it that you've been the victim of an account takeover. Be sure to insist that the card issuer also update any credit reports it furnished to the credit bureaus to delete any slow payment or overdraft history previously reported as a result of the fraudulent activity.

3. **True Identity Theft:** Someone, posing as you, opens one or more accounts in your name. They use your personally identifiable information, such as a Social Security number and other confidential information, to open up new accounts. They could be credit card accounts, automobile purchases they've financed in your name, cell phone accounts, or checking accounts. The bottom line is that someone is using your good name to get access to money, goods, or services.

Identity thieves will sometimes keep these accounts current and in good standing for months at a time, usually by obtaining new credit to pay the old credit. Often, it can be months before the victim discovers that these accounts have been opened. Maybe you learn about it when you start getting calls and letters from collectors about accounts you know nothing about. Maybe you learn about it when you apply for credit and get turned down because of negative information on your credit report. Maybe you learn about it when you order your free credit report. In at least one truly awful instance, a grandmother discovered she was the victim of identity theft only after she was arrested. A warrant for her arrest had been sworn out by a merchant after the ID thief had written a bad check on an account opened in the victim's name.

Because accounts established as the result of true identity theft are not yours and were never yours, you have no liability for any of them—not the first $50, not the first $500, not the first penny. And the creditors who established the accounts (who, like you have been victimized by the ID thief) should update their records so that these accounts are not reported to the credit bureaus in your name.

The rest of this chapter focuses on the laws dealing with true identity theft and what you can do to protect yourself from it.

THE WAYS AND MEANS OF IDENTITY THIEVES

It's pretty easy to steal someone's identity. If your credit card is ever in the hands of another person—for example, a waiter at a restaurant—that person could easily run it through a small device designed to read and store the magnetic strips on the backs of credit cards. Such devices, called "skimmers," are readily available, and sell for around $100. The thief could then load the data from your credit card onto another credit card and use it at his or her will.

Consumers need to realize that their personal information is a valuable commodity. Many identity thieves are resourceful, and will employ a variety of means to obtain information to wreak havoc on the unsuspecting, trusting, and unaware. If Social Security numbers, bank account numbers, or credit card numbers fall into the wrong hands, they can easily be used by imposters to rack up fraudulent charges in unheard-of amounts.

Identity thieves use a variety of methods to obtain information. Some will steal a person's mail to obtain his or her key information. Others will complete change-of-address forms to send an unsuspecting person's mail to a location that they can access. Sometimes thieves will steal records from victims' employers, hack into an organization's computers, or pose as employers themselves. Some identity thieves will even rummage through trash cans or dumpsters to locate account numbers in a practice called **dumpster diving.**

When they obtain this information, identity thieves may go on spending sprees, buying up lots of merchandise before finding new victims. Some identity thieves will open up new accounts, thus leaving their theft victims with damaged credit reports—through no fault of the victims. Thieves may even take out loans in a victim's name, or open up a bank account in a victim's name and use it to write bad checks.

PREVENTING IDENTITY THEFT

There are several steps you can take to minimize your exposure to identity thieves:

• Be careful to whom you reveal personally identifiable information such as your Social Security number. Do not give out this kind of information over the phone or online, unless you know the person or institution with whom you are dealing.

• Make a mental note of the dates each month you receive your regular bills. If you do not receive a bill from a regular creditor around the date you expect it, contact your creditor to make sure that it still has your current address. An identity thief may have changed your billing address so that he or she could use your account to run up charges without you noticing.

• Use passwords for your bank and credit card accounts. Do not use easily obtainable passwords such as your mother's maiden name or the name of your spouse. If you write your password down, keep it in a safe place.

• Guard your mail, and even your trash, from theft. When you throw away credit card and loan application offers, make sure that you thoroughly tear up all of the relevant paperwork. Don't make it easy for identity thieves. Inexpensive home shredding machines are readily available and are a good investment. Shred paper account statements, checks or other confidential information before disposing of them.

• Make sure that your computer is updated with the latest antivirus protection. Some viruses may cause your computer to release or send out your personal information or files. Use a firewall on your computer if you have access to the Internet. A firewall will make it much harder for a hacker to invade your computer and files.

ⓘ PHISHING

Consumers should be aware of a new type of identity theft called **phishing.** Phishing involves the fraudulent acquisition of someone's personally identifiable information from the Internet. A typical example involves an Internet user receiving an e-mail telling him or her to update his or her bank or credit card account information. Such e-mails typically contain a link. If the user clicks on this link, he or she will be directed to a copycat website (i.e., a website that looks like the bank or credit card issuer's website) that asks for personal account information. A user who provides his or her information as requested by the copycat website unwittingly provides an identity thief with the tools to commit his or her crime. This problem has become so widespread that Senator Patrick Leahy introduced an anti-phishing Act. For more information on this subject, see Anita Ramasastry's article, "The Anti-Phishing Act of 2004," at *writ. news.findlaw.com/ramasastry/20040816.html.*

• Avoid using automatic log-ins on sites that contain your personal information, such as Internet banking sites. While it might be easier to log in using automatic features, such features could also make it easier for unauthorized users to access your accounts. Make sure to log off every time you are done with a site.

• Pay attention to the privacy policies of various websites. Learn what personal information these sites acquire from you, and how that information is used.

• Be guarded about releasing your Social Security number and other confidential personal information. When asked to provide your Social Security number and other confidential information, ask why the person, business, or employer needs it, how it will be used, how the person or business will protect it, and what will happen if you refuse to provide it.

• As soon as you become aware that one of your credit or debit cards has been stolen, immediately notify the card issuer.

• Check your credit report at least annually to verify that no one has established accounts in your name. It's not unusual for an account opened by an identity thief to be active for several months before the unsuspecting victim discovers what has happened.

WHAT TO DO IF YOU ARE AN IDENTITY THEFT VICTIM

If you are the victim of identity theft, take the following steps as fast as you can:

- place a fraud alert on your credit reports and accounts;
- notify all creditors, banks, or other businesses where fraudulent accounts were opened in your name. Many of them will ask you to complete an affidavit swearing that the accounts are not yours, providing any information you might have about when or how the accounts were established or who the identity thief might be, and agreeing to cooperate with prosecution of the thief when and if he or she is found and brought to justice. (You'd be surprised how often the thief turns out to be a family member or close friend.)
- close any and all accounts that have been compromised by an identity thief. Ask for copies of the applications or other records related to the fraudulent accounts. The Fair and Accurate Credit Transactions Act (FACTA) requires creditors to furnish this information to you;
- notify the police;
- get a copy of your credit report so that you can determine how many other fraudulent accounts there might be; and
- notify the Federal Trade Commission's toll-free ID Theft hotline at: 1-877-IDTHEFT or online at *rn.ftc.gov/pls/dod/widtpubl$ .startup?Z_ORG_CODE=PU03.*

LEGISLATION COMBATING IDENTITY THEFT

There are numerous laws dealing with identity theft, both federal and state. Depending on the type of identity theft involved,

( ) TALKING TO A LAWYER

Q. How can I prove that I'm not a deadbeat but the victim of identity theft?

A. There are several things you can do. Request a copy of the account records, including the documents used to establish the account. The Fair and Accurate Credit Transactions Act (FACTA) entitles you to get these records from the company that opened the account. By reviewing those records, you'll probably find a number of ways to show that the account is fraudulent, for example the signature on the account agreement is not yours. File a police report and send a copy of the report to the company that opened the account. Contact the credit bureaus and make sure they put a fraud alert on your credit report. Creditors will usually request that victims of identity theft or other kinds of fraud complete a form affidavit. The affidavit asks you to swear that the account is not yours, was not established on your behalf and that you did not benefit from the account. The affidavit may also ask you to provide any information you might have about how the identity theft occurred (for example, your credit card was taken when wallet was stolen) or about who the thief is (for example, a former roommate who departed with some of your personal property and had access to your personal information). Finally, the creditor will ask you to verify in the affidavit that you will cooperate with authorities in prosecuting the ID thief if he or she is apprehended. The affidavit, because it is a sworn statement, is an additional indicator of your honesty and good faith in asserting that you have been a victim of identity theft.

—Answer by Robin K. Warren, Bank of America,
Charlotte, North Carolina

consumers can have different remedies. The law on identity theft continues to evolve, as more federal and state laws are passed to address the different forms of identity theft. Those who commit identity theft often will also be in violation of other federal laws, such as laws preventing identification fraud, credit card fraud, computer fraud, mail fraud, wire fraud, and mail theft.

You can contact a local consumer protection agency or attorney general's office to learn more about applicable laws in your jurisdiction. See the appendix of this book for a listing of state consumer protection agencies.

There are several federal laws that deal with the problem of identity theft. The **Identity Theft and Assumption Deterrence Act of 1998** provides that someone commits a crime when he or she "knowingly transfers or uses, without lawful authority, a means of identification of another person with the intent to commit, or to aid or abet, any unlawful activity that constitutes a violation of federal law, or that constitutes a felony under any applicable state or local law."

In December 2003, President George Bush signed into law the **Fair and Accurate Credit Transactions Act** (**FACTA**). We have discussed other provisions of that law in earlier chapters. Part of that law also addresses the problems created by identity theft. FACTA provides that consumers can issue a one-call fraud alert to one of the three nationwide consumer-reporting agencies. A military consumer going on active duty can issue an active duty alert. That agency must then notify the other nationwide agencies. Another provision of the law requires financial institutions and creditors to institute "reasonable policies and procedures" for "red-flag" guidelines regarding identity theft. This is to block the reporting of information identified as resulting from identity theft, and to allow a consumer free access to reports.

On July 15, 2004, President Bush signed into law the **Identity Theft Penalty Enhancement Act,** which provides greater penalties for identity thieves. It creates the crime of "aggravated identity theft," punishable by up to two years in prison when committed in connection with other felonies, and imposes a special five-year prison term for committing identity theft in connection with terrorism.

Many states have passed ID theft laws. Arizona passed the first such law in 1996. This law prohibits persons from "know-

( ) TALKING TO A LAWYER

Q. *What's the best way of not being burned by a phishing scam?*

A. Do not respond to e-mails asking for your personal or account information, and do not click on the link in the message. Delete the phony messages. Legitimate creditors will never e-mail or call you to ask you to confirm your confidential information. The reason they call it "phishing" is because the fraudsters know that if they cast out enough messages there are a few unsuspecting souls whom they'll reel in! Don't be one of them. Just say nothing. Silence is your best defense. If you feel you must do something, then forward the message to spam@uce.gov. The government uses this information to try to reel in the phishers. If you want to verify that the message is not legitimate, you can call the creditor with whom you have an account, using a phone number on an account statement, to confirm that they did not send the message to you.

—**Answer by Robin K. Warren, Bank of America,**
Charlotte, North Carolina

Q. *Can a computer firewall help prevent identity theft?*

A. A computer firewall can help keep cyber-snoopers from accessing confidential information stored on your computer. It is particularly important to maintain a firewall if you have a broadband connection and/or conduct financial transactions, such as online banking, via the Internet. A firewall is the equivalent of pulling the shades and locking the door to your house to keep snooping eyes and intruders from accessing your personal belongings.

A firewall doesn't replace other common sense steps you should take to protect yourself. Make sure that you do not give personal confidential information to anyone unless you know that they have a legitimate need for the information. Never give the information to anyone who initiates contact with you. Only give it in connection with transactions you've initiated by phone, the Internet (at secure sites, only) or in person. Never provide confidential information in an e-mail. E-mail is not secure. Use caution when disposing of confidential information, account statements, old checks, and pre-approved solicitations. Tear or shred these before disposing of them. If possible, use a locked mailbox. If your mailbox doesn't lock, be sure to remove your mail from the box daily. When paying bills by mail, don't put the envelopes with your personal checks in your unlocked mailbox. Drop them at the post office or put them in a U.S. Postal Service mailbox.

—Answer by Robin K. Warren, Bank of America, Charlotte, North Carolina

ingly tak[ing] or us[ing] any personal identifying information of another person, without the consent of that other person." State laws may give you greater protection than the federal laws; contact your consumer protection agency or state attorney general to find out what protections exist in your state.

THE WORLD AT YOUR FINGERTIPS

• For a good article that compares and contrasts several identity theft statutes, see "Identity Theft Statutes: Which Will Protect Americans the Most?" by Catherine Pastrikos, 67 Albany Law Review 1137 (2004).

• For another excellent article on identity theft, see Holly K. Towle, "Identity Theft: Myths, Methods, and New Law," 30 Rutgers Computer & Tech. Law Journal 237 (2004).

• For President Bush's statement about signing the Identity Theft Penalty Enhancement Act into law, visit *www.whitehouse. gov/news/releases/2004/07/20040715-3.html.*

• For a good overview of the identity theft provisions (and other provisions) of FACTA, visit *www.ftc.gov/opa/2004/ 06/factaidt.htm.*

• The Federal Trade Commission has published an informative booklet, "Identity Theft: What's It All About?," to warn consumers about the dangers of identity theft. This booklet is available online at *www.ftc.gov/bcp/conline/pubs/credit/id theftmini.pdf.*

REMEMBER THIS

- Identity theft is a growing problem. Guard your personally identifiable information, such as your Social Security number, and release it only when necessary.
- You can take many steps to reduce the threat of identity theft. These steps include installing a firewall on your computer system, not giving out your passwords to anyone, guarding your mail and trash from theft, and contacting creditors if you don't receive a recent bill.
- If you have been the victim of identity theft, take the following steps: (1) place a fraud alert on your credit reports and accounts; (2) close all accounts that have been compromised; (3) contact the police and report the problem; and (4) file a complaint with the Federal Trade Commission.

CHAPTER 9

Unfair Lending

How to Protect Yourself from Loans You Can't Afford

Bill Jones has faced some unexpected expenses this month. He has no way of getting money until his next payday, which is not for another two weeks. He has no family or friends who can lend him money. He walks into a "cash advance" establishment and writes a check for $380 that he postdates to his next payday. The check casher gives Mr. Jones $300, and tells him that he will hold his check until payday. On payday, however, Mr. Jones cannot afford to pay the entire $380 that he owes the check casher, so he has to pay an additional $20 "rollover" fee. It may be six months before he is able to repay his total debt. He needed money badly, but now he has a loan he can't pay back and the loan balance is increasing.

There are many opportunities for consumers to obtain cash advances that appear to be cheap and easy, but instead turn out to be expensive short-term loans. State and federal laws require comprehensive disclosures of costs and terms of loans, but these disclosures are highly technical and often are not available to the consumer until the consumer has already decided to enter into the transaction.

In some instances, even these disclosures are not required. Companies that offer these products may not be closely regulated by state or local laws, and the people who work for these outlets may not be required to be licensed or trained to offer these products to consumers.

In retrospect, the terms that the consumer agrees to may seem unfair or inappropriate. In the worst cases, the consumer may have been subjected to unfair treatment, such as "bait and switch," heavy sales pressure or even misrepresentation. These are instances of unfair lending, which are a byproduct of the

MORGAGE BROKERS

A mortgage broker is someone who helps a borrower find an appropriate mortgage. A mortgage broker does not make the loan or extend credit; he or she simply helps the borrower obtain the best possible mortgage by matching the borrower with a loan mortgage lender. The potential problem for borrowers is that mortgage brokers may collect their fees from the lender. It may not be clear to the borrower whether the broker is working for the lender or the borrower. In some cases the fees paid by lenders to brokers may be higher if the interest rates on the mortgage loans referred by the brokers are higher than prevailing market rates. Also, some mortgage brokers only refer to a limited number of mortgage lenders. In these cases, it is possible for an unscrupulous broker to work in tandem with lenders against the best interests of borrowers.

wide availability of high-priced credit arrangements aimed at unsophisticated consumers.

Consumers should be especially aware of the unfair lending practices often collectively referred to as "predatory lending." The problem of predatory lending has escalated within the past fifteen years. As Margot Sanders and Alys Cohen wrote in a 2004 piece published by the Joint Center for Housing Studies at Harvard University, "[w]hile abusive and fraudulent credit scams have always been a problem in a commercially oriented culture, the problems in the past fifteen years caused by the explosion of predatory lending are new in the history of personal credit." Groups such as the National Association of Consumer Advocates (*www.naca.net*) and the National Consumer Law Center (*www.nclc.org*) exist in order to protect consumers from unfair and deceptive practices. They attempt to provide financial and consumer credit advice, budget planning, debt counseling, and debt-consolidation strategies.

There is no universally accepted definition of "predatory

lending." Nonetheless, there are many accounts of predatory practices. As Tania Davenport writes in the 2003 article "An American Nightmare: Predatory Lending in the Subprime Home Mortgage Industry," unfair lending may involve "targeting, threatening, deceiving, manipulating, and defrauding the most vulnerable borrowers." A key element of the unfair-lending process involves targeting people most in need of money—people who often do not qualify for prime borrowing rates and terms. Unfortunately, some of the worst abuses may occur in home mortgage lending. Any consumer must be absolutely certain he or she can afford to repay any loan on his or her home, because the consequences of nonpayment may be loss of the consumer's most important asset.

Many states and even cities have passed laws that limit certain loan practices and terms. These outlawed practices include fraud and misrepresentation in soliciting or marketing loans, charging very high interest rates, imposing excessive prepayment penalties, and steering consumers into multiple refinances.

THE "SUBPRIME" MARKET

Consumers who cannot qualify for a conventional loan may find credit available on "subprime" terms. **Subprime lending** is defined as the provision of credit to borrowers with past credit problems, often at a higher cost or on less favorable terms than are available to borrowers in the "conventional" or "prime" market. In other words, a borrower who is deemed a credit risk is often charged a higher, "subprime" rate than those with better credit.

Theoretically, subprime lending helps people with credit problems to obtain homes and access to capital. In fact, in a 2000 study entitled "Curbing Predatory Home Mortgage Lending" (*www.hud.gov/library/bookshelf18/pressrel/subprime.html*), the Department of Housing and Urban Development (HUD) noted the widespread growth of subprime lending and remarked that subprime lending "can and does serve a critical role in the

Nation's economy" by providing credit to persons who cannot "meet the credit standards for the prime market."

Subprime lending makes loans available to homeowners who have blemished credit. Some homeowners, however, do not understand the terms of higher-cost home loans and the risks to themselves and their families. For example, the HUD study points out a downside to the widespread availability of credit to

---

ⓘ CONGRESS ON THE SUBPRIME MARKET

Congress is considering bills to strengthen federal laws that fight predatory or unfair lending in the mortgage industry, though such bills have not yet become law. For example, recent Congresses have seen the introduction of such bills as the Predatory Mortgage Lending Practices Reduction Act and the Prevention of Predatory Lending Through Education Act.

The Predatory Mortgage Lending Practices Reduction Act would establish a federal certification program requiring mortgage brokers to become certified and pass an exam on federal consumer protection laws. It would create civil penalties for violations of federal law pertaining to predatory lending, and it would also prohibit any charges in connection with a mortgage that had not been previously disclosed to the borrower.

The Prevention of Predatory Lending Through Education Act would establish a toll-free telephone number for predatory lending complaints and a Predatory Lending Advisory Council within the federal Department of Housing and Urban Development.

Finally, the Prohibit Predatory Lending Act, introduced in March of 2004, would impose a host of restrictions and limitations on high-cost mortgage loans and would prohibit balloon payments.

A recent regulatory development by the Office of the Comptroller of the Currency, a federal regulatory agency for national banks, broadly preempts state laws governing real estate predator lending, and replaces them with federal regulatory protection.

borrowers of all types of credit standing. That is, there may be unscrupulous lenders drawn into a business once dominated by community banks and savings associations:

> Since subprime lending often operates outside of the federal regulatory structure, it is a fertile ground for predatory lending activities, such as excessive fees, the imposition of single premium credit life insurance and prepayment penalties. . . . And predatory lending can have disastrous consequences for the unknowing borrower. At the very least, equity is stripped from the home. In more egregious cases, homeowners may lose their home altogether.

Disturbingly, predatory lending practices may target low-income persons and the elderly in the area of home mortgages. Congress has considered some new bills to provide protections to consumers victimized by such practices (see sidebar), though none have passed. State legislatures are also active in regulating high cost loans, and some of them have enacted consumer protection laws.

PREDATORY LENDING PRACTICES

There are many types of predatory lending practices, including flipping, packing, and stripping. We discuss these more fully in chapter 10, but briefly, loan **flipping** is a process in which a creditor encourages a consumer to refinance a loan several times in a relatively short period of time, each time adding higher points and fees. **Packing** involves adding fees to a new loan for services such as credit insurance (see chapter 3), or adding the borrower's old debt into the new loan. This tactic gets its name from the fact that lenders "pack" old debt into new loans, which can make it more difficult for borrowers to repay them. **Stripping** refers to the practice of basing the terms of a loan on a borrower's equity in his or her home, rather than on the borrower's ability to repay the debt. Eventually, foreclosure and sale of the property occurs, and the money derived from the equity is stripped from the homeowner and goes to the creditor in repayment.

Another example of predatory lending occurs when home improvement contractors go door-to-door, seeking to induce people to take out mortgages to pay for home improvements.

In many cases, consumers may not be aware that they are the victims of predatory lending practices. The Center for Responsible Lending (*www.responsiblelending.org*) has identified several possible initiatives to combat predatory lending, including:

• Prohibiting creditors from financing credit insurance as an up-front payment.

• Limiting direct and indirect fees charged to borrowers to three percent of the loan amount. The more fees imposed on a consumer to obtain a loan, the more likely the consumer's payments will be more than he or she can pay.

• Addressing the issue of "steering" by making sure that borrowers receive the lowest-cost loans for which they qualify. Borrowers must be aware that brokers can steer customers to particular finance companies with which they have a profitable arrangement. Borrowers should find out whether the broker is working for them or the finance company. Borrowers should only be guided toward the lowest-cost loans for which they qualify or to the most appropriate loan for their own financial circumstances.

• Avoiding mandatory arbitration clauses in home loan agreements. Arbitration can be a costly process, and many arbitration clauses have cost-splitting provisions, which require the parties to share the costs of the arbitrator. Companies can afford these fees, but many borrowers and individuals cannot.

• Prohibiting "flipping" of borrowers through repeated fee-loaded refinancings.

The Special Problem of "Payday Loans"

So-called "payday loans," formally known as **deferred-presentment check cashing**, may result in a borrower paying

( ) TALKING TO A LAWYER

Q. Are advances on tax refunds actually expensive loans? I'd always like the money earlier, but not if the cost is too much.

A. Rates charged in connection with "refund anticipation loans" or "refund anticipation checks" may be higher than for other loans, such as unsecured loans from finance companies. Be sure you review all of the documents and disclosures provided by your tax preparer that relate to the loan transactions.

—Answer by Donald C. Lampe, Womble Carlyle Sandridge & Rice, PLLC, Charlotte, North Carolina

Q. My bank offers bounce protection. What is that? Is it different from overdraft protection—and is it worth getting?

A. Overdraft protection or "bounce protection" is a feature that your bank may offer you to protect against overdraft fees and the consequences of bounced checks. These plans function like short-term loans, so be sure you understand the costs and charges, especially compared with the time that you have the use of the additional funds to cover overdrawn checks.

—Answer by Donald C. Lampe, Womble Carlyle Sandridge & Rice, PLLC, Charlotte, North Carolina

more for credit than is appropriate under the borrower's circumstances. In a common example of this practice, as detailed in the hypothetical at the beginning of this chapter, you have no money until your next payday, and you go to a check-cashing establishment and write a check for, say, $380 in order to obtain $300 cash. You must then pay back the $380 on payday, or be charged further fees. Check-cashing businesses may charge extremely high interest rates. Many commentators believe that they gouge low-income persons.

Nearly twenty states have laws that establish small-loan interest caps on payday loans. But in states that have no usury lim-its, the annual interest rate (APR) for such payday loans can be higher than 300 percent. As noted by Professor Creola Johnson in her *Minnesota Law Review* article "Payday Loans: Shrewd Business or Predatory Lending?," many studies have shown that payday lenders charge exorbitant fees for their services, some-times in violation of state laws.

In some cases, courts have ruled that check-cashing busi-nesses have violated the federal Truth in Lending Act by misrep-resenting the interest charges foisted upon consumers. For example, in *Turner v. E-Z Check Cashing of Cookeville, TN, Inc.*, a 1999 case that arose in Tennessee, a federal district court ruled that a check-cashing service violated the Truth in Lending Act by misstating its finance charges and APR. In that case, the check-cashing service stated the APR was 6 percent when it was actually 400.2 percent.

Professor Johnson writes that Congress should enact legisla-tion that accomplishes the following:

> (1) places a ceiling on the maximum interest rates and fees that lenders can charge; (2) prohibits banks from partnering with payday lenders; (3) forbids the collection of treble dam-ages from customers; (4) bans the criminal prosecution of customers; and (5) prohibits rollovers using the same or mul-tiple lenders.

The past several Congresses have considered (but not passed) such bills as the Payday Borrower Protection Act, which would limit annual interest rates to 36 percent and would prohibit the refinancing or "rolling over" of any loans. As Congressman Bobby Rush noted in introducing the legislation, "[m]ost loans made are small, usually no more than $100 to $500, but the interest rates can soar from 390 percent to 913 percent. Only loan sharks lend money with such high interest rates and loan sharking is illegal." (Of course, loans of small amounts for short periods must carry a rate of interest high enough to earn enough dollars to cover the lender's costs and some profit. Long-term large real estate loans can earn enough dollars at low rates to be profitable.)

(i) "SUBPRIME" CREDIT CARDS

As many as 40 million Americans have a hard time getting credit because of past bankruptcies, loan defaults, or low income. Some credit card issuers will give these high-risk borrowers credit cards, but at a price: high rates of interest and big up-front fees. And delinquency rates are high—as many as 20 percent of these cardholders ultimately can't pay their credit card bills, compared with 2-to-5 percent of lower-risk cardholders. Moreover, the card companies often go after delinquent accounts with very aggressive collection practices. For some consumers, easy credit may be turn out to be quite expensive and potentially very troublesome.

Consumers should avoid cash advances from check-cashing services and use them only as a last resort. The quick fix of a cash advance easily may result in costly credit on terms that may create further hardship for the consumer.

Other Types of Loans That Can Be Predatory

The term "predatory lending" refers to a series of lending practices; it does not refer only to one type of lending. Other types of loans susceptible to abuse include home improvement loans (discussed in chapter 10), rent-to-own purchases, and auto title loans.

Rent-to-own purchases are short-term, renewable rentals of property on a weekly or monthly basis. Consumers with limited resources often rent television sets, washers and dryers, or furniture because they don't have the money to pay for such items in full. If you renew your rental of a rent-to-own product enough times, you can actually purchase it; however, you will have paid far more than the purchase price by making multiple rental payments, which include finance charges. In fact, legislation in many states regulates these transactions, and a number of cases have treated them as extensions of secured credit, even though they are ostensibly in the form of a lease. Often, the ultimate cost of one of these rent-to-own contracts is not clear to the consumer.

Auto title loans are another type of loan ripe for abuse by unfair lenders. Auto title loan establishments are often located next to pawnshops, and often operate in ways that disadvantage the poor. In fact, they are structured as pawn transactions, and like them carry a high rate of interest. A person needing money can visit one of these establishments and turn over the title to his or her vehicle as collateral for a loan. The problem, however, is that the interest rates for auto title loans are high compared with other types of credit. In many states, auto title loan establishments face little state and local regulation. In Tennessee, for instance, it has been reported that some auto title loans have interest rates as high as 264 percent.

Your best defense against falling prey to such loans is being aware of the risks and, if you are forced to seriously consider one, examining its terms fully to understand what you will ultimately pay. When you see what an auto title loan really costs, you'll have extra incentive to find the money somewhere else, or find a way to get by without borrowing money.

THE WORLD AT YOUR FINGERTIPS

- The Federal Trade Commission has a publication on payday loans entitled "Payday Loans = Costly Cash" that is accessible online at *www.ftc.gov/bcp/conline/pubs/alerts/pdayalrt.htm*.
- The Federal Trade Commission also has congressional testimony from one of its officials regarding the dangers of predatory lending, available online at *www.ftc.gov/os/2000/05/predatorytestimony.htm*.
- The U.S. Department of Housing and Urban Development warns against predatory lending on its website, *www.hud.gov/*.
- The Joint Center for Housing Studies at Harvard University has an excellent white paper on the issue of whether federal regulation contributes to unfair lending, available online at

www.jchs.harvard.edu/publications/finance/babc/babc_04-21.pdf.

• The Center for Responsible Lending has information on predatory lending available online at *www.responsiblelending.org/lending_basics/signs.cfm.*

• The National Consumer Law Center has information available on its website about payday loans and mortgage reform; visit *www.consumerlaw.org/initiatives/payday_loans/index.shtml* or *www.consumerlaw.org/initiatives/predatory_mortgage/index. shtml.*

• The National Association of Attorney Generals' website also provides material concerning predatory lending at *www.naag.org/issues/issue-consumer.php.*

REMEMBER THIS

• Consumers should be especially careful of the unfair lending practices often collectively referred to as "predatory lending."

• Predatory lending takes many forms, including "flipping," "packing," "stripping," charging excessive interest rates, and misrepresenting the need for credit insurance.

• Avoid payday loans and cash advance loans if at all possible. Such loans often charge high interest rates for very short periods of time.

CHAPTER 10

Mortgage/Home Equity Loans

An Area Ripe for Abuse by Predatory Lenders

Two door-to-door salesmen knock on the door of the home of a 75-year-old woman living on a small fixed income. The salesmen convince the woman that she needs to make significant repairs to the siding and roofing of her house. The repairs will cost more than $10,000.

The salesmen, who work in conjunction with a mortgage broker, tell the woman that all is not lost if she does not have the funds immediately available to pay for the home improvements. They convince her to obtain a loan using the equity in her home as collateral. What they don't tell her is the monthly payments under the loan may be higher than her disposable monthly income, and that there is a large final payment, called a "balloon" payment, required at the end of the loan. She may well wind up losing her home.

The largest financial decision many people make in their lives is the decision to purchase a home. Unless you are wealthy, you'll probably have to finance the purchase—that is, take out a large loan, or mortgage, in order to have a home. This is a huge financial commitment for most of us, but the good news is that there are legal protections for consumers during the mortgage loan/home-buying process.

MORTGAGE LOANS

A mortgage is defined as giving a creditor rights in your real property (including land and the buildings and other improvements on the land) as security for the repayment of a debt. That means that if you don't make the required payments, the creditor has the right to take the property, sell it, and use the money in repayment. This is called **foreclosure.**

Not only is a mortgage home loan probably the single biggest extension of credit most people will ever take out in their lifetime, it can also result in your losing your home under a worst case scenario. Obviously it makes good sense to be very careful in making this commitment.

The Federal Trade Commission writes: "A mortgage—whether it's a home purchase, a refinancing, or a home equity loan—is a product, just like a car, so the price and terms may be negotiable." This means that consumers should pay close attention and read the fine print to make sure they are receiving a good deal. Consumer self-education is the best policy.

Consumers have rights during the mortgage/home-buying process. For example, the **Real Estate Settlement Procedures Act (RESPA)** requires that borrowers receive disclosures during the real estate settlement or closing process. RESPA requires mortgage brokers and/or lenders to provide borrowers applying for a loan with information on real estate settlement services, a good faith estimate of settlement costs (listing the actual charges the borrower is likely to pay) and a mortgage servicing disclosure statement.

Under RESPA, a mortgage lender/broker must deliver a good-faith estimate of the approximate costs of the loan at the time of closing within three days after the borrower completes an application for a mortgage loan.

RESPA also prohibits brokers and lenders from giving or accepting a fee or kickback in exchange for referrals of business involving mortgage servicing of federally-regulated mortgage loans. Another section of RESPA prohibits people from forcing home buyers to use a particular title insurance company.

Individuals can bring lawsuits under RESPA for violations of the law. The Department of Housing and Urban Development, state attorneys general, or state insurance officials may also bring actions to stop violations of RESPA. Those who believe they have a complaint under RESPA should send a complaint to:

Director, Office of RESPA and Interstate Land Sales

U.S. Department of Housing and Urban Development

Room 9154

451 7ᵗʰ Street, SW

Washington D.C. 20410

Consumers have rights in addition to those under RESPA. The federal Truth-in-Lending Act contains a provision giving consumers three business days to cancel most home equity/mortgage loans, as well as most transactions that are closed in your own home or somewhere other than the place of business of the company you're dealing with. This means that if something is bothering you about the loan or the lender has engaged in questionable behavior, you can release yourself from the obligations within the first three business days after the loan closing. This is called the **right of recission.**

 ## POINTS

Points are fees paid to the lender and/or broker for the loan at or before loan closing, and are usually a percentage of the principal amount of the loan. They are prepaid finance charges and can greatly increase the cost of credit. For example, one "point" is one percent of the principal amount of the loan. The total number of points you pay at or before loan closing is often linked to the interest rate of the loan. Normally, the more points you pay to the lender, the lower your interest rate will be. Many lenders quote loan interest rates that assume a certain number of points will also be paid. For instance, a lender might quote loan interest rates on the assumption that the borrower will also pay 1½ points (1.50 percent of the principal amount of the loan). If the borrower is willing to pay more points, the lender might quote a lower interest rate—but that does not mean the overall cost is less. If the borrower wants to pay fewer points (or no points at all), the lender might quote a higher interest rate.

Consumers should get information from several lenders or brokers. A mortgage broker may offer to shop for the best available mortgage deal with various lenders. Loan applicants usually pay the mortgage broker a fee for this service. It is important to ask a mortgage broker whether the broker only refers applicants to a limited number of specific mortgage lenders (using a "closed list" of lenders).

In some cases the mortgage broker may also be paid by the lender, and lenders in turn sometimes pay fees known as **yield spread premiums** to mortgage brokers. A yield spread premium is a fee paid by a lender to a mortgage broker if the interest rate on a mortgage loan referred by the broker is higher than a certain minimum interest rate set by the lender. The higher the loan's interest rate, the higher the yield spread premium the lender might pay to the mortgage broker.

Senator Paul S. Sarbanes described the potential positives and negatives of yield spread premiums at a January 2002 Senate committee hearing on predatory lending. He said:

> Yield spread premiums, properly used, can be a tool in helping a homebuyer or homeowner offset all or some of the closing costs associated with buying or refinancing a home. When used properly, the broker discloses his total fee to the consumer. The consumer may then choose to pay that fee, and perhaps other closing costs as well, by accepting a higher interest rate and having the lender pay the fee to the broker. In such cases, where the borrower makes an informed choice, the payment helps families overcome a barrier to homeownership—namely, the lack of funds for closing costs.
>
> It is very important that this be transparent and that the borrowers know exactly what their options are. But it appears that, in practice, perhaps in widespread practice, yield spread premiums are not used to offset closing costs or broker fees. Instead, these premiums are used to pad the profits of mortgage brokers without any regard to any services they may provide to borrowers.

Consumers should ask about the best available rates, determine whether the rates are fixed or variable (remember the importance of fixed rates versus variable rates in Chapter 4 on credit cards), and ask how variable mortgage interest rates are adjusted during the term of the loan.

Besides points, mortgage home loans also contain numerous other fees, including loan origination or underwriting fees, attorney fees, broker fees, recording fees, title insurance fees, appraisal and credit report fees, and other costs. Many of these fees do not have to be included in the Annual Percentage Rate of the loan. It is important to have an accurate idea of the total dollar amount of fees you will be required to pay at or before the loan closing. Also, some loan-related fees and other terms and conditions of a mortgage loan may be negotiable. For this reason, many consumers may want a lawyer or other representative on their side during these transactions.

The Federal Trade Commission has a "Mortgage Shopping Worksheet" that may help you compare various mortgage loan offers. See *www.ftc.gov/bcp/conline/pubs/homes/bestmorg.htm*.

AN AREA RIPE FOR ABUSE BY PREDATORY LENDERS

The largest single asset most of us have is the equity that we have built up in our homes through the years. Many mortgages these days are thirty-year mortgages. If you've owned your home for twenty years, you may have built up a significant amount of **equity** in the home—that is, the current value of your home minus the amount of any existing mortgages, liens and attachments on the home. Should you encounter tough financial times, you may need more money, and the equity in your home may be a promising source. But you need to understand the risk—if you fail to make the scheduled payments on a home equity loan, the lender may be able to foreclose on your home.

The Federal Trade Commission has useful pamphlets discussing the risks of using your home as collateral for a loan. See "Home Equity Loans: Borrowers Beware!" (*www.ftc.gov/bcp/*

conline/pubs/homes/eqscams.htm) and "Putting Your Home On the Loan Line Is Risky Business" (*www.ftc.gov/bcp/conline/pubs/credit/risky.htm*). As the Federal Trade Commission has said, "Remember, if you decide to get a home equity loan and can't make the payments, the lender could foreclose and you would lose your home."

It has been widely reported that many predatory lenders target certain homeowners—elderly widows, people with poor credit, and those with low incomes. Many of the practices identified in the predatory lending chapter (Chapter 9) surface with respect to home equity lending, including:

• **Equity Stripping:** The lender offers to make a mortgage loan with a loan repayment schedule at an amount the borrower cannot realistically meet. The idea of the predatory lender is to eventually foreclose on the property. If the property is sold at a foreclosure sale, there may not be any sale proceeds left to be paid to the homeowner after deducting the amounts owed on the mortgage loan and the mortgage lender's foreclosure costs. In such a case the homeowner would lose all of the equity in the home (with the lender having "stripped" the equity away).

• **Loan Flipping:** The lender calls the borrower to see if they would like to refinance an existing loan to obtain additional monies for more home improvements or for debt consolidation or other purposes. The lender makes it sound attractive but, in reality, the lender may be "flipping" an existing loan, charging the borrower points and fees on both the additional monies that would be lent under the new loan as well as the already outstanding unpaid amounts borrowed under the existing loan to be refinanced. If the principal amount of the existing loan to be refinanced included closing costs (such as points or other fees), then refinancing the existing loan could include paying new points and fees on previously borrowed points and fees.

• **The Big Balloon Payment:** Some lenders include in their loan contracts provisions by which the borrower has to make one huge payment at the end of the loan term. Sometimes this is because earlier required payments on the loan consisted primarily of interest and included only a very small amount to be applied to reduce principal. In other cases, the payments do not even cover interest, so it is added to the loan balance. (This is called **negative amortization**.) So this provision may in some cases require the borrower to pay close to the entire original principal amount of the loan at the end of the loan term, or even more than the principal. This is called a balloon payment. If the borrower is unable to pay the balloon payment due on a mortgage loan, and also unable to find a lender willing to refinance the **balloon payment**, the mortgage lender may foreclose on the borrower's home.

• **Credit Insurance Packing:** In this practice, the lender adds in, or packs, credit insurance and other benefits into the terms of the loan, sometimes without fully explaining the benefits to the borrower. The lender hopes the borrower will not realize that adding the cost of insurance and other benefits to the loan amount will increase the fees and payments due to the lender. Lenders may also earn a commission when they sell insurance and other benefits to borrowers, further increasing the total fees they may earn in connection with the loan.

REVERSE MORTGAGES

Reverse mortgages are also a potential risk for older people. At their best, they permit older people to take advantage of the equity they have built up in their home, using it for living expenses and other purposes. At their worst, they can have all the downsides of home equity loans.

Here is how they work. A **reverse mortgage** lets you borrow against the equity in your home, without having to repay the loan right away. You can get the money in a lump sum, in monthly cash payments for life, or by drawing on a line of credit, or you can choose a combination of these options (e.g., monthly payments plus a line of credit for emergencies). The amount you can borrow, and the size of the loan installments, are based on several factors, including: your age, the value of the home and of the equity you hold, the interest rate, and the kind of loan you select. These loans can be costly, but the relative costs

TALKING TO A LAWYER

Q. Our mortgage loan just got sold to a huge, out-of-state bank. I assume this is legal—but is there anything we can do about it? We'd rather deal with a bank in our community, where we know people and it would be easier to get the answers to our questions.

A. After a mortgage loan is closed (after the borrower has signed the loan agreement or the promissory note, and the mortgage or deed of trust on the real estate securing repayment of the loan has also been executed and recorded with the appropriate public official), and provided that the loan has not been rescinded (cancelled) during the first three business days after the closing (if the loan was secured by the borrower's primary residence and was not for the purpose of buying or constructing that residence), the lender who made the loan generally may sell the loan and/or the right to service the loan (in other words, the right to collect the loan payments required to be made by the borrower).

The loan is considered an asset (property) of the lender, and the lender may sell, assign, or even borrow against the loan (by using the loan as a type of collateral or security). The right to service the loan (the right to collect the loan payments required to be made by the borrower) is also an asset (property) of the lender, and the lender may sell or assign this right, with or without selling or assigning the loan itself.

Borrowers do not have the right to stop a lender from selling a loan, or from transferring the servicing of a loan to a third party. However, borrowers should receive notice if the servicing of their loan is being transferred (so that they can send their required loan payments to the new servicer of their loan).

—**Answer by Elizabeth C. Yen, Hudson Cook, LLP, New Haven, Connecticut**

lessen over time, and you will never owe more than the value of your home.

Most reverse mortgages have no restrictions on how you use the money. The loan usually does not have to be repaid until you sell, die, or move from your home, although some loans must be repaid at the end of a specified number of years. Some lenders combine a reverse mortgage with an annuity that allows you to receive loan payments under the annuity even after you sell your home and move.

When you sell your home or move, or at the end of the term, you must repay the money you have borrowed plus the accrued interest and fees. The house can be sold to repay the loan, or the funds collected some other way. The lender is not permitted to collect more than the appraised value of the house at the time the loan is repaid, even if the loan exceeds that amount.

The most widely available product is the federally insured **Home Equity Conversion Mortgage** (or **HECM**). Under this program, the Federal Housing Authority (FHA) provides insurance for reverse mortgages placed through private financial institutions. Another reverse mortgage program available nationally through private lenders is **Home Keeper Mortgage,** backed by Fannie Mae (the Federal National Mortgage Association). A few private companies also offer their own reverse mortgage products. These tend to be more costly, because the lender must charge customers more in order to self-insure against potential losses. Federal law requires all reverse mortgage lenders to inform you, before making the loan, of the total amount you will owe through the course of the loan. This enables you to compare the costs.

Eligibility. Eligibility depends on the individual product, but most have rules similar to the FHA and Fannie Mae programs. The borrower and every other person whose name is on the deed must:

• be at least sixty-two and
• own the property free and clear, except for liens or mortgages that can be paid off with proceeds from the loan

In addition, the property must be:

• the borrower's primary residence (that is, not a vacation home)
• a single-family residence

The decision to take out a reverse mortgage is complex. Reverse mortgages allow you to spend your home equity while you are alive. You may end up using all of your equity, and not have any left to pass down to your heirs. Some plans allow you to set aside some of the equity, so that it is not used.

HECM requires all potential borrowers to receive counseling from an agency certified by the U.S. Department of Housing and Urban Development. Some state laws require counseling for all borrowers, no matter what the product, but borrowers looking at private products generally are not required to have counseling.

Reverse mortgages are very complex, and involve difficult financial, legal, and personal decisions. Examine them carefully, and look for alternatives that may suit your needs. You should have professional advice in making this decision. Talk to a lawyer who is familiar with the issues, and discuss your aims and concerns with family.

Consumer information about reverse mortgages, including booklets, information about loan costs, and an interactive loan guide, is available from AARP at *www.aarp.org/revmort*. Additional information is available from the National Center for Home Equity Conversion at *www.reverse.org/*.

PROTECTIONS AGAINST PREDATORY
HOME EQUITY LOANS

In 1994, Congress passed the **Home Equity Ownership and Equity Protection Act (HOEPA)**. This law amends the Truth in Lending Act and establishes requirements for certain high-cost loans secured by the borrower's primary residence. However, HOEPA does not apply to revolving (open-end) lines of credit, and also does not apply to closed-end loans taken for the purpose of financing the purchase or initial construction of the borrower's primary residence. Furthermore, for HOEPA to apply, the Annual Percentage Rate (APR) or the fees paid by the borrower must exceed a certain level.

If a loan falls within the scope of HOEPA, the lender must meet certain requirements, as well as make extra disclosures. Specifically, HOEPA restricts prepayment penalties, post-default interest rate increases, balloon payments, negative amortization, prepaid monthly payments, and due-on-demand clauses, in which the lender has the right to demand that the loan be repaid in full at any time.

HOEPA prohibits lenders from engaging in a pattern or practice of making high-cost mortgage loans to consumers based on the value of their homes without regard to consumers' ability to repay. The law prohibits creditors from engaging "in a pattern or practice of extending credit . . . based on the consumers' collateral without regard to the consumers' repayment ability, including the consumers' current and expected income, current

◖◗ TALKING TO A LAWYER

Q. How do you know when you've taken on too much indebtedness on a home equity loan?

A. You've taken on too much debt if, after making a payment, you are short, or if you need to resort to payday loans or credit advances to make the payments.

—**Answer by Marc S. Stern, Law Offices of Marc S. Stern, Seattle, Washington**

Q. I'm older but I've got the credit needs of a younger person. I just got remarried at age 62, and I'd like to buy a new house for us, fix it up, etc. Can I get mortgage loans and a big amount of credit at my age? After all, I don't plan to work forever.

A. Yes, even though you are older, you can still qualify for a mortgage loan. Mortgage loans are often for larger amounts of money and are often for terms as long as thirty years. In addition to having a generally good credit record, you will need to show the creditor that your income will be sufficient to make your mortgage payments. This might require that you be able to show what income you will have (including Social Security and any pension funds) after you retire. As with all mortgage loans, the creditor will also want to ascertain the value of your house and the amount of your equity in the house (the total value of the house minus the amount of any other mortgages or other debts secured by the house) to be sure that the equity will support the loan amount requested.

—Answer by Robin K. Warren, Bank of America, Charlotte, North Carolina

A. Before making these decisions, you need to figure out if you are going to be able to make the payments. As you indicate, you are not going to work forever. If you are not going to work and if your retirement income will not support the payments, do you want to do this? It seems to me that you are setting yourself up for a bankruptcy.

—Answer by Marc S. Stern, Law Offices of Marc S. Stern, Seattle, Washington

obligations and employment." HOEPA was passed in part to prevent a form of "reverse redlining"—targeting residents in certain low- or moderate-income areas for credit at above-market rates, fees, and other terms. As one court has explained, "the legislative history of HOEPA demonstrates that Congress enacted HOEPA to force the high-cost mortgage market to police itself."

THE WORLD AT YOUR FINGERTIPS

• The Federal Trade Commission has an excellent publication on mortgages entitled "Looking for the Best Mortgage: Shop, Compare, Negotiate." See *www.ftc.gov/bcp/conline/pubs/homes/bestmorg.htm.*

• The U.S. Department of Housing and Urban Development (HUD) has an excellent resource page devoted to the Real Estate Settlement Procedures Act. See *www.hud.gov/offices/hsg/sfh/res/respa_hm.cfm.*

- The Federal Trade Commission has numerous publications regarding home equity loans. These include:
  - "Home Equity Credit Lines" *www.ftc.gov/bcp/conline/pubs/homes/homequt.htm*.
  - "Home Equity Loans: The Three-Day Cancellation Rule" *www.ftc.gov/bcp/conline/pubs/alerts/3dayalrt.htm*.
  - "Home Equity Loans: Borrowers Beware!" *www.ftc.gov/bcp/conline/pubs/homes/eqscams.pdf* or *www.ftc.gov/bcp/conline/pubs/homes/eqscams.htm*.
  - "Shopping for a Home Equity Loan?" *www.ftc.gov/bcp/conline/pubs/alerts/shopeqtyalrt.htm*.
  - "Need a Loan? Think Twice about Using Your Home as Collateral," *www.ftc.gov/bcp/conline/pubs/homes/hoepa.htm*.
  - "Putting Your Home On the Loan Line Is Risky Business," *www.ftc.gov/bcp/conline/pubs/credit/risky.htm*.

REMEMBER THIS

- Shop around for the best deal with respect to credit. Many consumer credit laws, including the federal Truth in Lending Act, require lenders to disclose the terms of the deal to you. If a lender is being evasive, avoid the lender at all cost.
- Be careful when taking a home equity loan. Carefully research the lender and the terms of the loan. You don't want to fall victim to a predatory lender.
- Federal law gives you three business days to cancel for any reason a loan that is secured by property used as your principal dwelling. That covers most home equity loans. If something is bothering you about the loan or the lender has engaged in questionable behavior, you may still have time to release yourself from the obligations within the first three business days after the loan closing. This is called the **right of recission.**
- Mortgage loans are complicated transactions in which consumers must be informed of myriad costs. As the FTC says, "shop, compare, and negotiate."

CHAPTER 11

Auto Financing and Leasing

The Lowdown on Buying, Financing, and Leasing a Car

Your old clunker just completely clunked. You don't have access to reliable public transportation. You need another car, but the problem is that you don't have enough money to pay for one. You'll have to finance or lease your vehicle. You go to a car dealership and they say it would be best for you to obtain financing through the dealership. They also tell you it would be even better to lease a vehicle from them. What should you know about auto financing before taking this plunge?

Buying an automobile may be your biggest financial purchase other than buying a home. Before going to the dealership, you should do some research. You should: (a) know how much you can afford to spend on a monthly basis; (b) identify the price range of the car you wish to buy; and (c) learn the APRs offered by various banks and other alternative sources of credit so that you can compare them with the APR offered by the dealership.

DEALERSHIP FINANCING

The most common type of financing is "dealership financing." In this arrangement, a buyer and a dealership enter into a retail installment sale contract where the buyer agrees to pay the dealership the amount financed, plus an agreed-upon finance charge, over a period of time. The dealership may retain the installment sale contract, but usually sells it to an **assignee** (such as a bank, finance company, or credit union), which services the account and collects the payments.

Most dealerships have a Finance and Insurance (F&I) Department, which provides one-stop shopping for financing. The

F&I Department manager will ask you to complete a credit application. The dealership may obtain a copy of your credit report, which contains information about current and past credit obligations, your payment record, and data from public records (for example, a bankruptcy filing obtained from court documents).

As noted above, if you enter into a retail installment sale contract with a dealership, the dealership typically will sell your retail installment sale contract to an assignee, such as a bank, finance company, or credit union. Accordingly, the dealership submits your credit application to one or more potential assignees to determine their willingness to purchase a retail installment sale contract between you and the dealer. These potential assignees will usually evaluate your credit application using automated techniques such as credit scoring, where a variety of factors, like your credit history, length of employment, income, and expenses may be weighted and scored.

Since the bank, finance company, or credit union does not deal directly with the prospective vehicle purchaser, it bases its evaluation upon what appears on the individual's credit report and score, the completed credit application, and the terms of the sale, such as the amount of the down payment. Each finance company or other potential assignee decides whether it is willing to buy the retail installment sale contract, notifies the dealership of its decision and, if applicable, offers the dealership a wholesale rate at which the assignee would be willing to buy the retail installment sale contract, often called the "buy rate."

Your dealer may be able to offer you manufacturer-sponsored incentives, such as reduced finance rates or cash back on certain models. You may see these specials advertised in your area. Make sure you ask your dealer if there are any special financing offers or rebates with respect to the model in which you are interested. Generally, these discounted rates are not negotiable and may be limited by a consumer's credit history, and are available only for certain models, makes, or model-year vehicles.

When there are no special financing offers available, you can negotiate the annual percentage rate (APR) and the terms for payment with the dealership, just as you negotiate the price of the vehicle. The APR that you negotiate with the dealer is usually higher than the wholesale rate at which a potential assignee would be willing to purchase your retail installment sale contract with the dealership. This negotiation can occur before or after the dealership accepts and processes your credit application.

DIRECT LOANS

An alternative type of vehicle financing is "direct lending." In the case of direct lending, the buyer obtains a loan directly from a finance company, bank, or credit union. The buyer enters into a loan agreement with the lender and agrees to pay the lender the amount financed, plus an agreed-upon finance charge, over a period of time. Once a buyer and a vehicle dealership enter into a contract of sale and the buyer agrees to a vehicle price, the buyer uses the loan proceeds from the lender to pay the dealership for the vehicle. Consumers also may arrange for their own vehicle loan over the Internet.

DEALER-ASSISTED LOANS

A dealer-assisted loan is a type of direct loan in which the dealership arranges for the buyer to obtain a loan directly from a finance company, bank, or credit union. If the dealership has attempted to arrange a loan for you, each lender to whom the dealer submitted your credit application decides whether it is willing to make you a loan, notifies the dealership of its decision and, if applicable, informs the dealership of the base rate required by the lender.

You may negotiate the annual percentage rate (APR) and the terms for payment with the dealership if the dealership has arranged for your loan, just as you negotiate the price of the vehicle. The APR you negotiate with the dealer is usually higher than the base rate required by a lender with whom the dealer has arranged a loan for you. This negotiation can occur before or after the dealership accepts and processes your credit application. As with any other direct loan, if the dealership succeeds in arranging for a loan, the buyer enters into a loan agreement with the lender and agrees to pay the lender the amount financed, plus an agreed-upon finance charge, over a period of time.

PRICE OF THE VEHICLE

Buyers should be aware of the terminology employed to describe the price of the vehicle. There is the **invoice price,** which refers to the manufacturer's charge to the dealer. Sometimes, you will hear salespeople refer to the price of a car as "five percent above invoice" or "$200 above invoice." The **base price** refers to the cost of the car without any special options. The base price includes the standard equipment and factory warranty. The "**Monroney**" **sticker price** is the price that federal law requires be attached to the car window. It includes the base price, manufacturer-installed options and their retail prices, transportation (destination) charges, and the total manufacturer's suggested retail price. It is named after U.S. Senator Michael Monroney, who in 1958 spurred the passage of the law that mandated auto sellers to place this sticker on cars. Finally, the **dealer sticker price** is the regular sticker price plus the suggested retail price with the dealer-installed upgrades and options.

Consumers should carefully do research on base car prices before dealing with the auto salesperson. Some dealerships will also add dealer **mark-ups.** These are simply additional fees that the dealer adds to the car price to increase its profit.

This is not to suggest that the auto-buying world is never friendly to consumers. In fact, due to the law of supply and demand, there are often great incentives on the part of dealerships to sell cars at reasonable prices. Consumers should check carefully for special rebates (money paid back to the consumer).

(i) INCENTIVE FINANCING/LOW-COST FINANCING

Many car dealers offer low-cost financing as a promotion. One example would be **incentive financing** with an APR that is below the rate being offered by, say, your credit union for the same term. How do you decide if these promotions are a good deal? All other things being equal, the incentive financing rate offer is probably good deal.

Answering the question is more complicated if the auto dealer or manufacturer is offering a cash rebate as an alternative to the incentive financing rate if you buy the car for cash or you arrange your own financing through your bank, credit union, or someone else. To see whether the incentive financing rate or the cash rebate is the better deal, you need to compare financing through the dealer at the low rate versus financing through your bank or credit union at the rate they will offer you for the same term using the cash rebate as an additional down payment. Generally, the better deal is the one with the lowest monthly payment over the same term. But consider also the convenience of dealership financing and whether you will need your bank/credit union credit lines for other needs. For example, a major car maker once offered a choice of a $1,500 cash rebate or 5.8 percent financing for four years on certain models. Assume that the car you would like to buy costs $16,000. If you have $2,000 for a down payment, you have the following choices:

1. If you finance with the dealer, your $2,000 down payment leaves $14,000 ($16,000 – $2,000) to be financed over four years at 5.8 percent. The monthly payments would be $327.51.

2. If you finance with your bank, credit union, or another credit grantor, the $1,500 cash rebate from the dealer plus your $2,000 gives you a total down payment of $3,500. This leaves $12,500 to borrow ($16,000 – $3,500.) If you borrow $12,500 for four years at 11.17 percent, your monthly payments would be $324.10, which, all other things being equal, is a slightly better deal.

If the rebate in the above example were available in combination with the low finance rate, the low finance rate would clearly be the better deal.

PURCHASE CONTRACT AND
LEASE AGREEMENT

If you are financing the purchase of a car from the dealer, you will receive a contract that governs the terms and conditions of the sale and financing of your vehicle. The contract is different from the "buyer's order" that you will receive if you order a new car. The contents of the contract will vary some depending on the state in which you sign the contract. At a minimum, the contract should include a description of the make and model of the car and its vehicle identification number, or VIN. The contract also should include: whether the car is new or used; the agreed-upon price of the car; details on the value of the trade-in vehicle (if you traded in a vehicle as part of your purchase), including the amount that you still may owe on the traded-in vehicle; and the financing terms. The financing terms should include the vehicle price, amount of the down payment, trade-in value, less any amount owed to another person on the trade-in, cost of any other ancillary products (like an optional service contract, extended warranty, credit insurance), finance charge, annual percentage rate, and the length of the financing.

Read the contract carefully. If there are any terms you disagree with, discuss them with the dealership's representatives before you sign the contract. Do not sign the contract if you don't understand what you are signing or believe that there is a mistake. Do not simply mark through terms you disagree with. That won't eliminate them from the contract unless both you and the dealership's authorized representative initial the change to signify that both parties accept it.

If you are leasing a car from the dealer, you will receive a vehicle lease agreement that governs the terms and conditions of the leasing of your vehicle. The lease agreement is different from the "order" that you may receive that describes the features of your leased car. The contents of the lease agreement will vary some depending on the state you live in or the state in which you sign the lease agreement. At a minimum, the lease agreement should include a description of the make and model of the car and its vehicle identification number, or VIN. The lease agreement also should include:

- whether the car is new or used;
- the agreed-upon price of the car and other amortized amounts such as a lease acquisition fee and the cost of a service contract (called the "capitalized cost");
- details on the value of the traded-in vehicle (if you traded in a vehicle as part of your lease), including the amount that you still may owe on the traded-in vehicle;
- the amount of any down payment (called the "capitalized cost reduction");
- the term of the lease;
- the mileage included in the lease and cost to you for excess mileage at the end of the lease term;

(i) LEMON LAWS

Every state, including the District of Columbia, has a lemon law designed to protect consumers when they purchase a car that simply does not perform well and constantly needs repairs. Under many state laws, if a vehicle's nonconformity or defect is subject to repair three or more times within a certain time period and the defect continues to exist or if the vehicle is inoperable for thirty days or more, the car is deemed a "lemon."

Under many laws, if the car is deemed a lemon, the manufacturer must pay you the full purchase price of the vehicle and all collateral charges (such as license and registration fees) associated with the purchase of the vehicle.

For information on various states' lemon laws, consult autopedia, an encyclopedia on automobiles, located online at *utopedia.com/html/HotLinks_Lemon2.html*.

The Better Business Bureau also has a section on lemon laws at *www.lemonlaw.bbb.org/*.

• a description of your responsibility for excess wear and tear on the leased vehicle;

• a description of your liability to the lessor in case you or the lessor terminate the lease before the scheduled lease term; and

• whether you have the right to purchase the vehicle at the end of the lease and, if so, the amount or method of determining the amount of the purchase option price. The lease agreement will also include a formula that shows how the dealer calculated your monthly lease payment.

Read the lease agreement carefully. If there are any terms you disagree with, discuss them with the dealership's representatives before you sign the lease agreement. Do not sign the lease agreement if you don't understand what you are signing or believe that there is a mistake. Do not mark through terms you disagree with.

MAKING PAYMENTS

You must make your scheduled payments on your contract or lease agreement. If the dealer has assigned (sold) your contract or lease agreement to a finance company, bank, or other financial institution (these companies are called "holders"), you must make your payments to the holder. If you do not make your payments when they are due, the holder may repossess your vehicle. The holder has the right to repossess your vehicle until your contract or lease agreement is paid in full. In most states, the holder can repossess the car without giving you any notice. The only caveat is that they cannot breach the peace in obtaining the car from you, meaning that they probably couldn't break into your garage to get it, or take it from you while you were in it.

Repossession rights vary from state to state. Once a holder repossesses your car, it may be able to sell the car to fulfill your obligations under your contract or lease agreement. If the sale doesn't cover everything you owe plus related expenses, like the repossession and sale, the holder may have the right to hold you responsible for the rest of the debt, often referred to as the "deficiency balance." If the sale brings in more than you owed plus the holder's expenses, the creditor should give the extra money, known as the **surplus,** to you. (A lessee is not entitled to any surplus because the lessee has no ownership interest in the leased vehicle.)

In some states, the purchaser of the vehicle will be given the option to reclaim the car before it is sold by paying the entire amount owed, plus additional costs incurred by the holder in repossessing the car. This is called the right of **redemption.**

THE "NEGATIVE EQUITY" PROBLEM

Most consumers do not write a check or pay cash for the entire car purchase. Most people finance their car through monthly payments as discussed earlier. Some payment plans now stretch for five or six years. As a result, a vehicle's value may decline more quickly than the balance owed under a retail installment sale contract or a loan agreement. This leads to a condition where you could owe more on your contract or loan than the vehicle is worth for several years after your purchase. This condition is sometimes called **negative equity.** It is also referred to as being "upside down" or "underwater." This is important during trade-in time.

Edmunds.com, a leading tracker of the auto industry, has reported that more than 30 percent of car buyers are in a negative equity situation.

You can avoid a negative equity situation by making a larger down payment and making your payment plan shorter. If you find yourself in a negative equity situation, a dealer may be willing to finance the negative equity on your trade-in as part of your purchase or lease of a new vehicle. However, this will increase your payments unless you make a larger down payment on the new transaction.

LEASING A VEHICLE

Many consumers lease their vehicles rather than purchase them. Under a lease, you pay a certain amount each month to drive a

( ) TALKING TO A LAWYER

Q. What is spot delivery, and how it is tied in to financing?

A. Spot delivery is a term used to describe a sale of a vehicle when the buyer takes delivery of the vehicle "on the spot," before the dealer has finalized a sale of its installment sale contract to a finance company, bank, or other financial institution. The buyer will sign an installment sale contract for the vehicle and the dealer will agree to let the buyer take the vehicle even though the dealer has not found a finance company, bank, or other financial institution to purchase the contract or there are certain items that the buyer still needs to provide to the dealer as a part of the credit application process (like an insurance policy, pay stub, or utility bill). In addition to the installment sale contract, the buyer usually signs a conditional sales rider or addendum to the contract that says that the dealer can cancel the installment sale contract if either the dealer does not assign (sell) it within a certain number of days or the customer does not provide the required information.

If the dealer is unable to find a buyer for the installment sale contract with the financing terms originally agreed to by the buyer, the dealer may cancel the contract. The buyer has a number of options. The buyer may enter into a new contract on different financial terms, the buyer can pay the entire balance due on the contract, or the buyer can return the vehicle and receive a return of any down payment and any traded-in vehicle.

—Answer by Mark S. Edelman, McGlinchey Stafford, PLLC, Cleveland, Ohio

Q. We're looking into leasing a car, and trying to compare one offer to another, but we're thoroughly confused by the terms. I know that in theory the law requires dealers to show the terms so that we can make sense of them, but I'm lost. Is there any practical advice you can give? What are the most important terms to look for?

A. Information on leasing is available from the Federal Trade Commission and perhaps from individual state agencies. Carefully studying lease disclosures required by law, which must be made clearly and in standard form, will also help you understand this information.

—**Answer by Frederick H. Miller, George L. Cross Research Professor, Kenneth McAfee Centennial Professor, McAfee Chair in Law, University of Oklahoma College of Law**

Q. *Is there subprime car financing? How does it differ from the financing offered to people with better credit?*

A. Subprime financing is the term that is used to describe financing made available to people with a history of credit problems. As a result of credit difficulties (prior bankruptcies, bad payment history, lack of credit history), these individuals pose a greater credit risk for dealers and for finance companies, banks, and other financial institutions who may purchase their contracts from the dealers. Customarily, the increase in risk is reflected in a higher finance charge. In addition, persons with increased credit risk may be required to pay a down payment that is a greater percentage of the amount financed than those with better credit.

—**Answer by Mark S. Edelman, McGlinchey Stafford, PLLC, Cleveland, Ohio**

vehicle over a period of time, normally two to four years. You must return the vehicle at the end of the lease. Most leases also give you the right to purchase the vehicle at the end of the lease.

The most common form of consumer lease is a **closed-end lease.** Under a closed-end lease, you may return the vehicle at the scheduled end of the lease term, pay any scheduled end-of-lease costs, and walk away. An **open-end lease** is a lease agreement in which the amount you owe at the end of the scheduled lease term is based on the difference between the residual value of the vehicle and its actual value at lease end. The remainder of this discussion focuses on closed-end leases because they are much more common than open-end leases.

There are several reasons people may prefer to lease. Leasing a vehicle allows you to drive a newer automobile more often than if you purchase for a similar monthly payment. Lease payments are smaller per month than installment purchase payments for the same contract term. Leasing may also give you a chance to drive a more expensive vehicle than you could buy. This is possible because the base monthly lease payments do not recoup the estimated residual value of the leased vehicle. Additionally, sometimes dealers will offer consumers a special subsidized, or **subvented,** lease that is favorable to the consumer.

However, there can be several disadvantages to leasing cars. These include the fact that leasing cars leads to never-ending car payments unless you purchase a car at the end of the lease. If you want to own your car free and clear, it can be better to finance a purchase rather than lease a vehicle. When you lease a car, you build up no equity in the car (unless you later purchase it).

Furthermore, most leases limit the number of miles you may drive (often 12,000–15,000 per year). You can negotiate a higher mileage limit and pay a higher monthly payment. You will have to pay charges for exceeding the allowable mileage if you return the vehicle. Most leases also assess a charge if you return the vehicle with excess wear and tear (as defined in the lease).

See chapter 1 for a brief discussion of rights you may have under a federal law governing leases.

THE WORLD AT YOUR FINGERTIPS

• There are several informative websites available to consumers that provide information about car values and prices. These include: *www.autosite.com, www.edmunds.com,* and *car prices.com.*

• The Federal Trade Commission has published several booklets that help consumers learn more about the purchase of automobiles. These include:

  • "Buying a New Car" *www.ftc.gov/bcp/conline/pubs/autos/ newcar.htm.*

- "Understanding Vehicle Financing" *www.ftc.gov/bcp/conline/pubs/autos/vehfine.htm.*
- "Keys to Vehicle Leasing: Quick Consumer Guide" *www.federalreserve.gov/pubs/leasing/.*
- "Vehicle Repossession" *www.ftc.gov/bcp/conline/pubs/autos/carrepo.htm.*
- For information about the value of your trade-in vehicle and how much you can expect to get for it, consult the Kelley Blue Book value: *www.kbb.com.*

REMEMBER THIS

- Before going to the dealership, you should do some research. You should: (a) know how much you can afford to spend on a monthly basis; (b) identify the price range of the vehicle you wish to buy; and (c) compare the finance rates offered by various banks with the finance rate offered by the dealership.
- You must make your monthly payments to the holder of the loan or contract. If you fall far enough behind on your payments, the holder of the loan or contract may repossess your vehicle.
- The Federal Consumer Leasing Act, which is part of the Consumer Credit Protection Act, is a disclosure law that protects consumers. It applies to any lease of consumer goods that lasts more than four months and in which the total contractual obligation does not exceed $25,000. There also may be state legislation regarding consumer leases, including variation of such leases known as "rent to own" transactions, which may be treated more like installment sales than leases. Chapter 1 contains more information about protections for consumers who lease products.

CHAPTER 12

Dealing with Debt

Tips on How to Get Control of Your Finances

Every month, you notice that your bills get larger and your disposable income gets smaller. You send minimum payments to your credit card companies, but are not making any headway with your debts. You don't really know where your money is going; you just know that it's not in your checkbook.

This type of scenario is all too familiar to millions of Americans. To avoid it, you must learn to achieve what author Dave Ramsey calls "financial peace"—or, at the very least, you must learn to budget. Many people exacerbate their financial situations by living beyond their means. It is essential that you take control of your finances—or at least accurately assess your financial state.

There are many costs associated with debt, aside from the financial cost of the debt itself. First, as we learned in chapter 6, your creditors will report your credit-related delinquencies to credit bureaus. As a result, you may have trouble getting more credit or maintaining the current lines of credit on your credit cards. Some cards may be canceled, or not renewed on their renewal dates. If you are already overindebted, having fewer credit cards may not be entirely bad. But when you really need a good credit record to rent an apartment, get a home mortgage loan, or get a new job, having a bad or even weak credit report can hurt.

Also, as you will see in the next chapter, debt may make you the target of collection efforts from your creditors and ultimately from professional collection agencies. These institutions naturally want to recover the money that you owe. They'll probably write and telephone you frequently.

Finally, debt raises the ultimate possibility of bankruptcy, which is discussed in Part II of this book. Regardless of what you might have heard, bankruptcy is not a pleasant experience. Congress passed a new bankruptcy law in 2005 that many experts say will make bankruptcy even tougher for debtors. Moreover, bankruptcy stays on your credit record for up to ten years and can handicap your access to various forms of credit for much of that period of time.

HOW MUCH DEBT CAN YOU HANDLE?

As a rough guideline, one long-standing rule is that if your monthly payments on debts, excluding your home mortgage payment, exceed 20 percent of your after-tax or take-home income (or 30 percent of your pretax income), you have most likely reached your debt limit. Since less than 3 percent of American families spend 30 percent or more of their gross income on debt payments, you can see that relatively few families permit their debt burdens to reach or exceed their debt limits.

With respect to debt, there are several reliable signs of danger. You might be in more debt than you can handle if you

• can only afford to make minimum monthly payments on your credit card accounts;

• have to use credit for expenditures for which you once paid cash;

• have used a series of consolidation loans, home equity loans, or other types of loans to pay overdue bills;

• are borrowing from one creditor to pay another—for example, taking a cash advance on your credit card to pay amounts owed to other banks or retailers;

• begin to run a few days late on critical payments, such as your rent or mortgage payment, or are consistently late with all your bill payments so that late fees are piling up; or

• dip into savings for normal living expenses.

RESPONSE TO DEBT DANGER SIGNS

If you recognize that any of these danger signs apply to you and your family, you need to take action. The worst thing you can do is nothing. If you fail to change your spending habits and fall deeper into debt, bill collectors will beset you, and you will find your options limited. You might even be forced into bankruptcy.

The first step toward taking control is slowing down your use of credit. If you are going shopping, take only the one credit card that you will need, or try using cash instead of credit cards. Cut up excess credit cards and return them to your creditors, asking them to notify the credit bureaus that *you* have closed the accounts; it is important that your credit report reflect that each account was closed at your request, and not at the demand of creditors.

▶ PRIORITIZE YOUR DEBTS

Nolo has published an excellent book, *Money Troubles: Legal Strategies to Cope with Your Debts* (8th ed., 2002), aimed at helping consumers take control of their debts. In this book, authors Robin Leonard and Deanne Loonin recommend that you prioritize your debts by grouping debts into "essential" and "nonessential" categories.

Essential debts include rent or mortgage, utility bills, child support payments, car payments, other secured loans, and unpaid taxes. Essential debts must be paid if at all possible; you must prioritize them. In particular, secured loans must be paid because, when you obtained these loans, you pledged certain collateral as a promise to repay them.

Nonessential debts include credit and charge card bills, department store and gasoline card bills, loans from friends and relatives (unless secured), magazine subscriptions, legal and medical bills, and other unsecured loans.

As a first step toward taking control of your finances, make a list of your essential and nonessential debts so you know exactly what you owe.

DEVELOPING A BUDGET

Next, find out where your money is going by keeping track of household purchases for two weeks. Make a note of all your expenditures. For example, if you start the day with $30 in cash and end it with only $5, make a note of where you spent the missing $25. In addition to recording your cash expenditures, make note of all credit purchases made during the same two-week period. When the two weeks are up, examine your expenditures, and hold a household or family conference to discuss how those expenditures can best be reduced. Now is the time to begin educating teenagers, and even younger children, about the value of money.

Above all, you must learn to live within your means. In other words, you must stop spending more than you can afford. Many people spend money—often through the overuse of credit cards—without really thinking about it; spending comes naturally in our culture of immediate gratification. But, as we have seen throughout this book, there is a steep price to be paid for living beyond one's means. Developing a budget can help you stay on track.

There are many different types of budgets, but most people benefit from a monthly budget that carefully lists their income and bills for the month. When keeping a monthly budget, you should keep track of all your expenses, including food, housing, transportation, utilities, insurance, education, taxes, and clothing. Many of these expenses will be fixed, in the sense that you can anticipate the amounts you will owe each month before you actually owe them. For example, your rent or mortgage will be the same each month, as will your cable bill (unless you order pay-per-view events that increase the amount of your bill).

Once you have a good understanding of where your money is going, you may find it useful for your household or family to prepare a cash budget indicating the highest monthly payments you can afford to make on each of your debts. Such a budget might look something like this, though it can be as fancy or simple as you want:

Family Budget

A. Monthly Income:
  1. Your and your spouse's
      monthly take-home pay   _____
  2. Other income   _____

                    Total monthly income: _____

B. Monthly Expenses:
  1. Food   _____
  2. Rent or mortgage payments   _____
  3. Utilities   _____
  4. Telephone   _____
  5. Transportation (gasoline,
      mass transit costs)   _____
  6. Regular Monthly Savings   _____
  7. Other Major Categories (itemize) _____

                    Total monthly expenses: _____

C. Annual Expenses:
  1. Taxes   _____
  2. Insurance (not paid monthly)   _____
  3. Medical and dental bills   _____
  4. School costs   _____
  5. Entertainment   _____
  6. Clothing   _____
  7. Other Major Categories (itemize) _____

                    Total annual expenses: _____

                    Divided by 12:   _____

D. Monthly income available for payments on debts (A −B+C): _____

E. Committed Income (i.e., income already committed to
    monthly payments):
  1. Personal loans   _____
  2. Extensions of credit to
      buy a car or truck   _____

                    Total committed income: _____

F. Discretionary income (D–E):   _____

Note that the above budget includes an "Annual Expenses" section. It is important to allow for annual expenses in your budget; otherwise, you may be unprepared if a bill that you don't think about on a monthly basis, such as an insurance bill or a bill for real estate taxes, suddenly becomes due. Also, it is generally easier to decide on an annual budget for such categories as clothing and recreation, and then divide that annual total by twelve to determine your acceptable monthly outlays in each category. The trick is not to spend your annual budget in the first few months of the year; calculating acceptable monthly outlays may help you to achieve this. Each month, allot a certain amount of money for each expense—for example, allow yourself a set amount of money for dining out, a set amount of money for clothing, and so forth—and do your best not to exceed that amount.

Note that savings are budgeted as a monthly expense. If you don't budget for savings, you won't save, and saving is important for two reasons. First, savings serve as an emergency fund in case somebody is laid off or becomes ill. A good rule of thumb is that an emergency fund in the form of savings or other readily accessible assets should equal three to five months of your household's after-tax income. Second, once you have set up an adequate emergency fund, savings can serve as a retirement fund (in conjunction with any retirement-savings programs you enjoy through your employer), a college tuition fund, or a fund for meeting other long-term goals that your household or family may have.

In the sample budget provided above, you may have wondered why the "Committed Income" section does not list credit card payments as one of its categories. The answer is that such payments are assumed to be included as part of your expenditures for clothes, entertainment, and whatever else you pay for using credit cards. If you are living within your budget, you should be able to make these payments using funds from the existing categories in your budget, so they won't require a separate line item.

After examining their budgets, many families may find that

◯ TALKING TO A LAWYER

Q. *Is it more important to make payments on secured loans than it is to pay off credit card debt?*

A. Yes. When you incur secured debt, you pledge collateral—for example, your house—in exchange for a loan. If you fail to make payments on secured debts, the creditor is entitled to take and sell the collateral you pledged—usually for an amount that is much less than what you owe. This means that, in addition to paying off the balance of your loan, you'll also have to replace the collateral sold by the creditor.

—Answer by Marc S. Stern, Law Offices of Marc S. Stern, Seattle, Washington

A. To the extent that you have pledged important assets as collateral for secured loans, such as a primary car or primary residence, then you may want to give these loans priority in order to preserve these assets. However, each debtor's situation is unique. You will need to set priorities based on your own particular needs and circumstances and the particular options that may be available to you—for example, borrowing temporarily from relatives; selling nonessential items or assets such as a second car (where, for example, public transportation is a viable option); moving in with family, friends, or relatives; or finding a roommate or boarder with whom to share living expenses. (This is where seeking professional advice may be of particular assistance to you in helping you sort out your priorities and looking at all your options.)

You may also want to think twice about not paying down your credit card debt. Some credit agreements governing so-called nonessential loans, like credit cards, include onerous default terms. Such terms may impose high finance charges if you are delinquent with payments; others known as "cross-default provisions" may allow satisfaction of your credit card debt with collateral that you have offered to the same creditor for an entirely different loan. Such provisions can dramatically increase your interest payments, fees and/or payment burdens or cause you to default under the terms of a secured loan, potentially placing your secured credit—and the assets securing that credit—at risk. Some credit card agreements now also contain so-called universal default provisions. Pursuant to such provisions, a default with one creditor (such as a missed payment) constitutes a default with any other creditors. This means that your card issuer (or another creditor) may impose delinquency pricing terms—for example, a higher finance charge rate—even if you have not missed a single payment.

In such a case, giving low priority to a seemingly nonessential loan may dramatically change your monthly obligations or inadvertently put a secured loan or asset at risk. You need to read the terms of each credit agreement carefully in order to make the best decision for your situation. You may be better served by trying to renegotiate credit terms or by asking about payment deferral or skip-a-payment options before missing a payment.

—Answer by Michael C. Tomkies, Dreher Langer & Tomkies LLP, Columbus, Ohio

the amount of money they have available each month to pay their debts is not sufficient—in the above budget, for example, the total from section D ("Monthly income available for payments on debts") might be less than the total from section E ("Committed Income"). If this is the case, income must be increased or expenditures must be reduced in order to free up money for paying the monthly bills. Go back and examine your two-week record of cash outflows and see where you can cut spending. Eliminate the costs of, say, going bowling once a week or pursuing some other hobby. Consider writing letters or e-mails rather than making long-distance calls. Adopt the industry approach of zero-based budgeting: Show a real need for any expenditure above zero. In addition to cutting cash outflows, you may be able to improve cash inflows. For example, a spouse or teenager might take a part-time job.

If you are not able to pay your monthly bills, you may want to approach one or more of your creditors and try to reduce or defer your monthly payments without having to pay a penalty. Simply be honest: Explain your cash flow problem and ask your creditors if they can help you get back on your feet. While there is no guarantee that creditors will agree to help you, the worst thing that you can do is to try to avoid them or make promises to pay that you don't keep. If self-help efforts don't do the job, you may want to contact a consumer credit counseling service that can help you set up a new budget. These services are discussed in chapter 14, Credit Counselors.

One obvious advantage of a budget is that you will learn, perhaps for the first time, where your money really goes every month. It takes discipline and practice, but developing a budget is a must for many people.

THE WORLD AT YOUR FINGERTIPS

• The FTC has a publication entitled "Knee Deep in Debt" that is available online at *www.ftc.gov/bcp/conline/pubs/credit/kneedeep.htm*.

• Our Family Place provides information on developing a budget on its website at *www.ourfamilyplace.com/budget.html*.

• Author Dave Ramsey, the head of Financial Peace University, has a website that may be worth a look if you feel you need help in developing a budget and getting out of debt, at *www.daveramsey.com/*.

REMEMBER THIS

• If you can only afford to make minimum payments on your credit cards, you are headed for debt problems.

• There are several other danger signs with respect to debt. They include not knowing or wanting to know your debts, constantly making late payments, postdating your checks to cover your debts, and juggling your bills.

• If you are having debt problems, slow down the use of credit if possible. Keep careful track of your finances and try to create a budget.

CHAPTER 13

Debt Collection and the Law

Your Rights Under the Fair Debt Collection Practices Act

You order compact discs from a mail solicitation offer. Unfortunately, you run into hard times and do not have the money to pay for the additional CDs you've ordered. The company contracts with a debt collector to attempt to obtain its money. The debt collector is relentless. The collector calls you at work, early in the morning, and late at night. The collector's employees employ every means of verbal persuasion, including humiliation and outright threats, to shame you into paying the debt. Do you have any relief from such collection practices? Is this conduct legal?

Such conduct may very well violate a federal law known as the **Fair Debt Collection Practices Act** (**FDCPA**). First passed in 1977, the law amends the Consumer Credit Protection Act to prohibit certain conduct by "debt collectors." The United States Congress made findings that: "There is abundant evidence of the use of abusive, deceptive, and unfair debt collection practices by many debt collectors. Abusive debt collection practices contribute to the number of personal bankruptcies, to marital instability, to the loss of jobs, and to invasions of individual privacy."

CONSEQUENCES OF NOT PAYING DEBTS

Creditors are very likely to report your delinquencies to one or more credit bureaus, thus harming your credit record. Creditors may also file a lawsuit against you seeking a judgment (i.e., a determination by a court that you owe a certain amount to a creditor). You will always have a chance to appear in court to defend yourself.

ⓘ WHAT IF YOU DON'T PAY DEBTS AS PROMISED?

The law allows creditors various ways of collecting unpaid debts, some of which depend upon the law of the state in which you live. They may be able to seize part of your wages or the car that you purchased on credit. Or they may rely on debt collectors to get the money from you. The law attempts to balance the rights of the creditor who provided the credit and the rights of consumers who used it but did not fully pay for it. However, even if you have managed your finances successfully, as explained in the previous section, this chapter may still be useful to you, because the FDCPA also gives rights to people who are not responsible for the debt which the debt collector is trying to recover.

If the creditor obtains a judgment, and you do not pay that judgment, the creditor will likely be entitled to garnish your wages; that is, to direct your employer to pay some portion of your wages directly to the creditor. Federal law sets a limit on what portion may be taken, and many state laws are even more protective. But if you have a good income, the probability is that some of it is subject to garnishment. If a garnishment is used, the creditor will direct your employer to subtract a given amount from your paycheck each payday and pay that amount to the creditor until the debt is satisfied. Your employer cannot fire you because of garnishment by one creditor, but may be able to if another creditor also garnishes your wages.

If you purchased a car, truck, boat, home appliance or other item on credit, your creditor may have a **lien** on the item that you purchased. This is especially likely if you signed a "Retail Installment Sale" agreement with the creditor. Having a lien means that if you fail to pay as agreed, the creditor may **repossess** (recover) the item that you purchased with credit. Many state laws require that the creditor notify you, say two weeks in advance, that a default has occurred or that the creditor intends to repossess so that you may have a last chance to pay your outstanding debt on the item. The creditor may not breach the peace when repossessing items you bought on credit. For example, the creditor may not seize an item by force if you refuse to surrender it, or break into your garage to seize a car.

Remember, most agreements specify that, when you are in default, the entire debt, not just the monthly payment, is immediately due. In the event of a default, the creditor is usually not required to repossess the property you bought on credit; the creditor could simply file a suit to collect the entire amount due. However, even if the creditor does repossess of the property bought on credit, the repossession may not end your obligation to the creditor. If your unpaid balance and accumulated, unpaid finance charges, plus the creditor's costs repossessing the property, are more than the amount that the creditor obtains from the sale of the property, you may still be legally liable to the creditor for the shortage. If the creditor thinks that you may be able to pay something toward the shortage, the creditor can ask a court to assess a **deficiency judgment** against you for the shortage. If you have a deficiency judgment against you, the creditor can invoke the law to take your other property (unless it is exempt from creditor process, which depends on state law) or possibly garnish your wages to satisfy the judgment. Laws in a few states prevent deficiency judgments in some cases.

If you are sued on a debt and believe you shouldn't have to pay, consult a lawyer. If you do not contest the case, the court will accept the creditor's version of events. You should also consult a lawyer if you owe a debt but believe that the debt collector's techniques violate FDCPA or your state's laws. If you win against the debt collector, you will recover some money, but you will not be excused from paying the debt.

DEBT COLLECTORS

Under the federal Fair Debt Collection Practices Act, a **debt collector** is someone, other than a creditor or its employees, who regularly collects consumer debts on behalf of creditors.

( ) TALKING TO A LAWYER

Q. What are "time-barred" debts, and how does that time differ from state to state?

A. The statute of limitations says that a lawsuit must be filed within a specified period of time from the last payment or promise of payment. It varies from state to state. More importantly, the agreement that you signed may include a provision that the law of a specific state applies. That means that even if the lawsuit is time-barred in your state, it may not be time-barred under the agreement.

—Answer by Marc S. Stern, Law Offices of Marc S. Stern,
Seattle, Washington

A. After a certain amount of time after you have defaulted on a debt (often between four and ten years), the creditor no longer has the right to bring a lawsuit to recover the debt. When a creditor files a lawsuit after the statute of limitations has expired, the lawsuit is time-barred and may be immediately dismissed.

You should be aware that a debt is not eliminated just because it is time-barred. Courts have held that creditors may still pursue "time-barred" debts as long as they do not threaten to file a lawsuit against you. (*Freyermuth v. Credit Bureau Servs., Inc.*, 248 F.3d 767, 771 (8th Cir. 2001).)

—Answer by Bruce Menkes, Mandell Menkes & Surdyk, LLC,
Chicago, Illinois

Q. What kinds of debts are covered by the Fair Debt Collection Practices Act?

A. The FDCPA covers communications by debt collectors attempting to collect debts which were incurred by individuals for personal, family, or household purposes. The word "debt" includes any amount a consumer has agreed to pay, and has been held to include condominium assessments, student loans, and even NSF checks. However, the FDCPA does not apply to attempts to collect taxes.

—Answer by Bruce Menkes, Mandell Menkes & Surdyk, LLC, Chicago, Illinois

A. All debts being collected by a third-party collector or by a division of the bank that deals solely with bad debts.

—Answer by Marc S. Stern, Law Offices of Marc S. Stern, Seattle, Washington

A. Any obligation to pay money involving a loan, or a purchase of property, insurance, or services, for personal, family, or household purposes.

—Answer by Frederick H. Miller, George L. Cross Research Professor, Kenneth McAfee Centennial Professor, McAfee Chair in Law, University of Oklahoma College of Law

This federal law does not cover creditors per se (unless the creditor uses a false name in attempting to collect the debt), although your state laws may govern them. Thus, a retailer who attempts to collect unpaid debts owed to it would not be covered by the FDCPA, but may be covered by the laws of the state where the delinquent consumer resides. These laws are usually similar to the federal FDCPA. The rest of this section is based on that federal law.

A debt collector may contact you by mail, in person, or by telephone or telegram, but the debt collector may not contact you at times the debt collector knows are inconvenient for you, unless you agree (or a court specifically grants permission). Unless a debt collector has information to the contrary, the debt collector must assume that times before 8:00 A.M. or after 9:00 P.M. are not convenient. Also, a debt collector is not permitted to contact you at work if the collector knows or has reason to know that your employer forbids employees from being contacted by collectors at the workplace. You can tell the debt collector what times and places are inconvenient for you to receive calls.

Also, a debt collector is forbidden from contacting you if he or she knows that a lawyer represents you.

LIMITING CONTACT FROM DEBT COLLECTORS

You can stop a debt collector from contacting you by notifying the collector in writing. (However, the debt collector could still file a lawsuit against you.) After that, the attempts at contact must stop. There are two exceptions to this. The debt collector may tell you that there will be no more contact, and that some specific legal or other action may be or will be taken. However, debt collectors may state this only if they actually plan to take such action.

Debt collectors must also stop trying to contact you if you notify them, by mail, within 30 days after they send you the notice described in the next paragraph, that you dispute all or part of the debt or that you are requesting the name and address of the original creditor. However, debt collectors are permitted to begin collection activities again if they send you proof of the debt, such as a copy of the bill, or the information you requested about the original creditor.

The FDCPA requires debt collectors to give you a notice within five days of first contacting you, containing:

• the name of the creditor to whom you owe the money;

• the amount of money you owe;

• a statement to the effect that the debt collector will assume the debt is genuine unless you challenge all or part of it within 30 days; and

• a statement about what to do if you believe you do not owe the money—for example, if you dispute the validity of the debt, the agency will send you verification of the debt.

Debt collectors don't have to send a separate document with this information if they provided it in the initial communication or if you've paid the debt.

A debt collector may contact any person to locate you. However, in doing so, the collector usually may not talk to anyone

⚠️ GROWTH OF DEBT-BUYING BUSINESSES BAD NEWS FOR DEBTORS

A growing industry has exploded in the past few years that could affect millions of consumers. This industry is the debt-buying industry. Some companies buy up consumer debt from credit card companies, health clubs, and other businesses that give up pursuing consumer debt. The debt-acquiring companies often buy the consumer debt at a very large discounted price. These companies then aggressively pursue the individuals, including suing them in small claims and municipal courts. The *Wall Street Journal* reports that this is a "multibillion-dollar industry." One effect of this industry is that consumers can no longer assume that seemingly ignored consumer debts will be forgotten.

Source: Suein Hwang, "Once-Ignored Consumer Debts Are Focus of Booming Industry," *The Wall Street Journal,* 10/25/04, A1.

more than once or refer to the debt when talking to that person. If debt collectors use the mail to contact you or another person, they may not send letters in envelopes identifying themselves as bill collectors. They may not send a postcard. Once collectors know that you have hired a lawyer, they may communicate only with your lawyer, unless the debt collector cannot find the lawyer's name and address, or the lawyer fails to respond to the debt collector within a reasonable time.

PROHIBITED CONDUCT

A debt collector may not harass, oppress, or abuse any person. For example, a debt collector may not:
- use threats of violence to harm you, your property, or reputation;
- use obscene or profane language;
- repeatedly use the telephone to annoy you;
- make you accept collect calls or pay for telegrams; or

- publish a "shame list" or other roster of individuals who allegedly refuse to pay their debts (though the debt collector can still report you to a credit bureau).

A debt collector may not use false, deceptive, or misleading statements when trying to collect a debt. For example, a debt collector may not:

- misrepresent the amount of the debt;
- falsely imply that the debt collector is a lawyer;
- tell you that your property or wages will be seized, garnished, attached, or sold, unless the debt collector or the creditor intends to do so and it is legal;
- threaten any action unless the action is lawful and the debt collector (or creditor) intends to take that action.

A debt collector may not use unfair means to collect a debt, such as:

⚠️ "NONPROFIT" HOSPITALS AS AGGRESSIVE DEBT COLLECTORS

There are many aggressive debt collectors, including some nonprofit hospitals. A 2003 story by *The Wall Street Journal* showed that some hospitals were taking extreme measures to collect debts from those who had not paid their medical bills and who did not appear in court for certain hearings. The article described a tactic that some hospitals were using a known as "body attachment"—the arrest of a person who fails to show up for a court hearing. Some debtors who didn't attend a court hearing to determine their assets after a hospital had been awarded a judgment against them found themselves in jail. The article states that one hospital in Illinois sought 164 arrest warrants for debtors who missed this kind of court hearing. See Lucette Lagnano, "Hospitals Try Extreme Measures to Collect Their Own Debts," *The Wall Street Journal,* 10/30/03, pg. 1.

According to a *National Law Journal* article in July 2004, 31 lawsuits have been filed against 300 nonprofit hospitals in 17 states. See Leonard Post, "Hospitals hit with plague of lawsuits; Unfair billing practices alleged against nonprofits," *National Law Journal,* 7/19/04, pg. 1.

- accepting a check postdated by more than five days;
- collecting any amount as interest or a fee, charge, or expense unless authorized by agreement or law;
- taking or threatening to take nonjudicial action to seize property exempt by law from legal process; or
- bringing a lawsuit in an inconvenient court or location.

If Debt Collectors Break the Law

There are several steps you can take if you think a debt collector is breaking the law. If a creditor (for example, a retailer or bank) is making the collection effort, check the law with the consumer protection office of your state or your state attorney general's office and write that office a letter detailing your complaint (with a copy to the offending creditor). If the collection effort is by an independent debt collector, write to the nearest office of the Federal Trade Commission or the office in Washington, D.C. (The addresses can be found in the Appendix of this book or at the website: *www.ftc.gov*.) The FTC has been active in pursuing violators and may fine them heavily or even put them out of business.

In addition, if debt collectors violate the Fair Debt Collection Practices Act, you may sue them in a state or federal court. However, you may do so only within one year from the date they violated the law. You may recover money for the actual damage you suffered. The court may also award an additional amount up to $1,000 for each violation. You may also recover court costs and your lawyer's fees. Class action suits can be brought against debt collectors who violate the FDCPA. Such suits can recover actual damages, and can potentially recover additional amounts up to $500,000 or one percent of the debt collector's net worth—whichever is less.

Filing Complaints with Your State About Debt Collectors

As noted above, you should file complaints about consumer credit reporting agencies or debt collection agencies with the Federal Trade Commission. You should also consider filing a complaint with the applicable state agency that regulates collection agencies. For instance, if a collection agency located in Tennessee were violating your rights, you would contact the Division of Consumer Affairs at the Department of Commerce and Insurance in Nashville, Tennessee. We list state consumer protection agencies in this book's Appendix.

In addition, some states prohibit nonlicensed collection agencies from collecting debts in their state. To collect a debt in Washington state, for example, the collector needs to be licensed there, regardless of where the creditor is located. Failure to be licensed is an unfair and deceptive practice, and there are additional damages available.

If you believe that you have been the victim of unfair harassment, you might also consider consulting an attorney. Victims of

---

(i) STATE COMMON-LAW CAUSES OF ACTION

Federal law is not the only source of law available to consumers harmed by the unlawful conduct of debt collectors. A variety of common-law torts can be used against certain overreaching conduct of debt collectors. These include defamation, invasion of privacy, intentional infliction of emotional distress, abuse of process, and malicious prosecution.

Defamation seeks to protect people from false statements that impugn their reputation. Given the importance of credit in today's society, false information regarding someone's credit may give rise to an actionable claim for defamation. If a debt collector engages in overly intrusive conduct in the pursuit of collecting a debt, an **invasion of privacy suit** is possible. The specific privacy tort, called **intrusion,** protects against invasive conduct that would be highly offensive to a reasonable person. Particularly outrageous conduct by debt collectors could give rise to a common-law suit for **intentional infliction of emotional distress or outrageous conduct.** Such conduct would have to exceed all bounds of social decency and cause mental injury.

FDCPA abuse can recover actual damages, including attorneys' fees and court costs, and the additional damages described above.

EXCEPTION FOR NONPROFIT COUNSELING GROUPS

There is an exception in the Fair Debt Collection Practices Act of which consumers should be aware. The law does not apply to "any nonprofit organization which, at the request of consumers, performs bona fide consumer credit counseling and assists consumers in the liquidation of their debts by receiving payments from such consumers and distributing such amounts to creditors." This means that certain nonprofit organizations that style themselves as debt consolidation companies are not covered by the FDCPA.

As noted in the next chapter, a number of groups have sprung up that purport to be nonprofit, but actually exist to line their own pockets. They operate relatively freely because federal law does not cover them (although some state laws do). The U.S. Congress is aware of this loophole in the law and is considering closing it. In late 2003, a bill was introduced in Congress called the "Debt Counseling, Debt Consolidation, and Debt Settlement Practices Improvement Act." This measure would prohibit these debt counseling organizations from unreasonably disclosing consumer information to third parties, making fraudulent or deceptive statements in connection with providing services to consumers, and ["us[ing] any unconscionable means to obtain a contract with any consumer, to collect, or attempt to collect a debt owed to the seller."] Another provision of the law would prohibit these debt settlement groups from accepting payments in advance from consumers until the groups have performed their contractual obligations. As of this time of writing, the bill has not yet passed. However, an organization composed of representatives of the states, called the National Conference of Commissioners on Uniform State Laws, is completing work on a uniform law to regulate such organizations. This proposed law will be introduced in state

( ) TALKING TO A LAWYER

Q. How can having a lawyer help you deal with bill collectors?

A. There are a number of ways:

1. They can keep creditors from calling you.

2. They can negotiate a settlement and, more importantly, document it in such a way that it can't come back on you, so that there is no question that there is a settlement.

3. They can provide unbiased advice about what your options are, whether bankruptcy is a good idea, or whether there are other alternatives.

4. They can help you structure your financial situation so that creditors cannot collect from you.

—Answer by Marc S. Stern, Law Offices of Marc S. Stern,
Seattle, Washington

Q. What's the best way to get rid of pesky bill collectors?

A. 1. Hire legal counsel to deal with them.

2. Caller ID is a wonderful tool. Write letters telling them to contact you only via mail.

3. You can always pay them or negotiate something.

—Answer by Marc S. Stern, Law Offices of Marc S. Stern,
Seattle, Washington

Q. I understand that the federal law only protects you against certain debt collectors. How could I find out if my state law gives me greater protections?

A. You need to speak with a lawyer in your state who is familiar with the state laws. You can try to do the research yourself but, since laws are written for lawyers to read, unless you understand the language, you may miss several things.

—Answer by Marc S. Stern, Law Offices of Marc S. Stern,
Seattle, Washington

legislatures in the next few years. To find out more, go to *www.nccusl.org*.

THE WORLD AT YOUR FINGERTIPS

• The Federal Trade Commission provides simple information on the Federal Debt Collection Practices Act and what debt collectors can and cannot do at: *www.ftc.gov/bcp/conline/pubs/credit/fdc.htm*.

• Online, non-profit credit counseling services can be accessed at: *www.cccsintl.org/*.

• If you have a complaint about a debt collector or a consumer credit reporting agency, contact your state department of consumer affairs (see Appendix) or contact the FTC. You can mail your complaint to the Federal Trade Commission, Consumer Response Center, 6th Street and Pennsylvania Avenue, NW, Washington, DC 20580. Alternatively, you can call toll-free 877 FTC HELP (382 4357), or use the online complaint form on the FTC website at: *rn.ftc.gov/dod/wsolcq$.startup?Z_ORG_CODE=PU01*.

REMEMBER THIS

• Debt collectors can generally contact you at home or at work by mail, in person, or by telephone after 8:00 A.M. or before 9:00 P.M. If debt collectors are contacting you at other times, they are violating the Fair Debt Collection Practices Act, unless they have reason to know that these times are not inconvenient to you.

• You may notify a debt collector in writing to stop contacting you. You may also inform a debt collector to stop calling you at work.

• Debt collectors may not harass, oppress, or abuse you. They may not repeatedly call you on the telephone to annoy you. The federal law known as the Fair Debt Collections Practices Act (FDCPA) regulates the conduct of debt collectors. Read this law and become familiar with it if you believe a debt collector is using improper techniques to collect a debt or is trying to collect a debt that you do not owe.

CHAPTER 14

Credit Counselors:
A Potential Pitfall

Know Exactly What You're Getting Into

You've seen the advertisements: "Credit Problems No More!—We Can Erase Bad Credit Records, 100 Percent Guaranteed." Unfortunately, such promises often turn out to be gimmicks that only draw unwitting consumers further into financial trouble. You must be careful when choosing a credit counselor; a bad choice could plunge you further into debt.

In its online pamphlet "Credit Repair: Self-Help May Be Best," the Federal Trade Commission issues the following warning:

Everyday, companies nationwide appeal to consumers with poor credit histories. They promise, for a fee, to clean up your credit report so you can get a car loan, a home mortgage, insurance, or even a job. The truth is, they can't deliver. After you pay them hundreds or thousands of dollars in fees, these companies do nothing to improve your credit report; most simply vanish with your money.

MANY ORGANIZATIONS CAN HELP

Despite the FTC's warning, some organizations do provide quality services for debtors and consumers. To find a quality organization, contact the National Foundation for Credit Counseling (NFCC) at *www.nfcc.org*. Founded in 1951, the NFCC is the nation's largest and longest-serving national nonprofit credit-counseling network. Its members, which typically do business using the name "Consumer Credit Counseling Service," provide counseling services, debt management services, and homeowner counseling and educational services. Such a group could help you negotiate with your creditors and reduce your debt to a more

▶ CREDIT COUNSELING AGENCIES AND THE NEW BANKRUPTCY LAW

The importance of credit-counseling agencies has arguably increased since the passage of the new bankruptcy law in 2005. The new law provides that a debtor cannot file for bankruptcy unless he or she, in an individual or group setting, has completed mandatory credit counseling within 180 days prior to filing a bankruptcy petition.

According to the new law, the U.S. trustee must approve not-for-profit credit-counseling agencies that can provide such services, and a list of such approved agencies must be provided in a "publicly available list." Agencies will be approved only if they demonstrate that they

> will provide qualified counselors, maintain adequate provision for safekeeping and payment of client funds, provide adequate counseling with respect to client credit problems, and deal responsibly and effectively with other matters relating to the quality, effectiveness, and financial security of the services [they] provide.

Such credit-counseling agencies must charge only "reasonable fee[s]" and "provide services without regard to ability to pay the fee." These agencies can help debtors develop debt management plans. Once a debt management plan is developed, it must be filed with the applicable bankruptcy court along with a certificate from the agency that helped develop it. ·

manageable level. In addition, the NFCC has a program called DebtAdvice.org (*www.debtadvice.org*) that helps consumers manage a wide variety of credit problems.

SOME ORGANIZATIONS MAKE PROBLEMS WORSE

Unfortunately, not every organization operating as a debt consolidator, credit counselor, or credit repair group has altruistic

( ) TALKING TO A LAWYER

Q. What are debt management plans and negotiation programs? Are they a good idea?

A. If your self-help efforts have not been successful or you need the assistance of a professional debt counselor to establish a budget and negotiate better credit terms with your creditors, then debt management or debt negotiation plans offered by reputable organizations (like the Consumer Credit Counseling Service, as discussed above) may be a good idea. In many cases, these organizations have established payment plans with major creditors. They may be able to assist you, either by collecting a lump sum from you each month and distributing the funds to your creditors (debt management) or by helping you obtain better credit terms while you continue to make payments directly to your creditors (debt negotiation). In many cases, creditors may be willing to accept payments of outstanding principal and reduce or waive applicable fees and finance charges for as long as you make timely payments under a plan. In other cases, the creditor may be willing to report your debt as "current" as long as you remain in good standing under the plan; this is known as "re-aging." Upon completion of the plan or program, your debt may be reported as "settled," though you may lose future credit privileges. This can be a better outcome than default or bankruptcy, and may permit you to reapply for credit with your creditor at a later date. In the case of the Consumer Credit Counseling Service, your creditor may even pick up part of the cost of such a plan through a "Fair Share" contribution to the service. Importantly, however, such plans typically may be used to manage or negotiate only your unsecured debt.

Firms to be avoided are those that suggest you can stop making payments, refuse to communicate with your creditor, or pay only pennies on the dollar for your outstanding debt. Such strategies can have dire consequences: your creditors may continue to report you as delinquent in real time (i.e., no re-aging), may refuse to accept any settlement of your account, or may incur collection expenses for which you could ultimately become liable. Such firms may also charge hefty up-front fees that limit your ability to pay your creditors and eliminate your debt as quickly as possible.

Be careful in your selection of advisors. It's your reputation on the line; it's your money. Don't be fooled by promises of a quick fix. A good workout plan could take as long as forty-eight to sixty months to complete.

—Answer by Michael C. Tomkies, Dreher Langer & Tomkies L.L.P., Columbus, Ohio

motives. Some engage in the types of actions that caused the Federal Trade Commission to issue the stern warning quoted at the beginning of this chapter.

It was for this very reason that Congress passed the **Credit Repair Organizations Act** (**CROA**), which was signed into law by President Bill Clinton in 1996. The CROA amends the Consumer Credit Protection Act to protect consumers from credit repair scams and false promises. Congress passed the measure, in its own words, because "certain advertising and business practices of some companies engaged in the business of credit repair services have worked a financial hardship upon consumers, particularly those of limited economic means and who are inexperienced in credit matters."

The CROA provides that credit repair organizations cannot charge or receive monies until a service they provide is fully performed. It also provides a list of disclosures that credit repair organizations (CROs) must make to consumers, including disclosure of the fact that neither a consumer nor a CRO has the right to remove accurate, correct, and verifiable information from a customer's consumer report, which contains the consumer's credit history, unless it is old negative information as defined in the Fair Credit Reporting Act. (See chapter 6 for more information about consumer reports.) Furthermore, the CROA bars CROs from advising consumers to make untrue or misleading statements regarding their credit histories.

As noted in the previous chapter, some organizations that engage in harmful practices are, in name at least, "not for profit." They style themselves this way so that they can avoid the requirements of some federal consumer protection laws. This problem has become so great that one legal commentator warns consumers to "research the histories and reputability of not-for-profit corporations with the same care and vigor that they research a for-profit entity."

In late 2003, the Federal Trade Commission filed a lawsuit against Ameridebt, Inc., one of the leading nonprofit consumer

---

⚠ TIP-OFFS TO RIP-OFFS

The FTC warns consumers to steer clear of companies that

- guarantee they can erase your unsecured debt;
- promise that unsecured debts can be paid off for pennies on the dollar;
- claim that using their systems will let you avoid bankruptcy;
- require substantial monthly service fees;
- demand payment of a percentage of your savings;
- tell you to stop making payments to or communicating with your creditors;
- require you to make monthly payments to them, rather than to your creditors;
- claim that creditors never sue consumers for nonpayment of unsecured debt;
- promise that using their systems will have no negative impact on your credit report; or
- claim that they can remove accurate negative information from your credit report.

As noted in the last chapter, a new uniform state law will help to regulate these companies.

---

debt-counseling organizations, charging that the company had engaged in fraudulent and deceptive practices. "We will not allow consumers to be duped into 'contributing' hundreds of dollars to these so-called 'non-profits,' " said Howard Beales, director of the FTC's Bureau of Consumer Protection. "There was nothing voluntary and nothing charitable about these payments. Consumers' money didn't go to creditors, it just ended up lining the pockets of the defendants."

The Federal Trade Commission warns that consumers should pay close attention when choosing any credit counselor, whether the counselor is for-profit or nonprofit, as some such groups may simply create more problems for consumers. (See the "Tip-offs to Rip-offs" sidebar for some specific recommendations.)

CREDIT REPAIR ORGANIZATIONS

Credit repair organizations (CROs) deserve a special word of warning. Such organizations generally advertise that they can help you review and update your credit record and report; their fees are often as high as $1,000. If your credit report has an error or needs updating, however, you can deal directly with a credit bureau on your own, for free or at very little cost. If the negative information in your credit report is accurate, only better management of your debts can offset your negative record, and only the passage of time can remove it. Be very suspicious if a credit repair clinic promises that it can remove accurate records of bankruptcy and bad debts from your credit record, or if it promises to get you credit. If a credit program sounds too good to be true, it probably is.

Finally, remember that for-profit credit repair organizations are regulated by federal and some state laws, and federal law prevents a credit repair company from receiving any money from you before it has completed its services. However, you should be aware that not all credit repair groups are subject to the requirements of the Credit Repair Organizations Act; the law does not cover nonprofit organizations that are tax-exempt under Section 501(c)(3) of the Internal Revenue Code.

(i) FIGHTING BACK AGAINST BAD CREDIT REPAIR ORGANIZATIONS

FACTS

In *Limpert v. Cambridge Counseling Corporation,* two people filed a class action lawsuit against a credit-counseling company under the Fair Debt Collection Practices Act (FDCPA), the Racketeering Influenced and Corrupt Organization Act (RICO), and the Credit Repair Organizations Act (CROA). (328 F.Supp.2d 360 (E.D.N.Y. 2004)) The plaintiffs had enrolled in a debt management plan with the defendants. Under that plan, they gave money to the defendants to pay their unsecured debts, and the defendants then disbursed those payments to the plaintiffs' creditors. However, the plaintiffs later claimed that the company had also falsely promised them lower credit card balances, improved credit ratings, fewer late fees, and lower interest rates.

DECISION

The Court rejected the plaintiffs' FDCPA claim because the defendants were credit counselors, not debt collectors: The court found that, "while the distinction between credit counseling and debt collection is finely cut, it is nonetheless controlling. . . . Defendants are not debt collectors as they do not collect debts owed to others; rather, they assume such debts as part of their method, whatever its merits, of credit counseling."

However, the court refused to dismiss the CROA claim, noting that "there is a fine line, in advertising and soliciting for credit-counseling services to an unsophisticated audience of lower-income debtors, between promising future rewards for creditworthiness, and implying that existing bad credit records may be prematurely expunged." (As this book goes to press, the outcome of the *Limpert* case is still pending.)

The World At Your Fingertips

- The Federal Trade Commission's pamphlet "Fiscal Fitness," which informs consumers about credit counselors, is available online at *www.ftc.gov/bcp/conline/pubs/credit/fiscal.htm*.
- The Federal Trade Commission has a publication for consumers on credit repair, "Credit Repair: Self-Help May Be Best," available online at *www.ftc.gov/bcp/conline/pubs/credit/repair.htm*.
- Consumer Credit Counseling has an article on its website written in an informative, question-and-answer format, at *www.cc-bc.com/fact_or_fiction.htm*.

Remember This

- Credit counseling sounds like a good thing, but not all credit-counseling groups are the same. Some are rip-offs for consumers. Be very careful if you decide to select one.
- Credit counseling has become even more important with the passage of the new bankruptcy law. That law requires individuals to undergo mandatory credit counseling 180 days before filing for bankruptcy.
- The new law also requires debtors under Chapters 7 and 13 to complete an "instructional course concerning personal financial management." If you don't complete this course, a discharge of debts will not be granted—you will still owe them.
- The Federal Trade Commission provides a checklist of guarantees that credit repair companies should not make. In particular, such companies should not claim that their systems will let you avoid bankruptcy, and should not guarantee that they can erase all of your unsecured debt.

Where to Go for More Information

Throughout Part I of this book, we've provided you with information and resources to help you find additional information on a variety of topics associated with credit. But there are still other resources for you to explore. Some may have been mentioned in previous chapters, but we think they're still the best places for you to start. Also included are some reminders and tips you can use to go about finding additional information.

YOU OWE IT TO YOURSELF: TWELVE WEBSITES TO GET YOU STARTED

There's definitely no shortage of credit-related sites on the Internet, but finding good, credible sources can be tricky. So you owe it to yourself to check out the sources we've culled below. Some of these websites are housed within larger sites, but they do contain detailed sections on topics associated with credit and personal finance. You're bound to find what you're looking for at one of these sites, or from a link at one of these sites (please note that they are not arranged in order of preference):

Federal Citizen Information Center—www.pueblo.gsa.gov
Downloadable articles on topics ranging from disputing credit report errors to getting credit when you're over the age of sixty-two. Click on "Money," or do a search for "credit."

Federal Trade Commission—www.ftc.gov/bcp/menu-credit. htm
The FTC's credit section includes articles and information presented in a variety of ways, including downloadable .PDFs and

audio files. Topics include credit and divorce, consumer rights, credit scoring, credit for seniors, and much more. Some topics are also available in Spanish.

The 'Lectric Law Library Lawcopedia's Banking, Finance & Credit Topic Area—www.lectlaw.com/tban.htm
This area of the 'Lectric Law Library's website includes articles on debt, credit and credit cards, loans and lenders, and scams and schemes. Links to other pertinent areas of the 'Lectric Law Library are also included for easy reference.

Bankrate.com—www.bankrate.com
Bankrate.com offers one-stop shopping for tools and information to help consumers make the best financial decisions. The site includes information on credit cards and mortgages, as well as investments, banking, and taxes.

CNN/Money—money.cnn.com
This site from CNN and Money magazine features a large section on personal finance that includes articles and tips on salient topics, such as credit and debt and college. Also featured is "Money 101," an interactive course on managing all your finances.

Consumer World— www.consumerworld.org
This site, run by consumer lawyer/advocate/educator Edgar Dworsky, features numerous links to agencies, articles, and other resources on all things consumer-related. See the "Money" section for information on credit and banking, but also check out the general "Consumer Resources" area for a plethora of other pertinent information.

National Consumer Law Center—www.consumerlaw.org
The NCLC works to protect consumers and promote marketplace justice; publications and information about initiatives (such as credit discrimination, predatory mortgage reform, and student loans) abound at this site.

Suze Orman's Resource Center—www.suzeorman.com/resources.asp
The website of renowned personal-finance expert Suze Orman, the Resource Center includes a nice selection of links organized

by topic area and features "Suze's Dictionary," a glossary of terms.

SafeBorrowing.com—www.safeborrowing.com
Developed by the American Bar Association, this site is geared toward helping consumers borrow safely when shopping for mortgage loans and reducing unfair mortgage-lending practices through information and education.

Credit Info Center—www.creditinfocenter.com

This site was started by a software-engineer-turned-loan officer-turned-software-engineer-again, and contains many helpful articles and links on topics such as consumer information, credit cards, mortgages, and loans.

Open Directory's Personal Finance Information—www.dmoz.org/Home/Personal_Finance
The Open Directory Project's website features a vast number of links relating to personal finance. Topics include identity theft issues, mortgages, loans, and debt and bankruptcy.

About.com's Credit/Debt Management—credit.about.com
This site includes articles and resources on debt counseling, debt reduction, credit law, fraud, getting credit, and more.

A NOVEL IDEA: READ MORE ABOUT IT

While none of the books listed below is actually a novel, each one makes for informative and valuable reading. Here are a few picks with which to start—though there are many, many more—on a variety of topics having to do with credit. Don't forget to check out what your local library has to offer, in addition to Amazon.com and other online bookstores.

Your Credit Score: How to Fix, Improve, and Protect the 3-Digit Number that Shapes Your Financial Future *by Liz Pulliam Weston (Prentice Hall, 2004).*

Mortgages for Dummies *by Eric Tyson and Ray Brown (For Dummies, 1999).*

The Budget Kit: The Common Cents Money Management Workbook (Fourth Edition) *by Judy Lawrence (Dearborn Trade, A Kaplan Professional Company, 2004).*

Pay It Down! From Debt to Wealth on $10 a Day *by Jean Sherman Chatzky (Portfolio, 2004).*

Rich Dad's Advisors®: The ABC's of Getting Out of Debt: Turn Bad Debt into Good Debt and Bad Credit into Good Credit *by Garrett Sutton (Warner Business Books, 2004).*

The Fragile Middle Class *by Teresa A. Sullivan, Elizabeth Warren, Jay Lawrence Westbrook (Yale University Press, 2000). A revealing study of why consumers go bankrupt.*

Taming the Sharks *by Christopher L. Peterson (University of Akron Press, 2004). A study of consumers and the high cost of credit.*

IT'S TO YOUR CREDIT, DON'T FORGET IT . . .

While websites and books are great places to get information, you might also want to see if any local venues are offering courses, lectures, seminars, or expert panels relating to the topics of personal finance, credit, debt, and so forth. Check with your local library, bar association, colleges, and senior citizens' centers (to name just a few) to see if anything is in the works. Your local radio and TV stations might also provide some salient programming. And if you can, be sure to check out the plethora of informative programs on national TV; they can be found on such cable channels as CNBC and CNNfn, and often feature finance experts such as Lou Dobbs and Suze Orman. If you're not a cable subscriber, many of these shows and channels also have websites.

And don't forget to look beyond libraries, TV, and radio. Countless message boards, user groups, mailing lists, and chat rooms exist on the Internet—many of these could help you in your quest for knowledge and provide a "been there, done that" perspective from others about the issues you're facing. Communicating with others who have been in your position is a great way to learn about other avenues to explore, and what pitfalls to avoid. Some websites may also provide an area where you can send in your questions and get answers.

PART II

Bankruptcy

CHAPTER 16

Problem Debt

What to Do When You're Swimming in Red Ink

You notice that your debts far exceed your income. You can barely pay your mortgage and provide enough food for your family. You haven't made a credit card payment in three months, a car payment in two months, or a payment on your doctors' bills in several months. Creditors are calling your house from morning until night and writing aggressive collection letters threatening you with lawsuits. You feel you are running out of options. Should you file for bankruptcy? What should you do?

Many Americans find themselves in the type of situation described above: they are in serious debt trouble. The creditors keep calling, but the debts just keep growing. Historically, debtors who failed to pay their debts were sent to prison. But in America, we now have a uniform system of bankruptcy laws that provide relief and a fresh start to many individuals who are in financial trouble and distress.

Bankruptcy is one of the alternatives available for relieving financial distress, but it is a serious legal procedure with long-term consequences. Before you take the step of filing for bankruptcy, you should learn about bankruptcy and how it works, explore other options with a credit counselor, and decide which course of action is best for you.

Some people in financial trouble can improve their situations simply by contacting and negotiating directly with creditors. Others may get help from reputable local financial-counseling programs or reputable consumer credit counseling services, which have experience negotiating with creditors and formulating and establishing repayment plans. Remember, bankruptcy is a last resort, not a first resort. For some people, however, bankruptcy relief may be the only realistic alternative.

The choice of a remedy is not always easy. As a first step,

consider the pros and cons of filing for bankruptcy, and compare the two basic types of consumer bankruptcy: **Chapter 7 bankruptcy** ("straight bankruptcy") and **Chapter 13 bankruptcy** (sometimes called "wage-earner bankruptcy"). (These types of bankruptcy are compared and contrasted in chapters 18, 19, and 20 of this book.) Each of these types of bankruptcy is covered by a section of the federal **Bankruptcy Code,** under which bankruptcies are filed all over America.

In April 2005, President Bush signed into law **the Bankruptcy Abuse Prevention and Consumer Protection Act of 2005**. This law—which went into effect in large part on October 17, 2005—was the first major overhaul of bankruptcy legislation since 1978, and effected major changes in the existing bankruptcy system. One major change is that those who file for bankruptcy are required to consult with an "approved nonprofit budget and credit counseling agency" before filing. Other major changes make it more difficult for people to file for bankruptcy under Chapter 7, which means that more people will have to file under Chapter 13.

If you ultimately decide to seek relief in bankruptcy, you should hire a lawyer who is familiar with the federal bankruptcy laws. Given the new law, you will need an attorney who has stayed abreast of recent changes. Keep in mind that, since the new law is more complicated and imposes new duties on lawyers, it is possible that the cost of legal services for bankruptcies will increase.

ALTERNATIVES TO BANKRUPTCY

Before resorting to bankruptcy, you should explore alternatives for taking care of debts you cannot pay. For example, a creditor might be willing to settle its claim in exchange for a partial cash payment, or it might be willing to stretch out the term of its loan and reduce the size of the payments you owe each month. These concessions would allow you to pay off your debt by making smaller payments over a longer period of time; the creditor would eventually receive full payment. If you pursue this option, you should make sure you do not end up paying too much interest.

You may also find that you are **judgment proof,** in which case you do not need to file for bankruptcy to protect your property and wages. "Judgment proof" simply means that you have so little money, income, and property that you would be unable to pay a court judgment entered against you. In addition, under state and federal exemption laws, creditors are not allowed to seize certain income from judgment-proof debtors, such as Social Security income, wages below certain levels, and certain personal property. If there's no point in creditors going after you in court, there may be less reason for you to declare bankruptcy. If you believe that you may be judgment proof, discuss your situation with a credit counselor.

Keep in mind, however, that if you don't declare bankruptcy, creditors can foreclose on your home, repossess your car, and continue their collection efforts. Creditors will also be able to enforce court judgments against you if your financial situation improves.

Learn What You Owe

When considering filing for bankruptcy, a good first step is to assess your debt level as compared to your income level. Before

---

⚠ KEEPING CURRENT

Be aware that bankruptcy law has recently changed. A few provisions took effect in the spring of 2005; the rest became effective on October 17, 2005. The American Bankruptcy Institute (ABI) provides a wealth of information about the new law on its website (*www.abiworld.org*), including several analyses of the changes it effects. Of course, the best way to understand how the new law affects you is to seek advice tailored to your situation from a lawyer with experience in the area of bankruptcy.

---

you can make a plan as to your financial future, you need to determine what debts you owe and whether you can live within a strict budget. Many people can reduce their debt significantly simply by living within a self-imposed budget and not spending money on unnecessary items. They can learn to take charge of their lives and begin to reclaim their financial futures. For others, bankruptcy might be the only realistic option. But you can't make this decision until you figure out and carefully examine your income and debt.

Contacting Creditors

If you are behind on your payments, the debt collectors for each of your creditors may already be calling or writing you. You might be more successful if, acting on your own behalf without a lawyer, you phone each creditor, ask for the credit department, explain your sincere intent to repay the account, and express your need to stretch out the number of monthly payments and reduce the dollar amount of each payment. You might also offer to come to the collection department's office to further discuss your situation. Make sure you always ask for and write down the name of each person you talk to. Ask each creditor to agree to a voluntary plan for the repayment of your debts. This may help you avoid having to file for bankruptcy.

In dealing with creditors, ask them to reduce or drop late fees and interest, and get all agreements in writing before making payment. If you reach a settlement for a single payment, when making the full and final payment be sure to include the language "paid in full, final, and complete satisfaction of [your account, including account number]" on the face and back of your check. Never give creditors information that would enable them to directly access your checking account; maintain control over your payments.

One problem that often arises when dealing with multiple creditors is that some creditors may be unwilling to give you more time to pay without knowing what your other creditors are willing to do. In such cases, it may be difficult for you to arrange a meeting of your creditors to negotiate a collective reduction in your monthly payments or the amount of your debt. If this is the case, you can also seek the help of a lawyer to negotiate such an arrangement. Some universities, local courts, military bases, credit unions, and housing authorities have credit-counseling programs, but counselors affiliated with such programs may not have the ability or experience to meaningfully negotiate with your creditors to reduce your monthly payments.

Your best bet may be to seek the help of a reputable non-profit consumer credit counseling service (CCCS). You can find the nearest CCCS by calling 800-388-2227 or by visiting *www.nfcc.org*. Some CCCS establishments charge a small monthly service fee. In addition, you should be aware that creditors frequently provide most of the support for financial-counseling services. As a result, some observers believe that they tend to downplay bankruptcy as an option—though this is not necessarily a bad thing, since you are generally better off if you can avoid bankruptcy by reducing your debt to a manageable level.

In the repayment plans arranged through credit-counseling centers, you generally make monthly payments that are distributed among your creditors until your debts are paid in full. Creditors usually prefer this kind of plan, since it eventually allows them to get more of their money than they would if you filed for

---

⚠ A WORD OF WARNING

Be cautious when seeking out a for-profit counseling service. If you choose such a service, be sure you understand its fees and what it will do for you. Some services require long-term commitments. Investigate the service and its credentials carefully; consider calling the local Better Business Bureau for information. And always be on the lookout for predatory debt counselors. (See Chapter 14 for more information and advice about choosing a credit counselor.)

Chapter 7 bankruptcy. This approach may also benefit you, to the extent it prevents you from having to file for bankruptcy.

Under a repayment plan arranged through a financial-counseling service, you still might have to pay interest charges on some or all of your debts. However, in these types of situations, many creditors will agree to waive or reduce interest charges and delinquency fees if you ask them to do so.

Consolidating Debt

Occasionally you may buy time and avoid bankruptcy by consolidating your debts—that is, by taking out a big loan to pay off your smaller debts. However, the primary danger of consolidation is that you may find it very easy to use your credit cards to borrow even more money, which could leave you with even more total debt and no additional income to make the monthly payments. Indeed, if you have taken a second mortgage on your home to get a consolidation loan, failure to make payments on the loan could even put you at risk for losing your home. You should also analyze thoroughly the interest rates on such loans: make sure a loan's interest rate is lower than that of your credit cards.

( ) ASK A LAWYER

Q. I'm considering debt consolidation, but it sounds too good to be true. What should I be wary of? How can I protect myself in this process?

A. If it seems too good to be true, it probably is. What will your payments be? What is the interest rate? Is there a prepayment penalty? What would you have to give up? If you do consolidate, cut up your credit cards—or put them in a safe-deposit box, or even in the freezer in a plastic bag filled with water. If you lower your payments by consolidating, you will not accomplish anything if you continue to use your cards and run up more debt.

—Answer by Marc S. Stern, Law Offices of Marc S. Stern, Seattle, Washington

A. You might first consider meeting with a not-for-profit financial-counseling service or a bankruptcy lawyer about the pros and cons of debt consolidation, especially if your home is involved. Compare the interest rate to be paid if you consolidate your debts with your current interest rate. After the debt consolidation, do not abuse credit cards. Otherwise, you will find yourself in the same position that you were in before—but the second time around, there will be no equity in your home to justify consolidation. Be careful: You could lose your home if you use it as collateral for the consolidated debt. Remember that with debt consolidation you are trading in your unsecured credit card debt for a secured lien against your home—that's the trade-off for a lower interest rate! Maybe a Chapter 7 or Chapter 13 bankruptcy would be best for you instead of debt consolidation if the risks of relapsing into financial trouble are too high.

—Answer by Judge David S. Kennedy, United States Bankruptcy Court, Western District of Tennessee

A. You can try to consolidate your debts on your own, or through an agency. If you use an agency, be sure to check its references with the Better Business Bureau and ensure that it is approved by the U.S. trustee for credit counseling in the bankruptcy system. It is important to understand the fees, both up front and during the payment period, and what happens if you can't make a payment—for example, a drastic increase in your interest rate. Be careful if you take a second mortgage or a home equity loan: in either case, you place your home at risk, and your interest payments may not always be deductible in full.

—Answer by David Greer, Williams Mullen Hofheimer Nusbaum, Norfolk, Virginia

THE WORLD AT YOUR FINGERTIPS

- Myvesta.org, formerly known as Debt Counselors of America, offers an interactive website focusing on nonbankruptcy remedies such as debt consolidation; visit *www.myvesta.org*.

- Debt Advice is a major nonprofit site, affiliated with the National Foundation for Credit Counseling and offering much information for consumers; visit *www.debtadvice.org/index.html*.
- Another nonprofit site is American Consumer Credit Counseling; visit *www.consumercredit.com*.
- DebtReliefUSA.net is a for-profit site that can help you reduce your debt; visit *www.debtreliefusa.net*.
- The National Foundation for Credit Counseling provides debt relief advice, credit counseling, and related services at *www.nfcc.org*.

REMEMBER THIS

- Bankruptcy is one of many alternatives available for relieving financial distress. Examine all the options available to you for dealing with your financial problems and decide which course of action is best for you. Remember, under the new bankruptcy law, it may be more difficult than in the past for you to file for Chapter 7 bankruptcy; you may wish to speak to an attorney about the different types of bankruptcy available to you.
- Try negotiating directly with creditors to obtain some financial relief. Creditors may be willing to reduce their interest rates or allow a longer payment plan.
- You may also seek help from a reputable local financial-counseling program or a reputable consumer credit-counseling service. Such services may be able to help you consolidate—and reduce—your debt.
- If you do decide to file for bankruptcy, the new bankruptcy law requires you to undergo credit counseling through a non-profit credit-counseling agency in the six months before you file. You have nothing to lose by exploring this option, whether you eventually file for bankruptcy or not.
- Remember that not all for-profit and nonprofit credit-counseling services are equal; some are better than others. Contact the Better Business Bureau before dealing with such a service.
- In dealing with creditors, ask them to reduce or forgive late

fees and reduce interest. Get all agreements in writing before making payment. Never give creditors information that would enable them to directly access your checking account; maintain control over your payments.

• Occasionally, you may buy time by consolidating your debts—that is, by taking out a big loan to pay off your smaller debts. However, the primary danger of consolidation is that you may find it very easy to use your credit cards to borrow even more money, which could make the total amount of your debt even larger. Consolidating credit card debts by taking out a second mortage can also put you at risk of losing your home if you can't make the payments.

CHAPTER 17

Bankruptcy Defined

Your Guide to a Complicated Area of Law

You are mired in debt. You are essentially broke. You've assessed your income as compared to your debt level, you've tried to negotiate with creditors, you've tried to work with a nonprofit credit-counseling center, and you've tried to develop a workable budget. But your debt level is simply too high. You probably need to consult a lawyer and file bankruptcy. You need a fresh start.

Bankruptcy is a legal process through which people and businesses can seek to obtain fresh financial starts when they are in such financial difficulty that they cannot repay their debts as agreed. When a person files bankruptcy, a court eliminates all or a portion of that person's or business's existing debts under Chapter 7, or stretches out the monthly payments on those debts under the court's protection and supervision under Chapter 13.

⚠ NEW LAW MAKES FILING TOUGHER

As a result of the new bankruptcy law—the Bankruptcy Abuse Prevention and Consumer Protection Act of 2005, generally effective on October 17, 2005—it is harder to file Chapter 7 bankruptcy than it was in the past. Under the new law, Chapter 7 bankruptcies may increasingly be dismissed. In addition, some bankruptcies that would have been filed under Chapter 7 will now be filed under Chapter 13 at the outset, and others are more likely to be converted to Chapter 13 bankruptcies after being filed. Under Chapter 13, people will have to pay off a greater portion of their debts over a period of up to five years.

The bankruptcy process is also designed to provide a measure of protection to creditors. Secured creditors are often in a better position than unsecured creditors because they hold a lien—an interest in the property of the debtor that backs up the right to payment—on the debtor's assets. But sometimes even general unsecured creditors can obtain some money from a debtor's estate, and will share equally in whatever payments the debtor can afford to make.

While your bankruptcy case is pending, most creditors cannot try to collect their debts from you directly. Nor can they try to collect from you after the conclusion of the case for any and all discharged debts—that is, debts that the court has excused you from paying. Remember, however, that not all debts are discharged. There may still be debts for which you are liable after the conclusion of your bankruptcy case.

LEGAL FOUNDATIONS OF BANKRUPTCY

Article I, Section 8, Clause 4 of the Constitution authorizes the United States Congress to pass "uniform laws on the subject of bankruptcies throughout the United States." In keeping with this authorization, Congress has created an intricate body of law that

---

(i) WHAT CAUSES BANKRUPTCY?

There can be many causes of bankruptcy. Approximately 90 percent of bankruptcies are the result of unemployment, medical bills, or divorce. The remaining 10 percent are caused by a variety of factors—including the failure of a business or overuse of credit cards. Every individual situation is different, though a common feature of many bankruptcies is a large amount of debt on credit cards with high interest rates, and it is often a dramatic downward shift in financial circumstances that triggers the bankruptcy process.

governs bankruptcy, most recently the Bankruptcy Abuse Prevention and Consumer Protection Act of 2005. This law builds upon the Bankruptcy Code that Congress passed in 1978, which was generally effective on October 1, 1979. The Federal Rules of Bankruptcy govern the procedure used in bankruptcy cases and proceedings. Federal bankruptcy judges hear such cases and proceedings, and every federal judicial district has a bankruptcy court; there are ninety such courts in the United States.

FILING FOR BANKRUPTCY

Filing for bankruptcy is a very personal, very serious decision. Most people file when they have made a good-faith effort to repay their debts, but see no way out of debt other than filing for bankruptcy. Once the decision has been made, a person or business may declare bankruptcy by filing a petition with the U.S. Bankruptcy Court—that is, a request that the court provide protection and relief under the Bankruptcy Code. The person filing for bankruptcy—the debtor—must provide information about his or her assets, liabilities, income, and expenditures, a certificate to prove that he or she has undergone credit counseling within 180 days of filing, tax returns, a photo ID, and evidence

( ) TALKING TO A LAWYER

Q. *I'm pretty desperate and seriously considering bankruptcy, but I'm worried about the effect of bankruptcy on the rest of my life. What will happen to my credit cards? Will my neighbors and coworkers know I'm bankrupt?*

A. It depends. If you are current on one or more credit cards at the time you file a bankruptcy case, the likelihood is that you may keep them. If you owe debts on your credit cards, however, the likelihood is that the cards will be cancelled—although you can try to negotiate terms with the credit card companies. It is true that bankruptcy filing is a matter of public record; however, unless you owe debts to your neighbors and coworkers, they may not find out about it. If you owe them money, you will have to include them in your list of creditors, in which case they will receive formal notice of your bankruptcy filing. If a prospective landlord or employer asks about your bankruptcy, he or she may be sympathetic if you explain your reasons for filing—for example, medical problems, loss of a job, or divorce.

—Answer by Judge David S. Kennedy, United States
Bankruptcy Court, Western District of Tennessee

A. Bankruptcy is a serious measure to be utilized only as a last resort for serious debt problems. The bankruptcy will be a matter of public record, meaning that a record of the filing will be available for anyone to find if they want to look for it, including neighbors, mortgage companies, landlords, and future employers. If you file a Chapter 13 case, your credit cards should be torn up and will no longer be available to you. (This could be changed with court permission and the approval of the credit card companies, but don't count on it.) In a Chapter 7 case, you may be allowed to keep a credit card that has a zero balance, or one that you agree to reaffirm (continue to pay after the filing), but the interest rate may be significantly higher than it was before, and the company may wish to cancel your card in response to the bankruptcy filing. You need to be prepared to pay your monthly balances in full should you decide to keep an active credit card following a Chapter 7 filing. This will prevent you from getting back into the same situation that caused you to file in the first place. (There is now an eight-year wait between Chapter 7 filings.) Finally, an employer isn't allowed to discriminate against you for filing bankruptcy, but keep in mind that bankruptcy may nonetheless impact your employment in situations where financial stability is an issue—for example, if you seek to attain a new position or license.

—Answer by Shayna M. Steinfeld, Steinfeld & Steinfeld, P.C.,
Atlanta, Georgia

of recent payments from employers. Complete disclosure, candor, and honesty are required. Often, debtors have a lawyer prepare and file their bankruptcy petitions and other information for them, although some debtors do represent themselves. Bankruptcy relief is a privilege available to most people; full bankruptcy relief is not an absolute right.

Secured and Unsecured Debts

A **secured debt,** such as a home mortgage or a car loan, is a debt that a creditor is entitled to collect by repossessing and selling certain assets of the debtor if payments are missed. With a secured loan, the creditor extends credit but requires the debtor to put up certain collateral to guarantee the loan, such as a house,

---

⚠ USE BANKRUPTCY WITH CAUTION

Bankruptcy may be the best, or only, solution for extreme financial hardship. But as noted earlier, it should be used only as a last resort, since it always has long-lasting consequences. The record of a bankruptcy can remain in your credit files for as long as ten years; this is a long time in today's economic system, in which so much depends on having good credit. Moreover, there are limits on how often you can fully benefit from certain forms of bankruptcy. For example, you may lose any equity you have in your home or car, since that property might be sold and the equity realized for the benefit of your creditors.

Study the pros and cons carefully before resorting to bankruptcy as a means of solving your economic troubles, and be sure you understand the types of bankruptcy cases you can file. Do not wait until the last minute to seek help—the day before a foreclosure or court hearing may be too late to get good advice or to take advantage of nonbankruptcy options. Get advice when you find you cannot pay your monthly expenses in full for more than three months, or if you face a sudden large debt, such as a medical bill, for which you cannot make payment arrangements.

---

a car, or household goods. In other words, the creditor has "se-cured" the loan. Most consumer debts are **unsecured**, and cred-itors of such debts are not allowed to seize your assets if you miss payments.

Examples of secured debt include home loans, car loans, judgment liens (in which someone obtains a court judgment against you for failing to pay a debt), tax liens (in which the county, state, or federal government has a lien on your property because of failure to pay taxes), and second mortgages. Exam-ples of unsecured debt include most credit card debt, doctors' bills, legal bills, utility bills, and bills for various other miscella-neous purchases.

Advantages of Filing for Bankruptcy

There are several advantages to filing for bankruptcy. By far the most important advantage is that filing for bankruptcy allows the vast majority of filers a fresh financial start. As we shall see below, if you file for Chapter 7 bankruptcy you may be **dis-charged from** (forgiven from paying) most *un*secured debts. You may be able to **exempt** (that is, keep) many of your assets, al-though state exemption laws vary widely in their descriptions of which assets you may keep. Bear in mind that in some cases, the new bankruptcy law will make it harder to obtain a Chapter 7 bankruptcy discharge.

Another big advantage of filing for bankruptcy is that the mo-ment you file, most collection efforts must stop immediately. As soon as your bankruptcy petition is filed, there is by law an **auto-matic stay,** which stops most collection activity immediately, in-cluding home foreclosures and car repossessions. If a creditor continues to try to collect a debt, that creditor may be held in contempt of court or ordered to pay damages. The automatic stay applies even to the loan that you may have obtained to buy your car. If you are reasonably current on the payments and con-tinue to make payments on that secured debt, it is unlikely that your creditor will do anything to collect. If you miss payments, however, your creditor will probably petition the bankruptcy court to have the stay terminated in order either to repossess the car or to renegotiate the loan.

Federal law protects your right to file for bankruptcy—for example, you cannot be fired from your job *solely* because you have filed.

( ) **TALKING TO A LAWYER**

Q. I'm way behind in my rent payments and my residential landlord is threatening to evict me. Can I stop him from doing that if I file for bankruptcy?

A. Not necessarily. The answer depends upon whether your residential landlord has only threatened to evict you, or has actually begun eviction proceedings before you file for bankruptcy.

Under the new law, if your residential landlord has already begun eviction proceedings in state court and has obtained a judgment for possession of the residential premises before you file for bankruptcy, the landlord can evict you unless you, the debtor, do two things: (1) file a certification with the bankruptcy court, along with your bankruptcy petition, that there are circumstances under applicable non-bankruptcy law that would allow you to reinstate the residential lease and cure the monetary default; and (2) pay thirty days' rent to the bankruptcy court clerk to be transmitted to the landlord. The landlord can still object, in which case the bankruptcy court must decide within ten days of the filing of the objection whether the landlord can proceed with the eviction in order to gain possession of the rental property. Then you must also file a second certification with the bankruptcy court, within thirty days of filing your bankruptcy petition, stating that the pre-petition default that gave rise to the landlord's judgment for possession in state court has been cured—in other words, that you have paid all back rent. Even after you file this second certification, however, the landlord may still object, in which case the court must determine within ten days of the objection whether the landlord can proceed with the eviction action.

The new law also provides that, if the residential landlord has begun eviction proceedings before you file for bankruptcy on the grounds that you have endangered the rental property or have used or allowed others to use illegal substances on the property, all the landlord has to do is file a certification to this effect with the bankruptcy court clerk. The landlord can then proceed with the eviction process fifteen days later if the debtor does not object. Note that the law does allow you to object within fifteen days and, at a hearing, show the bankruptcy court that the situation has been remedied or never existed in the first place. At that point, it will be up to the bankruptcy court to decide whether your landlord can proceed or not. Bear in mind that the deadlines for these types of situations are very short. An experienced and qualified lawyer will be able to help you better understand your particular position.

—Answer by Judge David S. Kennedy, United States Bankruptcy Court, Western District of Tennessee

Q. I'm being sued by one of my creditors. If I file for bankruptcy, will filing stop the suit from proceeding? If so, how long in advance of the court date should I file?

A. Yes, the filing of bankruptcy will automatically stop the suit. Rely upon the advice of your lawyer regarding when your bankruptcy case is to be filed. Most, but not all, lawsuits will "go away" after a bankruptcy filing, as the defendant's debts will be subject to discharge in bankruptcy. If possible, file the bankruptcy case before a judgment is rendered against you in state court.

—Answer by Judge David S. Kennedy, United States Bankruptcy Court, Western District of Tennessee

A. Yes. There is an automatic stay in bankruptcy cases that immediately prohibits creditors from continuing such actions without getting the bankruptcy court's permission. You can file at any time before the date of the applicable hearing in order to stop a proceeding, even moments before if necessary, but the situation becomes much more complicated after a hearing has occurred.

—**Answer by Shayna M. Steinfeld, Steinfeld & Steinfeld, P.C., Atlanta, Georgia**

Q. My spouse and I are getting divorced. If I file for bankruptcy, will the automatic stay affect my divorce?

A. Yes. While some narrow exceptions to the automatic stay do apply to divorces involving a party to a bankruptcy, in most cases the stay will, as a practical matter, prevent completion of the divorce until the stay is lifted, expires, or is terminated. However, a spouse can file a motion with the bankruptcy court asking for relief from the stay so that certain aspects of the divorce and a division of the marital assets can proceed. Failure to obtain relief from the stay before proceeding with certain aspects of a divorce that are not exempt from the stay can lead to sanctions being entered for violations of the stay. The interaction of bankruptcy and divorce law is very complicated. You should consult with a lawyer who is knowledgeable in both areas of the law if you are contemplating filing for bankruptcy while your divorce is ongoing, or vice versa.

—**Answer by Gregory S. Mager, Ansay, O'Neil, Cannon, Hollman, DeJong, S.C., Port Washington, Wisconsin**

Getting Credit After Bankruptcy

A study by the Credit Research Center at Purdue University found that about one-third of consumers who filed for bankruptcy had obtained lines of credit within three years of filing. One-half had obtained them within five years. However, the terms of the new credit may be affected by the fact that a bankruptcy filing has occurred. For example, if you might have been eligible for a bank card with a 14 percent interest rate before bankruptcy, the best card that you can get after bankruptcy might carry a rate of 20 or 25 percent—or you might have to rely on a card secured by a deposit that you make with the credit card issuer. Use your cards only when absolutely necessary, and pay them off in full each month if possible.

Disadvantages of Filing for Bankruptcy

Perhaps the major disadvantage of filing for bankruptcy is that a record of the filing remains on your credit report for as long as ten years. Filing for bankruptcy will thus make it more difficult for you to obtain credit in the future. Another disadvantage of bankruptcy is that you might have to surrender some of your nonexempt personal property or your home to a bankruptcy trustee, who will then liquidate (sell) the assets and apply the money to debts you have with your creditors. Finally, there is still a stigma associated with bankruptcy in some circles, though that stigma has been reduced over the years as many people—including celebrities—have filed.

TYPES OF BANKRUPTCY

There are several types of bankruptcy, each addressed in a separate chapter of the federal Bankruptcy Code: Chapter 7, Chapter 9, Chapter 11, Chapter 12, and Chapter 13.

Chapter 7 and Chapter 13 are the types of bankruptcies available for individual consumers. Chapter 9 involves bankruptcies filed by cities and towns. Chapter 12 deals with the special cases of family farmers. Chapter 11 bankruptcy, called **reorganization**, is used primarily by commercial businesses that are restructuring or liquidating while continuing their operations. While an individual not engaged in business may file for Chapter 11 bankruptcy under some circumstances, such proceedings are expensive and complex, and consumer debtors nor-

⚠️ **KEEP UP INSURANCE PAYMENTS**

You should be sure to maintain adequate insurance coverage on your home and/or automobile during your bankruptcy case. If you don't maintain insurance coverage, a creditor may be able to get the automatic stay lifted and repossess your car or foreclose on your home.

mally use Chapter 7 or Chapter 13. This book will mainly address Chapter 7 and 13 bankruptcies, though we will also take a quick look at bankruptcy options for family farmers and family fishermen available under Chapter 12.

Proceedings under **Chapter 7** (straight bankruptcy) involve the borrower surrendering most of his or her nonexempt assets. A bankruptcy trustee is appointed in every Chapter 7 case to administer nonexempt assets (if any) and distribute to the creditors either the assets themselves or the proceeds from **liquidating** (selling) them. Some assets are exempt under Chapter 7, and cannot be sold to satisfy debts. The assets that are exempt depend on specific federal laws and on state laws that vary significantly around the country.

It used to be the case that all consumers were eligible to file for bankruptcy under Chapter 7; however, under the new law passed in 2005, an individual debtor who earns more than the median income in his or her state may, depending on the particular circumstances, be denied a Chapter 7 discharge. (You can find more information about Chapter 7 bankruptcy in the next chapter.)

Proceedings under **Chapter 13** (so-called wage-earner bankruptcy) require the debtor to propose a repayment plan for repaying all or a portion of his or her debt in installments from his or her future income. Chapter 13 plans can last for anywhere from three to five years. Of course, if a person can pay off all of his or her unsecured claims in less than three years, the repayment period can be shorter.

(i) YOU'LL STILL HAVE TO PAY THESE DEBTS

Ordinarily, you cannot discharge:

- fines and penalties imposed for violating the law, such as criminal court fines and criminal restitution;

- debts you forget to list in your bankruptcy papers, unless the creditor learns of your bankruptcy case or the creditor could no longer file a claim after learning of the bankruptcy;

- student loans, unless it would be an undue hardship for you to repay;

- child support and alimony;

- many property settlement obligations from a divorce or separation, including past due amounts;

- fraudulent debts (last-minute credit binges and/or cash advances);

- debts for personal injury or death caused by your intoxicated driving; and

- recent income tax debts and most other tax debts.

In general, the new law narrows the requirements for Chapter 13 discharge, meaning that more debts will be paid under Chapter 13 than were paid previously.

Under any bankruptcy chapter, once the bankruptcy case ends, most borrowers are discharged from—that is, no longer liable for—most of the debts they incurred before filing their bankruptcy petitions, called **pre-petition debts**. In other words, the court excuses such borrowers from having to repay most debts. The borrowers then start over again with substantially clean financial slates, except that a record of the bankruptcies will generally remain on their credit records for ten years.

You should understand, however, that with both Chapter 7 and Chapter 13 bankruptcies, a discharge does *not* automati-

⚠ TOUGH STANCE ON STUDENT LOANS

Whether it's because college seems so long ago, or because the money wasn't spent on anything tangible, many people forget that they have an obligation to repay student loans. However, student loans are one of the most difficult types of debt to escape: most student loans survive bankruptcy, and can still be collected decades after college because there is no statute of limitations on the repayment of such debts.

Most student loans are made by private banks, but are subsidized by the federal government so they have relatively low interest rates. According to the American Council on Education, two-thirds of students at private four-year colleges have student loans, which average $17,000 per student by graduation day. Students must start paying off their loans six months after graduation, and generally must repay over ten years.

The Department of Education has been pursuing student loan debtors aggressively over the last five years. It has the power to garnish paychecks and seize tax refunds and Social Security payments without a court order.

Under the old bankruptcy law, student loans from government agencies and not-for-profit entities could not be discharged in bankruptcy. The new bankruptcy law extends that prohibition to student loans from nongovernmental entitities and for-profit organizations. Now, no student loan is dischargeable unless the debtor can show an "undue hardship," which is a difficult standard to meet.

The lesson: don't forget about your student loans and assume you won't have to pay them. More than likely you'll be repaying what you owe for ten years or more after the golden days of college are over.

cally wipe out secured creditors' liens, most student loans, support payments to children, most recent taxes, debts for personal injury due to driving while intoxicated, some fines and penalties, or debts you forgot to list in your bankruptcy petition. Such debts will remain due and payable—along with, perhaps, certain other specifically nondischarged debts. In some cases, the court may deny a discharge altogether.

When Are Debts Discharged?

The bankruptcy court enters a discharge order relatively early in most Chapter 7 cases, usually from four to six months after you file your petition. In Chapter 13 cases, you make full or partial payment to creditors under a court-confirmed plan over a period of time, which can be as long as five years, and then receive a discharge. Under the new law, debtors cannot obtain a discharge under Chapter 7 or 13 until they have taken an approved course in personal financial management.

(i) AN ALTERNATIVE FOR FARMERS AND FISHERMEN: CHAPTER 12

Family farmers and family fishermen have the option of a special type of bankruptcy under Chapter 12 of the Bankruptcy Code. It is one of a series of special farm aid provisions enacted to help farmers and fishermen survive periodic economic slumps and save their family farms or commercial fishing operations.

Chapter 12 is for family farmers and family fishermen who have regular incomes. It allows family farmers and fishermen with commercial fishing operations to avoid foreclosure on their farms or fishing operations by pledging part of the profits from their future crops or catches to pay off their debts, particularly those secured by a farm or commercial fishing vessel.

Only farmers and fishermen acting in good faith have the right to adjust their debts under Chapter 12. In order for a petition to proceed quickly, as in other chapter filings, the debtor must submit to the bankruptcy court a list of creditors, a list of assets and liabilities, and a statement of financial affairs. The debtor usually will require legal help. The process is similar to that of a Chapter 13 case, but the discharge is the same as in a Chapter 7 case (subject to the same exceptions).

Chapter 12 of the Bankruptcy Code specifically defines "family farmer" and "family fisherman," and a debtor must fit this definition in order to file.

How Long Will Bankruptcy Remain
on a Credit Record?

Most Chapter 7 and Chapter 13 bankruptcies stay on your credit record for ten years from the date you file for bankruptcy. In some states, a Chapter 13 bankruptcy will remain on your record for only seven years, as an incentive for people to use Chapter 13 bankruptcy and pay off part of their debts instead of using Chapter 7 bankruptcy.

The consequences of having a bankruptcy on your credit record can be severe. Creditors may deny you credit in the future or charge you significantly higher interest rates. So long as your credit record includes unfavorable information, you may have credit problems. This means that you may have trouble renting an apartment, getting a loan to buy a car, or obtaining a mortgage to buy a house.

In one respect, however, bankruptcy may improve your chance for credit. Because Chapter 7 provides for a discharge of debts no more than once every eight years, lenders know that a credit applicant who has just emerged from Chapter 7 cannot soon repeat the process.

WORKING WITH A LAWYER

There are a number of ways for debtors to find bankruptcy attorneys to represent them:

• The American Board of Certification has certified some one thousand lawyers specializing in bankruptcy; you can get their names and locations from the ABI website at *www.abiworld.org*.

• In addition, some states certify lawyers as bankruptcy specialists when they have had significant experience in the field. Access the ABA Web page at *www.abanet.org/legalservices/ specialization/source.html* for a list of state certification programs, some of which encompass bankruptcy law.

• You could also ask a lawyer whom you know well to recommend a specialist.

• Suggestions from a friend, a relative, a neighbor, or an associate who has had a good experience with a particular lawyer may also help.

• Bar associations and groups operated for people with special needs, such as the elderly or persons with disabilities, often provide referral services. For a list of bar association referral programs, access the ABA Web page at *www.abanet.org/legal services/lris/directory.html*.

• You might also find a lawyer by looking in the yellow pages of your telephone directory or at advertisements in your local newspaper. If you hire a lawyer from the phone book or a direct-mail solicitation, be sure to check his or her references. Remember that phone book ads and direct-solicitation ads do not ensure that you will receive good service.

FILING ON YOUR OWN

It is perfectly legal to file your own bankruptcy petition without a lawyer; however, the more complicated your debt situation, the more risky it is to represent yourself. If you do decide to file for bankruptcy on your own, bear in mind that the law changed in 2005, and make sure that the information you rely upon is up-to-date. It is not advisable to hire a nonlawyer to help you file bankruptcy.

Be careful in your selection of a lawyer, and make sure your lawyer is familiar with bankruptcy laws and procedures and has a good reputation. When you have an initial talk with a prospective lawyer, ask yourself: Does he or she seem to understand your financial (and emotional) problems and offer solutions, or is he or she simply affiliated with a "factory" that does little more than process paper?

You can, and should, discuss your lawyer's professional fees in advance and understand what procedures are covered by these fees. This will give you as clear an idea as possible of what the bankruptcy procedure will cost. You do not need to be surprised later on.

In addition, discuss with your lawyer whether he or she will charge additional fees if there are proceedings required other than the filing of the case. Your lawyer's responsibilities in a basic case will include preparing and filing the petitions and additional schedules and attending the creditors' meeting. (Note that the filing requirements have increased under the new 2005 bankruptcy law.) In some states, filing for bankruptcy may also include preparing and filing a homestead deed. In addition, in the case of a Chapter 7 bankruptcy, there may be reaffirmation agreements to negotiate, sign, and file; objections to exemptions; homestead declarations to complete; or objections to the discharge of some or all of your debts. In a Chapter 13 case, your lawyer may have to deal with objections to approval of your repayment plan or the way you have valued your assets. In either chapter, your lawyer may have to respond to your creditors' **motions for relief from the automatic stay**, which seek court approval to repossess property or foreclose on real estate.

In some Chapter 13 cases, you can pay your lawyer from the assets of your estate, which is administered by the court in a bankruptcy case. This is not the case, however, with lawyer fees under Chapter 7. In 2004, the Supreme Court decided in the case of *Lamie v. United States Trustee* that bankruptcy attorneys are not entitled to receive compensation from the bankruptcy estate in Chapter 7 cases. Depending upon the complexity of your case, your legal fees might range from $400 to $5,000. Chapter 13 cases are usually more expensive than Chapter 7 cases, though it helps that such fees may be included in your repayment plan.

THE WORLD AT YOUR FINGERTIPS

• To find a certified bankruptcy lawyer, access the American Board of Certification website at *www.abcworld.org/abchome.html*.

• To understand more about bankruptcy, access the U.S. Bankruptcy Code and bankruptcy rules at *www.thebankruptcysite.com/bankruptcy_law.htm*.

- For bankruptcy basics and forms, access the site of the U.S. Bankruptcy Courts at *www.uscourts.gov/bankruptcycourts.html*.
- To find out what exemptions you are entitled to in your state, and whether you can choose between state or federal exemptions, click on "bankruptcy exemptions" at *www.bankruptcyaction.com*.
- Bankrate.com has an informative article entitled "12 Myths about Bankruptcy." It is accessible online at *www.bankrate.com/brm/news/debt/debt_manage_2004/bankruptcy-misconceptions.asp*.
- The American Bankruptcy Institute has an informative publication on its website entitled "25 Changes to Personal Bankruptcy Law." It is accessible online at *abiworld.net/bank bill/changes.html*.

REMEMBER THIS

- Bankruptcy is a legal process through which people and businesses can obtain fresh financial starts. It is for people who are not in a financial position to repay their debts.
- In many cases, bankruptcy could be your only realistic option. If you think this may be the case, consult a lawyer for advice.
- There are different types of bankruptcy. Two major types for consumers are Chapter 7 (straight/liquidation bankruptcies) and Chapter 13 ("wage-earner" bankruptcies). Your lawyer will help you decide under which chapters you are eligible to file, and which one is best for you.
- Select a bankruptcy lawyer with care. Do not rely solely on advertisements. You may contact your local bar association, refer to the American Board of Certification, or take one of the other steps recommended in this chapter. Do not hire a nonlawyer to file your bankruptcy.
- Bankruptcy cases begin with the filing of a petition with the U.S. Bankruptcy Court.
- During bankruptcy, creditors cannot call you to collect debts. Once a bankruptcy petition is filed, an automatic stay prohibits most collection activities.

- Most consumer debts are unsecured. Some creditors are called "secured creditors" because they have the right to seize and sell the collateral for a loan, such as a car or your home, if payments are missed. Secured creditors have more protection in a bankruptcy than unsecured creditors.

- Use bankruptcy with caution; a record of the filing remains in your credit record for as long as ten years.

- Your bankruptcy must include all of your debts and property; you cannot file bankruptcy only for a certain debt or type of debt. If you have your own business as a sole proprietor, it must be included in the filing. However, if your business is incorporated, it is considered a separate entity and does not have to be included.

- The new bankruptcy law, which took effect in October 2005, imposes even more requirements on those filing for bankruptcy. It will result in some Chapter 7 cases being dismissed or converted to Chapter 13 cases. If anything, this new law makes the selection of a qualified bankruptcy attorney even more important.

CHAPTER 18

Straight Bankruptcy:
Chapter 7

The Most Common Form of Bankruptcy

Mr. Smith makes a modest income and has few significant assets. He rents an apartment. He is struggling to pay his rent because of his mounting credit card bills and other debts. He defaults on payments to many creditors, and receives collection letters and phone calls every day at home and on the job. He has consulted with a credit-counseling service, and they have told him his best option is to file bankruptcy. What type should he file?

Bankruptcy law, like many aspects of the legal system, can be quite complicated. It is intimidating to the average consumer, who simply knows that he or she cannot pay the bills. You hear lawyers talk in legal jargon about Chapter 7, Chapter 11, and Chapter 13. What do they mean? The following section explains the most common type of bankruptcy available to the average consumer: Chapter 7. This is the type of bankruptcy usually best suited to a person who has a modest income, few assets, and comparatively high debts.

Straight bankruptcy under Chapter 7 is available if less drastic remedies will not solve your financial problems. It allows you to discharge (eliminate) most of your debts. About 70 percent of all consumer bankruptcy filings nationwide are Chapter 7 cases. However, given the newer and more stringent requirements of the Bankruptcy Abuse Prevention and Consumer Protection Act of 2005, it remains an open question whether people will continue to file for Chapter 7 bankruptcy in such high numbers. In fact, some commentators predict that a major effect of the new law will be to increase the number of Chapter 13 cases filed. (Chapter 13 is discussed in later chapters.)

As noted in the previous chapter of this book, Chapter 7

ⓘ THE CASE OF STUDENT LOANS

In most bankruptcy cases, student loans are not dischargeable, which means that the debtor still has to pay them. They may be discharged, however, if a debtor can show that his or her student loan debt would constitute an **undue hardship.**

Because the Bankruptcy Code does not define "undue hardship," various courts have developed tests aimed at determining what does and does not constitute undue hardship for bankruptcy purposes. For example, the United States Court of Appeals for the Seventh Circuit has developed a three-part test. Under this test, a debtor must show: (1) that he or she cannot maintain, based on his or her current financial situation, a minimal standard of living for himself or herself and his or her dependents if forced to repay the loans; (2) that other circumstances exist indicating that the debtor will remain in the same financial situation for a significant period of time; and (3) that the debtor has made good-faith efforts to repay the loans.

The debtor carries the burden of proof to establish these factors demonstrating undue hardship. In *Goulet v. Educational Credit Management Corp.*, the Seventh Circuit rejected the claims of a fifty-five-year-old debtor that he had an undue hardship defense to paying his student loans. The debtor argued that his substantial debt, a prior felony conviction, and a substance-abuse problem constituted extraordinary circumstances sufficient for a finding of undue hardship. The Seventh Circuit disagreed, focusing on the fact that the debtor had obtained a quality education with the money borrowed through his student loans. "The natural conclusion, when considering his exemplary educational record and nearly-completed graduate work, is that Goulet can apply himself when he desires to do so," the court wrote. "The record does not demonstrate that he lacks the capacity to work, only that he does not seem anxious to do so." (284 F.3d 773 (7th Cir. 2002))

A federal district court in Florida reached a similar result in *In Re Mallinckrodt*, which involved a forty-two-year-old debtor who had more than $70,000 in student loan debt. The debtor had a master's degree in psychology and had worked as a tennis instructor, but had a very small income. The court determined that the debtor failed the "other circumstances" prong of the undue-hardship test, on account of the fact that the debtor "has nothing but opportunities to earn more income." (274 B.R. 560 (S.D. Fla. 2002))

bankruptcy does not result in a discharge of all types of debt. If a debt is excepted from discharge, you remain legally responsible for it.

CHAPTER 7 EXPLAINED

The Beginning of a Chapter 7 Case

The new bankruptcy law requires debtors to receive credit counseling within 180 days before filing for bankruptcy. Debtors must present to the bankruptcy court a certificate that they received such credit counseling. The counseling must be "from an

( ) TALKING TO A LAWYER

Q. Will I be able to get out of the obligations I was socked with during my divorce last year?

A. Not in a Chapter 7 case. Any and all support-related debt—for example, child support, alimony, medical expenses for a child or ex-spouse, ex-spouse's attorney's fees, guardian ad litem fees, and possibly the debt for your ex-spouse's car, credit cards, or mortgage, depending on the specific facts of your case—are never dischargeable in bankruptcy. The 2005 changes mean that even nonsupport debt (e.g., some credit cards or a property settlement debt) will not be discharged in Chapter 7. In a Chapter 13 case, you may be able to discharge nonsupport debt.

—Answer by Marianne Culhane,
Creighton University School of Law

approved nonprofit budget and credit counseling agency." Such agencies must be "approved" or accredited by the U.S. bankruptcy trustee or bankruptcy administrator. (In North Carolina and Alabama, such officials are known as "administrators" rather than "trustees.")

Credit counseling can take place individually or in a group, in person, on the telephone, or on the Internet. Such counseling assists individuals by "outlining the opportunities for available credit counseling and assisting such individuals in performing a related budget analysis." (Undergoing credit counseling is the bankruptcy equivalent of providing informed consent—in other words, it serves as proof that the person filing for bankruptcy is fully apprised of his or her financial situation and the ramifications of his or her actions.)

A Chapter 7 bankruptcy case begins when you file a petition with the U.S. Bankruptcy Court asking it to relieve you (or you and your spouse, if you are both filing) from your dischargeable

---

▶ **HOW TO FIND OUT IF A CREDIT COUNSELING AGENCY IS "APPROVED"**

Section 111 of the new law provides that the bankruptcy court clerk shall "maintain a publicly available list" of approved agencies and "instructional courses" for would-be bankruptcy filers. The U.S. trustee or bankruptcy administrator must review the qualifications of nonprofit credit agencies to ensure that they meet certain standards. For example, the law requires that an agency be approved only if it can demonstrate that it

> will provide qualified counselors, maintain adequate provision for safekeeping and payment of client funds, provide adequate counseling with respect to client credit problems, and deal effectively with other matters relating to the quality, effectiveness, and financial security of the services it provides.

The law also gives federal district courts the power to review the qualifications of these agencies to ensure they are meeting the applicable standards.

▶ **A NEW TEST TO DETERMINE WHETHER CHAPTER 7 IS AVAILABLE TO THE DEBTOR**

The new bankruptcy law provides for a **means test** to determine whether a debtor qualifies for Chapter 7 relief. According to this test, if a debtor's income is below the state's median income level, the debtor is probably eligible to file Chapter 7. However, if the debtor's income is above the state's median income level, then the court applies a complex formula to determine whether the debtor's current monthly income minus presumed deductions is less than $100. If the debtor's income is less than $100 a month, then the debtor can file for bankruptcy under Chapter 7. However, if the debtor's monthly income after allowed deductions is more than $166, the debtor must file under Chapter 13. Debtors whose monthly income after deductions is between $100 and $166 may need to file under Chapter 13, depending on the percentage of their unsecured debt they could repay using disposable income over a five-year period. Visit *www.census.gov/hhes/income/4person.html* for information on the median income in each state.

The new law also makes it tougher for debtors when computing their "applicable monthly expense amounts." That's because, under the new law, the amount of those monthly expenses is calculated based on "National Standards and Local Standards" published by the Internal Revenue Service. Make sure to consult with your attorney about these changes.

If a debtor's Chapter 7 case is dismissed, the debtor may refile under Chapter 13 or consent to a conversion under Chapter 13. In order to repay creditors in part or completely, the debtor will then have to pay his or her extra monthly income to creditors under Chapter 13 for up to five years.

debts. The bankruptcy court clerk or the Bankruptcy Noticing Center will notify your listed creditors that you have filed a bankruptcy petition, and creditors must immediately stop most efforts to collect the debts you owe. A bankruptcy trustee will be appointed, usually a local private lawyer approved by the Justice

Department who performs bankruptcy work in the normal course of his or her legal practice. Your bankruptcy case is a federal court action.

As of the date you file your bankruptcy petition, your assets will be under the protection of the court. In addition, as noted above, the law imposes an **automatic stay**, which immediately prohibits most creditor collection efforts against you. Note, however, that if someone has co-signed a loan for you, the automatic stay does not stop creditors from seeking payment from your cosigner in a Chapter 7 or Chapter 11 case.

When you file a petition for bankruptcy, you have to fill out and file many forms. Under Section 521 of the new bankruptcy law, these forms include:

- A list of creditors;
- A schedule of assets and liabilities;
- A schedule of current income and expenditures;
- A statement of your financial affairs;
- Copies of all payment advices or other evidence of payment received within sixty days before the date of the bankruptcy filing;
- A statement of your monthly net income, itemized to show how the amount is calculated;
- A statement disclosing any reasonably anticipated increase in your income or expenditures over the twelve-month period following the date of the bankruptcy filing; and
- A certificate from an approved nonprofit credit-counseling agency.

If requested by a creditor or the trustee, you will also have to provide tax returns and a photo ID. If you are self-employed, a statement of your business affairs must also be included. The required schedules are quite detailed, and the information you provide must be complete and accurate.

All of these forms will provide the bankruptcy court and parties in interest—that is, your creditors and the trustee—with a complete picture of what is called your **bankruptcy estate**. Specifically, the information contained on these forms should

▶ **A BREAK FOR DISABLED VETERANS**

A section of the new bankruptcy law deals with dismissal of Chapter 7 cases or conversion of such cases to Chapter 13 cases upon a finding of abuse—that is, a finding that the debtor has too much income to qualify for Chapter 7 bankruptcy under the means test. However, an exception exists for disabled veterans whose indebtedness arose during active duty or while such debtors were "performing a homeland defense activity."

Federal law (38 U.S.C. § 3741) defines a "disabled veteran" as follows:

> The term "disabled veteran" means (A) a veteran who is entitled to compensation under laws administered by the Secretary for a disability rated at 30 percent or more, or (B) a veteran whose discharge or release from active duty was for a disability incurred or aggravated in the line of duty.

This means that if you are a disabled veteran, it is likely that your bankruptcy case will remain a Chapter 7 case and will not be converted to a Chapter 13 case. However, note that these provisions of the law are new; as a result, you may need the advice of an experienced bankruptcy attorney familiar with the new law to determine whether you fit within this exception.

---

include a list of all your creditors and the amounts of their claims, the sources and amounts of your income, a list of all your property (both real [land and real estate] and personal), and a detailed list of your monthly expenses. In essence, these forms describe your financial history, listing all of your income, all of your debts, and all of your assets.

As of October 17, 2005, in order to file the necessary forms, debtors must pay a Chapter 7 statutory case-filing fee of $220, an administrative fee of $39, and a trustee surcharge fee of $15, for a total of $274 in fees. Individuals may pay the $274 in

⚠ LIST ALL OF YOUR ASSETS!

When filing for bankruptcy, don't engage in fraud by failing to list an asset or by giving an asset away to someone just before filing. Such behavior could lead to the denial of the bankruptcy discharge, perjury charges, or possibly even to jail time for bankruptcy fraud.

installments within 120 days after the Chapter 7 case is filed; in certain circumstances, the court may also extend the length of this period to 180 days. Failure to pay the necessary fees could result in the dismissal of a bankruptcy petition, unless the court waives the fees, which it may do if the debtor's income is less than 150 percent of the poverty level and the debtor cannot pay the fees in installments.

Liabilities and Schedules

For purposes of a bankruptcy filing, your liabilities typically include

• your priority debts (such as taxes and past-due support payments);

• your debts to secured creditors (bills from auto and furniture dealers, home mortgages, and so on); and

• your debts to unsecured creditors (bills for department store credit cards, medical bills, and the like).

Be sure to list all of your creditors and their correct names and addresses. Remember, liabilities can also include any lawsuits in which you are a defendant or a potential defendant—for example, a personal injury claim against you arising out of a car accident. Even if you are current with your bills, if you omit some creditors from your filing or provide incorrect addresses for them, you might not be discharged from the applicable debts. It may be very helpful to access your credit report before filing to ensure that you have listed all of your outstanding debts. (Chapter 6,

Credit Records, explains how to access your credit report.) Also, make sure to give your lawyer copies of all your bills and collection letters.

Should you fail to list all of your creditors in your filing, the Federal Rules of Bankruptcy Procedure typically allow debtors to amend their petitions. See *www.tnwb.uscourts.gov/forms/localforms/MISC008.pdf* for an example of a court order granting debtors the ability to amend their petitions to add previously omitted creditors.

Assets

When filing for bankruptcy, you should list all of your assets, which generally include

- all of your real property (for example, your home), including any real property you own together with your spouse or other persons;
- all of your personal property (such as household goods, cars, clothing, cash, retirement funds, bank accounts, accrued net wages, and tax refunds to which you may be entitled); and
- any lawsuits in which you are a plaintiff or a potential plaintiff (e.g., workers' compensation claims and/or personal injury claims).

In addition, you will need to designate which of the real or personal property listed above you want to exempt from creditors.

Note that your post-petition earnings from your job are not part of the Chapter 7 bankruptcy estate. Also note that, under Chapter 7, you might well have to turn over many, if not all, of your nonexempt assets to the trustee who is appointed to supervise your case, depending upon the classification (value) of such assets, and on state or federal law exemptions.

Encumbered Assets

Assets pledged as collateral on a loan are known as **encumbered assets**. When you have borrowed money to buy a car, a boat, household furniture, an appliance, or other durable items, the lender commonly has a lien (legal claim) on that property to secure the debt until the loan is fully repaid. In order to obtain a new loan, you may also have given a creditor a lien on property you already owned, as in the case of a second mortgage obtained to finance home improvements. Some creditors may obtain liens without the debtor's agreement, either because they have won a lawsuit against the debtor or because the law automatically provides a lien for certain claims, such as for duly assessed taxes or purchases that haven't been paid for in full.

In bankruptcy, a claim generally is secured to the extent that it is backed up by collateral. Often the collateral is worth less than the amount of the debt it secures, such as a $1,200 item of collateral securing a loan balance of $3,000. In that case, the lender is **undersecured** and is treated as holding two claims: a $1,200 secured claim and an $1,800 unsecured claim. On the other hand, sometimes a debt is secured by collateral having a value that exceeds the loan balance at the time of bankruptcy, such as a $65,000 home subject to a $30,000 mortgage. In that case, the lender is **oversecured**. In this example, the oversecured lender is entitled to no more than the $30,000 it is owed. The excess value of $35,000 is referred to as the **debtor's equity**.

If you cannot make the required payments on a secured claim (and also cannot catch up on any overdue back payments), the creditor ordinarily has a right to take back the collateral after having the automatic stay lifted or after the discharge. However, you may be able to keep your car, boat, or other encumbered item by redeeming it or reaffirming your debt. These concepts are explained later in this chapter.

Unencumbered Assets

Unencumbered assets include (1) assets on which there is no lien at all; and (2) the debtor's equity in assets that are collateral for oversecured claims. You retain unencumbered assets to the extent that they are exempt; otherwise, they must be surrendered for distribution among those creditors holding unsecured claims, or the equivalent value of the unencumbered assets must be paid to the trustee. However, if your unencumbered assets are worth less than a certain amount, or would be difficult to sell, the trustee might abandon them (i.e. return them to you) if he or she decides it would not be cost-effective to sell them and distribute the money to the creditors.

Exempt Assets

Some of your property may be exempt from the reach of the bankruptcy trustee and your creditors—in other words, the law may allow you to keep it. **Exempt assets** are assets that you must list on your schedules (specifically **Schedule C**), and that you may shield from your unsecured creditors. Federal and state laws define the assets that you may protect in this way. For the most part, state law determines what you can exempt; however, some states do allow you to follow the federal exemptions if you prefer them to the state exemptions. (Remember that your state's exemptions may differ widely from federal exemptions, and from exemptions allowed by other states, and that federal exemptions are not available in all states.) Section 522 of the Bankruptcy Code provides a detailed list of exemptions available to debtors under federal law. In brief, these exemptions include:

(1) $18,450 in your home or burial plot

(2) $2,950 in one motor vehicle

(3) $475 per item, up to $9,850 total, in household furnishings, household goods, apparel, appliances, etc.

(4) Jewelry with a fair market value of up to $1225

(5) $975 in any property, plus up to $9,250 of any unused amount of the exemption for your home/burial plot

(6) $1,850 in any implements, professional books, or tools of your trade

(7) Any unmatured life insurance contract you own, other than a credit life insurance contract

(8) Professionally prescribed health aids

(9) Your right to receive:

- a Social Security benefit, unemployment compensation, or a local public assistance benefit;
- a veterans' benefit;
- a disability, illness, or unemployment benefit;
- alimony, support, or separate maintenance, to the extent reasonably necessary for your support and the support of your dependents; or
- a payment under a stock bonus, pension, profit-sharing, annuity, or similar plan or contract on account of illness, disability, death, age, or length of service, to the extent reasonably necessary for your support and the support of any of your dependents. Based on a recent ruling by the U.S. Supreme Court, this includes Individual Retirement Accounts (IRAs). The new law also codifies this ruling—that is, writes it into the statute—by exempting retirement funds in a tax-exempt fund or account.

(10) Your right to receive property that is traceable to

- an award under a crime victim's reparation law;
- a payment for the wrongful death of an individual of whom you were a dependent;
- a payment under a life insurance contract that insured the life of an individual of whom you were a dependent on the date of such individual's death;
- a payment, not to exceed $15,000, on account of personal bodily injury of you or an individual of whom you are a dependent; or
- a payment in compensation for the loss of future earnings of you or an individual of whom you are or were a dependent.

Let's use the example of your home to see how this works. As noted above, under the federal statute you can exempt from bankruptcy up to $18,450 of the equity in your home. A couple filing a joint Chapter 7 case may exempt twice this much—a total of $36,900 worth of equity in their home. This is called

ⓘ WHICH LAW APPLIES?

In seventeen states, you may elect to exempt assets under either federal or state law. In most states, however, you may use only the state exemptions. Federal law has become more complicated as to which state exemptions are available to debtors. The new bankruptcy law provides that debtors can choose state exemptions in a state in which they lived for 730 days prior to filing for bankruptcy. If the debtor has lived in more than one state during that 730-day period, then the debtor can choose the exemptions of the state in which he or she lived during the majority of the 180 days before the 730-day period. These exemptions, particularly the homestead exemption, are subject to ultimate limits under federal law.

their **homestead exemption.** If the home is worth $65,000 and has a $25,000 mortgage, then the couple has $40,000 worth of equity in their home ($65,000 − $25,000 = $40,000). Since $36,900 is exempt by federal law, the couple's creditors can claim only $3,100 (the difference between the couple's equity of $40,000 and the $36,900 exemption). As a matter of practice, the couple would probably keep their home—perhaps at the cost of paying that $3,100 in nonexempt equity to the bankruptcy trustee—rather than have it sold for the benefit of their creditors. (Note that the couple may also be able to exempt the equity in their home under another statutory category, or under applicable state law.)

State-by-State Exemptions

Allowable asset exemptions vary widely from state to state. For example, variations among the states are found with respect to a broad array of exempt assets such as cars, jewelry, household furnishings, books, and tools of the debtor's trade.

Home exemptions also vary by state. The federal exemption

for a home is $18,450, but Florida, along with six other states, has no dollar cap on homestead exemptions. Florida allows a homestead exemption that protects from creditors a debtor's home and property so long as the size of that property does not exceed half an acre in a municipality or 160 acres elsewhere. As a result, under the old law, investment bankers and Hollywood stars who filed for bankruptcy could retain beachfront homes in Florida worth millions of dollars. A number of other states have high caps on homesteads, in effect enabling debtors, under the old law, to shield considerable amounts of money from creditors under the right circumstances. In Georgia, in contrast, the homestead exemption is limited to $5,000.

The new federal bankruptcy law makes it harder to shield money, even in those states with high homestead exemptions. The new law establishes that, regardless of state law, debtors may exempt no more than $125,000 of interest in a homestead that was purchased within forty months (1,215 days) of a bankruptcy filing. However, you may still shelter more than $125,000 (if state law permits) if you bought your home (or a prior home) more than forty months before filing.

Married versus Single Debtors

In cases involving an individual married debtor or joint debtors, several specific points about exemptions are worth noting.

First, in joint cases, each spouse must claim exemptions under the same law, with both relying either on state law or on federal law. If they each want to claim exemptions under different law, they need to file separate cases.

Second, when married debtors elect to apply federal exemptions (and often when they elect to apply state exemptions), each spouse can claim the full exempt amount on his or her own behalf, in effect doubling the amount of exemptions to which a single person would be entitled.

Third, in some cases, such as when one spouse has debts and the other is debt-free and has assets, it might be preferable for only the spouse with debts to file for bankruptcy. In about a third of the states, creditors of only one spouse are barred either completely or in large part from reaching real and/or personal property owned by a debtor and nondebtor spouse as joint tenants or tenants by the entirety. Such prohibitions generally apply in any bankruptcy case in which state law exemptions govern. The way your property is titled may determine the appropriate exemption; give your lawyer copies of your deeds, bank account statements, and car titles to find out whether your creditors can reach your assets.

The Case of Secured Lenders and Exemptions

As mentioned above, exempt assets are beyond the reach of *unsecured* creditors and the bankruptcy trustee. However, exemptions do not ordinarily affect the rights of creditors to assets on which they have liens. For example, a homestead exemption generally does not affect the right of a mortgage lender to foreclose

---

(i) WHAT THE TRUSTEE CAN LIQUIDATE

The Bankruptcy Code requires that you give all nonexempt unencumbered assets to the bankruptcy trustee—that is, all the assets that aren't exempted by law and aren't secured as collateral to a loan. Unless it would be too costly, the trustee will then liquidate (sell off) these nonexempt assets to help pay your creditors.

In actual practice, over 95 percent of Chapter 7 filings are **no-asset filings**—that is, filings in which there are no nonexempt assets with value left for unsecured creditors after the exempt assets have been claimed and the secured assets returned to the creditors. No-asset filings are often the result of careful planning by an experienced bankruptcy attorney.

on your home. Similarly, furniture bought on store credit may be subject to a **purchase money security interest**, and some credit card companies may attempt to create liens on items you purchase with their cards, in which case such creditors may have rights to your assets even in bankruptcy. Under some specific circumstances, the Bankruptcy Code may permit you to undo a lien and then assert exemption rights. This is a matter about which it is best to consult a lawyer.

CHAPTER 7 IN ACTION

Keeping Assets

If you are required to surrender some nonexempt property that you wish to keep—for example, a car—you may under certain circumstances arrange to **redeem** it (buy it back) for a price no greater than its current **redemption value**. Redemption value is the amount for which a retailer could sell the item, taking into consideration the item's age and condition. For example, if you owe $3,000 on your car, but its redemption value is only $1,200, you can recover the car by paying a lump sum of $1,200 to the creditor who has a lien on it at the time of redemption, which should be within forty-five days of the first creditors' meeting. The redemption price must be paid in full; this differs from past practice, which allowed a lender to accept the redemption price in installments over an extended period of time.

In the real world, of course, it may be very hard to come up with $1,200, which must be paid from your personal assets, and not from property that has been set aside for distribution to creditors. Possible sources of funds would include your post-petition salary, proceeds from the voluntary sale of exempt assets, or loans from relatives or friends. Some companies specialize in making redemption loans on automobiles. Sometimes you can negotiate a short payment plan, but it is up to the creditor whether or not to allow this.

Another Way to Keep Your Property:
Reaffirming Debt

You may **reaffirm** a debt, if the applicable creditor is willing to allow it. By reaffirming a debt, you promise to pay the creditor (usually, but not always, in full), and you may keep the property involved, so long as you keep your promise. But if you later default, the creditor can repossess the property and the remaining balance will not be discharged.

The new bankruptcy law provides some protections for consumers considering reaffirmation of their debts. It imposes certain obligations on creditors. Under the new law, creditors must provide extensive disclosures to debtors, including the following statements:

• "Reaffirming a debt is a serious financial decision. The law requires you to take certain steps to make sure the decision is in your best interest. If these steps are not completed, the reaffirmation agreement is not effective, even though you have signed it."

• "You may rescind (cancel) your reaffirmation agreement at any time before the bankruptcy court enters a discharge order, or before the expiration of the 60-day period that begins on the date your reaffirmation is filed with the court, whichever occurs later."

If a debtor reaffirms a debt, the creditor must inform the debtor as to the amount of debt reaffirmed, the applicable interest rates, when payments will begin, and filing requirements with the court.

Reaffimation of debts other than home mortgages must be approved by the debtor's lawyer or the court.

The new law also prohibits debtors from retaining property without redeeming or reaffirming the debt by making installment payments. In other words, even if you are current on, say, your car loan, you still must reaffirm or redeem that loan in order to keep the car. This is a change from what used to be permissible in some parts of the country.

Chapter 7 debtors must redeem or reaffirm promptly, within forty-five days of the first creditors' meeting; if they don't meet

⟨⟩ TALKING TO A LAWYER

Q. I think I've got a tax refund coming. What happens to that refund in bankruptcy?

A. The tax refund will have to be disclosed in your list of assets. Depending on the amount of the refund, you may be able to claim all or a substantial portion of it as part of the exemptions to which you are entitled. To the extent you are unable to claim all of the tax refund as an exemption, the excess amount will be turned over to the bankruptcy trustee for distribution to creditors after payment of administrative costs.

> —**Answer by Judge David S. Kennedy, United States Bankruptcy Court, Western District of Tennessee**

A. Under state and federal law, you are entitled to exemption of certain assets. (Exemptions are a way to "shield" certain amounts and types of assets from liquidation, and vary tremendously by state.) The Chapter 7 trustee will be entitled to any portion of the refund that is not exempt under applicable state or federal law. The issue becomes slightly more complicated if the refund is in two names, and if only one of you files the bankruptcy case. In that case, it is possible that the trustee would get only a portion of the nonexempt refund. Courts in different states rule in very different ways on this issue, so it is best to assume that the trustee would get all or most of the refund.

> —**Answer by Shayna M. Steinfeld, Steinfeld & Steinfeld, P.C., Atlanta, Georgia**

Q. I'm behind in my car payments. Can a bankruptcy stop the dealer from repossessing my car?

A. Yes. Upon the filing of a bankruptcy case, an automatic stay takes effect that will stop the dealer from repossessing the car. But unless you can work out a consensual agreement with the creditor or redeem the car (pay it off) for the redemption amount, in a Chapter 7 case the likelihood is that you will eventually lose the car. In a Chapter

13 case, you may be able to keep the car under a repayment plan. Chapter 13 offers broader relief and more options for debtors than does Chapter 7 when dealing with secured claims.

—Answer by Judge David S. Kennedy, United States Bankruptcy Court, Western District of Tennessee

this deadline, they can lose the property: the automatic stay will end, and the creditor could repossess the collateral.

Reaffirmation is not always in your best interest, especially when the reaffirmed debt relates to property worth far less than the debt being reaffirmed. Most reaffirmations relate to mortgage loans and loans for personal property that is especially valued by the debtor—for example, a car or a boat.

If you can, it is a good idea to use a reaffirmation negotiation as an opportunity to renegotiate the loan, especially on personal property that has **depreciated** (i.e., decreased in value). If you want to retain items that are worth less than the secured debt against them, then either redemption or a Chapter 13 reorganization may make more sense.

After discharge, it is too late to reaffirm, and the creditor may repossess the property, but cannot collect the balance due.

Leased Automobiles

If you are leasing a car and wish to retain it during and after a Chapter 7 bankruptcy, you must notify the lessor in writing that

▶ **YOUR INTENTIONS**

Within thirty days of filing for bankruptcy, and usually as part of the papers you file, you must use a court form to advise your secured creditors whether you intend to surrender or redeem any collateral, or reaffirm any debt. You can address the issue of reaffirmation at the creditors' meeting.

you want to assume the lease. The lessor will then tell you whether it is willing to let you keep the car, and on what conditions—for example, the lessor may require that you make up back payments. In order to keep the car, you must then agree to the lessor's offer within thirty days. Your liability under the lease will not be discharged if you assume it, so the effect is like that of a reaffirmation, but without the requirement of attorney or court approval.

Other Ways to Keep Property

In the case of a loan securing personal property—for example, a loan for a computer or furniture—you may be able to keep the item and simply continue making payments. Creditors cannot be forced to allow this, but some creditors may decide not to repossess if they continue to receive full payment and if you were current with your payments when your bankruptcy case was filed.

Transferring Property Prior to Filing Bankruptcy

Bankruptcy trustees will look carefully at any attempts to hide assets or to avoid disclosing the true identity and value of your assets. In particular, they will look at transfers of property, and won't allow transfers of property in return for nothing, or in return for far less than the property was worth. You will be asked whether you have transferred property within two years prior to filing. If you have transferred property without getting enough in return, a trustee can cancel the transfer and recover the property for your bankruptcy estate and creditors. Moreover, if the trustee discovers that you made the transfer with the intention of defrauding any creditor, you may be denied discharge and also face federal criminal charges for committing a fraudulent transfer. The greater the period of time between a transfer and your bankruptcy filing, the less likely it is that the transfer will be perceived as fraudulent.

The bottom line is that you cannot keep any debts or assets out of bankruptcy, and failing to disclose all of your assets may expose you to criminal charges or the denial of discharge, even after liquidation.

Other Steps for Filing Bankruptcy

Procedures for filing bankruptcy vary greatly by state, but you may be required to take the following steps:

• In some states, you may have to file a homestead deed in the appropriate state court; such a filing must generally be made by a specific deadline. A **homestead deed**, also called a **declaration of homestead**, is a document intended to protect your property from creditors. Generally, it describes the property and assigns an approximate value to it. The document may also have to be recorded in the appropriate office (such as a land record office) in the county in which you live. (In some states, you may be required to take this step *before* you file for bankruptcy.)

• You will be required to appear at a first meeting of creditors, where the trustee will examine you under oath about your petition, statement of financial affairs, and schedules. Creditors can also question you about your debts and assets, and will often attend this meeting to discuss reaffirmation, surrender of property, and related issues. Later, the trustee will determine whether to challenge any of your claimed exemptions or your right to a discharge.

• If you disagree with the trustee's decision, you may protest to the court, which will make the final decision.

( ) TALKING TO A LAWYER

Q. I'm confused. I hear people who've been in bankruptcy referring to a "341 meeting." What is that? If I file for bankruptcy, is it a big deal?

A. A 341 hearing is a hearing required by Section 341 of the Bankruptcy Code. It is also known as a "first meeting of creditors," a name first used in the Bankruptcy Act of 1898. (For lawyers, old nicknames die hard!)

At a 341 hearing, the trustee and any creditor who wishes to attend (most don't) will question you about your assets, liabilities, and problematic financial situation. Though the hearing is not a big deal for most debtors, there can be exceptions; your lawyer should be able to prepare and warn you if anything extraordinary is expected.

—Answer by Marc S. Stern, Law Offices of Marc S. Stern, Seattle, Washington

A. This is a question-and-answer session, conducted under oath and subject to the penalty of perjury, before the trustee (not a judge). In a Chapter 7 case, the hearing is conducted by the Chapter 7 trustee; in a Chapter 13 case, it is conducted by the Chapter 13 trustee. Creditors have an opportunity to ask you questions about the debts you owe them and their collateral—for example, they might request insurance information, ask you to specifically identify components of your car, or inquire about the purchase of your home or other property. These questions will generally be formulated based on your bankruptcy paperwork; thus, it is critical that the paperwork contain accurate and complete information. The meeting will usually last less than ten minutes, and there will usually be a waiting room full of other debtors who are there for their own meetings. If you haven't participated in any fraudulent or other "shady" activity, the 341 meeting of creditors really should not be a big deal—though an exception may exist if a creditor or ex-spouse is very angry at you, in which case the meeting may be more complicated.

—Answer by Shayna M. Steinfeld, Steinfeld & Steinfeld, P.C., Atlanta, Georgia

Q. *What happens at the end of a bankruptcy case? Do I go to court? How do I know which debts have been discharged and which have not?*

A. The 2005 changes to the law require you to complete a personal-financial-management instructional course before you can obtain a discharge in either a Chapter 7 or Chapter 13 case. The clerk of court will have a list of approved courses. At the conclusion of your case, you will receive a piece of paper called a "discharge", which will state that all pre-petition debts are discharged except for a generic statutory list of debts that are excluded. This will mean that your creditors may no longer collect the discharged debts from you personally—though if they have a lien on your property, such as your house or car or stereo, they may take back their collateral if you still owe them money. Your attorney should be able to tell you which specific debts were or were not discharged. In general, if no creditor files an adversary proceeding seeking to challenge your discharge, and your case is seen through to conclusion—in a Chapter 13 case, for example, this means that your case is not dismissed for nonpayment of monthly trustee fees—you will be discharged from most debts that you incurred prior to filing. (Keep in mind, however, that if you fail to list a creditor in your bankruptcy paperwork, that creditor's debt may be excluded from the discharge.) Debts that automatically remain due include support obligations to an ex-spouse or child, student loans, certain taxes, and restitution and debts incurred while driving intoxicated. There may be other exceptions to the discharge, which also vary by bankruptcy chapter, but most of those require the filing of a lawsuit. Finally, student loans may be discharged if you file a complaint and prove that their repayment will be an "undue hardship" on you and your family. This is a difficult thing to prove.

—**Answer by Shayna M. Steinfeld, Steinfeld & Steinfeld, P.C., Atlanta, Georgia**

A. In most Chapter 7 cases, the debtor will receive in the mail a written discharge of his or her debts. The discharge should arrive roughly sixty days after the debtor appears at the meeting of creditors. A discharge will also be granted after the successful completion of a three- to five-year Chapter 13 plan, and a copy of the discharge order will be mailed to the debtor.

—**Answer by Judge David S. Kennedy, United States Bankruptcy Court, Western District of Tennessee**

The Role of the Bankruptcy Trustees

After determining your exemptions, the bankruptcy trustee will assemble, liquidate (sell), and distribute the value of your non-

▶ ## SHOULD BOTH SPOUSES FILE FOR BANKRUPTCY?

Whether married couples in debt should both file for bankruptcy depends on the nature of the debt. A debt may be a **separate debt** if it is in your name only. If you have been married for a short time, your debts are more likely to be considered separate debts. A debt may be a **joint debt** if both spouses signed a contract for the debt, as in the case of a home loan or credit card agreement.

In most states, a bankruptcy filing by one spouse wipes out the bankrupt spouse's separate debts. The separate property of the nonbankrupt spouse will not be affected. However, if spouses have co-signed for a loan, the bankruptcy of one spouse does not relieve the other of the obligation to pay the debt. After a bankruptcy filing, the creditor may look to the nonbankrupt spouse for payment, unless the bankruptcy case was filed under Chapter 13 and the bankrupt spouse plans to pay back 100 percent of the debt.

If you live in a community property jurisdiction, then the situation is a little different. Arizona, California, Idaho, Louisiana, Nevada, New Mexico, Texas, Washington, and the Commonwealth of Puerto Rico are community property jurisdictions. Alaska and Wisconsin also have community property features in their law. In community property jurisdictions, the separate property of the nonfiling spouse—property owned before the marriage, for example—is not affected. However, in community property states, the general rule is that the income of both spouses is considered community property, as is any property they acquire during the marriage. Since all of the community property is available to pay community creditors and any other creditors of the spouse who has filed for bankruptcy, the filing of one spouse could have a significant impact on the other.

Filing by one spouse may be noted on the nonbankrupt spouse's credit record.

If you and your spouse both file for bankruptcy, then the bankruptcy will eliminate each spouse's debts as well as all jointly held marital debts.

When two spouses file together on a joint petition, their bankruptcy estates remain separate, unless the court orders them to be consolidated.

You should be wary of a joint filing if you have marital problems that appear to be leading to divorce court. Your best bet is to seek the counsel of a bankruptcy lawyer well versed in the laws of your state.

If both you and your spouse file for bankruptcy at the same time, only one case-filing fee with required charges (in all, about $270) will have to be paid to the court in a Chapter 7 or 13 case. State law may, however, require separate homestead deeds.

exempt assets (if there are any). The trustee might "abandon"— that is, return to you—property that would bring no value to your unsecured creditors. This will include nonexempt assets with minimal resale value.

The first creditors to be paid are the secured creditors. The trustee will first distribute to secured creditors the value of their collateral, or the collateral itself if the collateral is worth no more than the debt. So the bank will get your house back if you have no equity; it could keep it (unlikely) or sell it, but in neither case will your unsecured creditors benefit.

Next, the trustee will pay unsecured priority claims, such as most taxes and past-due support, such as alimony and child support. If any funds are left, the trustee will distribute them to your general unsecured creditors, such as credit card companies and hospitals, on a pro rata (proportionate) basis. Say, for example, that after the payment of secured and priority claims, the proceeds from the sale by the trustee of your nonexempt assets equal 20 percent of your remaining debts. Then the trustee will pay each general creditor 20 percent of what you owe. In return, the court will discharge you from paying any remaining balance on your general unsecured debts.

The trustee will also pay the administrative claims, such as his or her commission fees (ranging between 3 percent and 25 percent, depending on the value the trustee recovers), and the fees of professionals, such as lawyers and accountants.

THE WORLD AT YOUR FINGERTIPS

• To obtain statement-of-financial-affairs forms, access *www.uscourts.gov/rules/comment2002/b7.pdf.*

• For a list of exemptions in different states, visit Bankruptcy Site.com at *www.thebankruptcysite.com/what_do_i_keep.htm.*

• The Nolo website features information on states with large homestead exemptions. Visit *www.nolo.com/lawcenter/index.cfm* and click on "Keeping Your Home During Tough Times."

• For a Q & A on bankruptcy debts, access *www.debtwipe-out.com.*

• A law firm from Arizona provides a detailed list of bankruptcy FAQs at *www.doney.net/faq.htm.*

• For a discussion of reaffirmation of debt in bankruptcy cases, visit *www.mauilaw.com/article5.htm.*

• You can download official bankruptcy forms for all types of bankruptcy from the U.S. Courts website at *www.uscourts.gov/bankruptcycourts.html.*

• In addition, visit *www.census.gov/hhes/income/4person.html* for information on the median income in each state. (This is now an important factor that can determine your eligibility for Chapter 7 bankruptcy.) Bankruptcy forms are long and detailed, and you may need a lawyer to help you complete them.

REMEMBER THIS

• Chapter 7 bankruptcy allows you to discharge most of your debts. It is the most common form of bankruptcy used by individual consumers. In a Chapter 7 bankruptcy case, a trustee is appointed to investigate and supervise your case.

• When you file a Chapter 7 bankruptcy, you must file schedules and a statement of financial affairs. Information you must list on these forms includes your financial history, income, debts, and assets; the forms are quite detailed. On your schedules, list all of your debts, including priority debts, debts to secured creditors, and debts to unsecured creditors.

- Remember that if you are seeking to file for bankruptcy, you must file a certificate showing that you have received credit counseling and a budget plan from an approved nonprofit credit-counseling service.

- Under either federal or state law, some of your assets may be exempt from creditors during bankruptcy. States have different exemptions. Exempt assets are beyond the reach of unsecured creditors and the bankruptcy trustee.

- The Bankruptcy Code requires that you give all nonexempt, unencumbered assets to your trustee. If these assets have sufficient value to make a sale worthwhile, the trustee will liquidate them to pay creditors.

- You may be able to reaffirm some debts—that is, promise to pay them—in order to keep certain assets, subject to the approval of the affected creditor.

- You cannot avoid the reach of creditors during bankruptcy simply by transferring title to property that you own. Generally, this restriction applies to transfers made within two years of a bankruptcy filing, but, depending on the circumstances and state law, transfers made even earlier than that may also be undone.

- Bankruptcy does not discharge all debts. You are still liable for some tax claims, alimony, child support, fraudulent debts, student loans, and criminal obligations.

- Husbands and wives, depending on state law and the status of joint debt, may want to file jointly for bankruptcy.

CHAPTER 19

Wage-Earner Bankruptcy: Chapter 13

A Form of Bankruptcy for People with Regular Incomes

Mr. and Mrs. Jones make an excellent combined salary. Unfortunately, they have underestimated the effect of the declining stock market, the cost of college for their children, extreme and unexpected medical costs, and other expenses. They have substantial nonexempt assets that they don't wish to see swallowed up by creditors. They want to discharge some of their debts, but can still afford to make some payments to creditors; they just need some relief in the form of reduced or restructured payment plans. The Joneses might find that they are ineligible for a Chapter 7 bankruptcy because of their high income. However, a Chapter 13 bankruptcy might suit them better, because it will enable them to preserve some assets.

Chapter 13 allows individuals with regular incomes to pay a portion of their debts under a court-approved payment plan and keep both their exempt and nonexempt assets. This chapter will explain the basic features of a Chapter 13 bankruptcy plan.

CHAPTER 13 IN ACTION

The Basics of Chapter 13

In certain ways, a Chapter 13 bankruptcy is similar to a Chapter 7 bankruptcy. For each type of bankruptcy, debtors must obtain credit counseling within 180 days before filing for bankruptcy and complete a personal-financial-management course in order to secure a discharge. In addition, with each type of bankruptcy, you must list with the court all of your assets and debts. In each, you obtain an automatic stay upon the filing of the case, limiting creditor action against you. And in each, you can obtain a discharge that will eliminate personal liability for most debts.

However, Chapter 13 bankruptcies also have many differences from Chapter 7 bankruptcies. A typical Chapter 7 bankruptcy usually lasts about four to six months before the discharge is granted, while a Chapter 13 case can last three to five years and the discharge is delayed until the end of the case. Under Chapter 7, you do not make payments to your creditors, though your nonexempt assets may be sold and the proceeds split among your creditors. Under Chapter 13, on the other hand, you make monthly payments under a repayment plan.

If you have a steady income, Chapter 13 allows you to pay all or a portion of your debts under the protection and supervision of the U.S. Bankruptcy Court, with which you file a bankruptcy petition and a proposed payment plan. The law requires that your payments to creditors be no less than they would have been if you had filed a Chapter 7 case. An important feature of Chapter 13 is that you will be permitted to keep all your assets (both exempt and nonexempt) while the plan is in effect and after you have successfully completed it.

Eligibility for Chapter 13

Chapter 13 is available to almost everyone who has a regular income. The only other requirement is that you have less than $307,675 in unsecured debts (such as credit card debts) *and* less than $922,975 in secured debts (such as home mortgages and car loans). These figures are not doubled when husband and wife file a joint case, and are subject to periodic adjustments; the new law provides that they will be modified every three years. Anyone with greater debts usually must declare bankruptcy under Chapters 7 or 11 of the Bankruptcy Code.

Differences from Chapter 7

The major difference between Chapters 7 and 13 is that in Chapter 7 you pay debts out of your *nonexempt assets*, while in Chapter 13 you pay debts out of your *future income*. As a result, a repayment plan under Chapter 13 normally allows you more time to pay your debts than does a Chapter 7 plan, involves you paying off more of those debts, and allows you to deal more easily with secured creditors (e.g., home mortgage lenders and companies providing financing for your purchase of a car or truck). The permitted repayment period is usually three years for people with a low income, and five years for those debtors whose disposable income is above the median in their state.

Under the bankruptcy law passed in 2005, not everyone is eligible for relief under Chapter 7. As a result, more people may file under Chapter 13.

Typically, the amount that you repay under a Chapter 13 plan is equal to the total of your planned monthly payments over three to five years, assuming a good-faith effort to repay your debts. Thus, your payments represent either (1) full satisfaction of your debts; or (2) all of your disposable income for a three- to five-year period. **Disposable income** consists of whatever is left over from your total income after you have paid for taxes and reasonable and necessary living expenses, as determined on a monthly basis. Note, however, that the new bankruptcy law changes the definition of "reasonable and necessary living expenses" for some above-median-income debtors. For these debtors, allowable expenses are determined in large part by IRS regulations. It will be important for you to consult with your attorney to determine what expenses are permitted. Under a Chapter 13 plan, debtors must also pay secured creditors the values of their liens over time, and cannot change the terms of their home mortgage loans.

Mechanics of Filing Chapter 13

To file Chapter 13 bankruptcy under the old law, you had to file a petition and the required schedules that accompanied it, including a statement of financial affairs. This meant that you had to list all your assets, debts, and creditors, including all sources of income, all of your property, and your monthly living expenses, just as you would when filing a Chapter 7 petition. Under the law passed in 2005, you need to provide more detailed information, including a statement of monthly net income itemized to show how the amount was calculated, copies of all payments received sixty days before the filing of the petition, copies of federal tax returns, and a photo ID. As noted above, you will also have to file a certificate showing that you received credit counseling within 180 days before your bankruptcy filing.

You will also need to file a repayment plan within fifteen days of filing your petition. In your payment plan, you agree to pay a certain amount each month to your creditors. Your plan will indicate the amount of money you propose to pay each month, the total amount to be paid, the percentage return you propose to pay to your creditors, and the expected length of the plan. You must make your first payment on this plan within thirty days after you file it.

After you submit your plan to the court, a Chapter 13 trustee is appointed to handle your case. The trustee will verify the accuracy and reasonableness of your plan. The plan will then be distributed to your creditors, who will have the opportunity at a creditors' meeting to challenge your repayment proposal

▶ **COUNSELING NOW MANDATORY**

Before you can obtain a discharge under Chapter 13, you must submit a certification with your bankruptcy petition indicating that you have completed a financial-education course. One major purpose of the new bankruptcy law is to encourage greater personal responsibility. The thinking behind this new requirement is that the mandatory course requirement will engender greater responsibility and help ensure that debtors will not have to return to bankruptcy.

(i) CHAPTER 13 TRUSTEES

The role of a Chapter 13 trustee varies among judicial districts. Most trustees work with debtors to help them learn to manage their finances. Often a trustee will arrange for (or require) monthly payments to be automatically deducted from a debtor's paycheck and credited directly to the trustee's account for disbursement to the various creditors. Generally, a small part of the debtor's monthly payments goes to the trustee as compensation for these services.

if they believe it doesn't meet the specific requirements of the Bankruptcy Code. You must attend the creditors' meeting and answer questions under oath from your creditors and the trustee regarding your financial affairs and the proposed terms of the plan. The Chapter 13 trustee attends this meeting, but the bankruptcy judge does not.

The trustee will want to be sure that your plan provides enough money for you to live on, but will also challenge living expenses that seem unreasonably high. One issue will be whether you are making a good-faith and sincere effort to repay your debts, even if that effort means reducing your living standards, such as by eliminating entertainment expenses. Since the trustee's recommendation will carry considerable weight with the court, it pays to be honest and open with the information that you provide.

There are several positive features of a Chapter 13 plan. For one thing, under some circumstances, you can propose to repay a creditor at a lower interest rate than the rate stipulated in your original contract with that creditor (except in the case of a home mortgage). Moreover, your proposed repayment plan needn't provide that you pay back the entire amount you owe. Instead, you can reorganize your debts and submit a reasonable payback plan proposing that debts to secured creditors be paid back on your own schedule, without exorbitant interest. This flexibility can be a great advantage for Chapter 13 debtors. For example, if a person is stuck in a particularly bad car contract and wants to keep his car, he may be allowed to pay only the fair market value of his car, rather than the entire (often much higher) amount stipulated in the original contract. However, this option has been greatly limited by the new law (see the section below on the value of secured collateral). Also, keep in mind that you still must put forth your best effort to repay your debts.

A creditor might file an objection to a Chapter 13 plan if it will receive less under the plan than it would have under Chapter 7. Unsecured creditors are entitled to receive at least as much as they would have received under a Chapter 7 bankruptcy. This is called the "**best interest of the creditors**" **rule**. Another common objection is that the plan, in essence, does not require you to commit enough of your projected disposable income to repayment.

After a meeting of your creditors is held, the bankruptcy judge will hold a confirmation hearing, and either confirm your plan or deny it. The confirmation hearing must be held twenty to forty-five days after the creditors' meeting. If the judge rejects the plan, you can propose another plan. If you are eligible to file Chapter 7, you could also convert your Chapter 13 bankruptcy into a Chapter 7 filing.

Bear in mind that under the new law you must start making payments to the trustee, your landlord, and on your secured debts within thirty days of filing, regardless of whether the plan has been confirmed by a judge or not.

Value of Secured Collateral

The new law limits the practice of stripping, or dramatically reducing the value of, certain secured loans. Under the old law, you had the right to propose a new value for the property you owed money on. For example, if the blue-book value of your car was less than what you owed, you could propose to pay only the blue book value in satisfaction of your debt. The new law, however, prohibits the stripping down of security interests in motor

▶ **IF YOU'RE SELF-EMPLOYED**

Chapter 13 can also be an effective tool for self-employed individuals. If you are self-employed and filing under Chapter 13, you should list your average monthly business expenses, business income, and business debts when filing your payment plan and schedules. You should also include incidental income, such as part-time wages for babysitting, alimony and support income, and rental income.

vehicles acquired within 910 days of the petition filing, and of other secured debts incurred within one year of the bankruptcy. You must repay the full amount of the loans on such property. This limit on lien stripping is one of the major changes effected by the new federal law.

CHAPTER 13 PAYMENT PLANS

Preparing Your Plan

As has been discussed throughout this chapter, you have some flexibility in preparing a Chapter 13 bankruptcy plan, provided that your creditors raise no objections. The plan that you prepare for review by your lawyer should take into account your income from all sources and your reasonable necessary expenses. It should also anticipate any known future changes in your income or expenses, such as retirement or a rent increase. What is left from your income after paying living expenses will be available for disbursement to your creditors. Note that some items, like child support payments and money used to pay certain debts, are excluded from "available income."

Your plan must provide for payment in full of all **priority claims**—that is, certain taxes and family support obligations, including overdue child support and alimony. The new bankruptcy law makes domestic-support obligations a top priority. A debtor can lose the protections of a Chapter 13 plan if he or she does not remain current with his or her family support obligations.

Besides keeping up with such current obligations, you'll have to "cure"—that is, make up for—payments you have missed in the past. You can arrange to pay such overdue debts over the life of your repayment plan. If your disposable income is above the median in your state, your plan may have to run for five years. As noted above, a creditor or the trustee might object to your plan. If this happens and the court disapproves the plan, you must redraft your plan to address the objection.

After the Plan Is Approved

Once the court confirms your payment plan, you must continue to make regular monthly plan payments to the trustee. Bear in mind that these payments must begin within thirty days after filing the plan or the initial bankruptcy petition, whichever is earlier, and both dates might precede the confirmation of your plan. The trustee usually distributes payments among your creditors in accordance with your confirmed repayment plan. You will continue, of course, to pay for your ongoing utility and grocery bills, and other everyday expenses. The court will grant you a Chapter 13 discharge after you complete the payments specified in your plan, usually in three to five years. If you are unable to complete the payments, you will not obtain a discharge of any of your debts unless you qualify for a hardship discharge, which requires proof of special circumstances beyond your control that made it impossible for you to make further plan payments (see below).

New Filing Requirements

Chapter 13 now imposes additional filing requirements on debtors during the lives of their repayment plans. Upon request from the judge or a party in interest (e.g., a trustee or creditor), debtors must submit annual financial statements showing the "the amount and sources of income" and expenditures.

◖◗ TALKING TO A LAWYER

Q. *What percentage of my debts do I have to pay in a Chapter 13 case? Is it the same percentage for all debts, or do I have to pay a greater percentage of certain debts?*

A. This is a matter of local practice. The law provides that under certain circumstances you can pay as little as zero percent to unsecured creditors; however, you must provide full payment to priority creditors. Priority debts are specified in Section 507 of the Bankruptcy Code and include, among other things, child support and some taxes.

—**Answer by Marc S. Stern, Law Offices of Marc S. Stern, Seattle, Washington**

A. There is no fixed percentage amount of debts that have to be paid under Chapter 13 plans. Some plans may pay 100 percent to unsecured creditors while others may pay 70 percent, 40 percent, 20 percent, 10 percent, or even zero percent, depending on the particular facts and circumstances. Generally, all unsecured nonpriority creditors—for example, credit card companies—will be treated the same and receive the same percentage of repayment. If an unsecured creditor objects to confirmation of a Chapter 13 plan, the debtor must submit all of his or her disposable income for a period of at least thirty-six months to pay whatever percentage of the debt can be paid during that period. For cause, the court may allow some creditors to be treated differently. If the debtor's income exceeds the state's median income, the plan may have to last five years.

—**Answer by Judge David S. Kennedy, United States Bankruptcy Court, Western District of Tennessee**

Q. *This is not my first time being deep in debt. I had many debts discharged three years ago under Chapter 7, but now I've got new ones. Can I file a Chapter 13 bankruptcy?*

A. No. The eight-year discharge bar in Chapter 7 cases does not apply in Chapter 13 cases. However, a discharge would not be granted in a

Chapter 13 case if the discharge in the Chapter 7 case was granted within four years of the filing of the subsequent Chapter 13 case. So-called serial filings are allowed in Chapter 13 cases; however, Chapter 13 plans must be filed in good faith. Good-faith requirements are often said to be the "gatekeepers" of Chapter 13.

—Answer by Judge David S. Kennedy, United States Bankruptcy Court, Western District of Tennessee

Payments under Chapter 13 Plans

You must do all you can to make the payments required under a Chapter 13 bankruptcy plan. If you don't make the required payments, the ramifications can be severe. If you fail to take the initiative in dealing with defaults under your Chapter 13 plan—for example, by seeking a change in the plan or a hardship discharge (discussed below)—a creditor or the trustee may seek to have your case either converted to Chapter 7, or dismissed outright. If the case is dismissed, the automatic stay that arose upon the filing of the Chapter 13 case is dissolved. This means that the collection calls will begin again, and your car could be repossessed or your home foreclosed upon as if there had been no bankruptcy. If you are eligible for Chapter 7, conversion to Chapter 7 could be good or bad for you, depending on the circumstances. For some debtors, conversion to a Chapter 7 case might be a good result. If you have little or no equity, Chapter 7 isn't much of a threat, so you might seek to have your Chapter 13 case converted to Chapter 7 on your own if you are having problems making the Chapter 13 plan payments. However, if you have a lot of equity in your home or your car that you want to retain, Chapter 7 could be something you'd prefer to avoid, since it would give your creditors a chance to recover nonexempt assets that you wish to protect. In that case, you'd have every reason to keep up with your Chapter 13 plan. Be aware, however, that conversion to Chapter 7 does not necessarily mean that you are eligible for a Chapter 7 discharge; conversion and eligibility for discharge are different matters entirely.

Sometimes, special circumstances can qualify a debtor for

temporary relief from the requirements of a Chapter 13 plan. For example, if you have an accident that causes you to lose time from work temporarily, you may be able to arrange a moratorium, which means that you can miss a payment and catch up later. Furthermore, if there is a major permanent reduction in your income—for example, from lost hours due to a chronic illness—the trustee may support a modification in the plan if you meet certain legal requirements. Modification might entail stretching payments out over a longer period (not to exceed five years) and reducing the amount of each payment accordingly, or perhaps giving up some asset for which you had planned to make payments. If you complete performance of your modified plan, you are entitled to a full Chapter 13 type discharge, provided you have satisfied the other requirements as well (i.e., completed debtor counseling and stayed current on all post-petition domestic-support obligations).

Hardship Discharge

If there is no modification of your plan but you have defaulted on your plan payments as a result of circumstances for which you "should not justly be held accountable," and if your unsecured creditors have already received as much as they would have received under Chapter 7, you may qualify for a **hardship discharge** if you can show that a modification of the plan would be impractical. This is a Chapter 7 type discharge.

WHICH DEBTS ARE DISCHARGEABLE UNDER CHAPTER 13?

Before 2005, a Chapter 13 discharge covered many more types of debt than did a Chapter 7 discharge, and that broader discharge was a major advantage of filing under Chapter 13. Under the new law, the Chapter 13 discharge granted upon completion of a plan still covers more types of debt than the Chapter 7 discharge, but the difference is much smaller than it was before.

Debts not discharged by Chapter 13 include:

- Taxes, where returns either were not filed or were fraudulent;
- Debts left off the bankruptcy schedules;
- Support debts;
- Student loans;
- Debts for personal injuries caused by drunk driving;
- Criminal fines;
- Some restitution orders;
- Debts for money obtained under false pretenses;
- Debts for luxury goods bought on credit within ninety days of filing;
- Cash advances over $750 obtained within seventy days of filing; and
- Funds obtained by embezzlement.

Note that debts for property settlement and willful property

(i) CONVERSION TO CHAPTER 7

Sometimes Chapter 13 bankruptcies are converted to Chapter 7 bankruptcies. If there is neither a modification nor a hardship discharge of your Chapter 13 obligations, and if your income is low enough that you are eligible for Chapter 7, you may choose to convert your case to Chapter 7. Following conversion you would presumably receive a Chapter 7 discharge, unless you have already received such a discharge within the preceding eight years. (Of course, in a Chapter 7 case, you must surrender all your nonexempt unencumbered assets.) Sometimes the conversion to Chapter 7 is forced upon you because you simply cannot meet the obligations of the Chapter 13 payment plan.

Representative Sensenbrenner, the Chairman of the House Judiciary Committee, said on the House floor that the right to convert from Chapter 13 to Chapter 7 was not changed by the new bankruptcy law. However, under the new law, if you do convert to Chapter 7, you do not get credit for payments you made on secured debt under Chapter 13.

damage are still dischargeable under Chapter 13, even though they would not be discharged under Chapter 7. The Chapter 13 hardship discharge, as discussed above, covers only debts that would be dischargeable under Chapter 7.

The World at Your Fingertips

• The required forms for filing a Chapter 13 bankruptcy are available online at *www.uscourts.gov/bankruptcycourts.html*. Each judicial district has its own form of Chapter 13 plan. You should use the Chapter 13 plan form that applies in your district.

• You can find more information and FAQs about Chapter 13 bankruptcy at the Nolo website (*www.nolo.com*). Just click on "Bankruptcy" and follow the links for more information on Chapter 13.

Remember This

• Chapter 13 allows individuals with regular incomes to pay all or a portion of their debts under the protection and supervision of a court. Under Chapter 13, you file a bankruptcy petition and a proposed payment plan, which can extend from three to five years, with the U.S. Bankruptcy Court.

• Chapter 13 filings may increase in the wake of the bankruptcy law passed in 2005; fewer people will be eligible to file under Chapter 7, and some Chapter 7 bankruptcies will be converted to Chapter 13.

• The bankruptcy trustee will typically distribute your proposed payment plan to your creditors. Creditors will have a chance to challenge your proposals. Once the payment plan is approved by the court, you make monthly payments to the trustee, who then disburses the money among your creditors in accordance with the plan.

• If you cannot make payments under a Chapter 13 plan, you may be able to convert to a Chapter 7 plan or seek a dismissal of the Chapter 13 case.

• The new bankruptcy law makes some major changes for those filing bankruptcy under Chapter 13. These changes include severely limiting the stripping down of auto liens, increasing the length of many plans to five years, providing that plans will not be confirmed if domestic-support obligations are not met, and making fewer debts dischargeable under Chapter 13.

CHAPTER 20

Chapter 13 or Chapter 7?

Which Should You Choose?
Advantages and Disadvantages

Laurel has large credit card debts that she cannot pay and is considering filing for bankruptcy. She has $50,000 of equity in her home, is paying off a car, and would like to keep both. But she can't stand the idea of committing her hard-earned wages to creditors for up to five years through a Chapter 13 bankruptcy. How can she decide what kind of bankruptcy is right for her?

Choosing the best form of bankruptcy for a particular situation is often difficult. The chart on pages 267–269 summarizes the differences between the two most common types of consumer bankruptcy—Chapter 7 and Chapter 13—and provides a quick overview of your options with respect to each. To assist you in making an informed decision, this chapter will explore more thoroughly the advantages and disadvantages of both types. Bear in mind, however, that the bankruptcy law passed in 2005 may make you ineligible for Chapter 7 bankruptcy if you earn more than the median income in your state and have disposable income.

ADVANTAGES OF CHAPTER 13

Chapter 13 bankruptcy plans have several advantages over Chapter 7 plans. Perhaps the most important advantage is that Chapter 13 plans allow you to retain and use all of your assets, so long as you make payments to your trustee as agreed in your court-approved repayment plan.

Another distinction between Chapters 7 and 13 is that a few debts are dischargeable in a Chapter 13 case that are not dischargeable in a Chapter 7 case (such as property settlement debts and debts for willful property damage). However, divorce-related alimony and child support payments are not discharge-able in either chapter—you have to pay them. Whether a debt is for support or property settlement is a question of federal, not state, law. Chapter 19 of this book contains more information about the kinds of debt that are not dischargeable under either chapter.

Chapter 13 may also be preferable if you are a party to one or more co-signed loans. Under Chapter 13, if you had people co-sign any of your consumer loans or other credit representing consumer debts, and the collateral for such loans is in your possession, your creditors cannot collect from these cosigners until it is clear that the Chapter 13 plan will not pay the entire amount owed to the creditors. This is called a "co-debtor automatic stay." In contrast, if you file Chapter 7, your creditors will have the right to demand payment from your cosigners immediately.

Another advantage of Chapter 13 is that you can use it more often than Chapter 7. The law forbids you to receive a discharge under Chapter 7 more than once every eight years. However, Chapter 13 allows you to file Chapter 13 repeatedly, and receive the benefits of the automatic stay, though each filing will appear on your credit record and will be reviewed by the trustee to prevent abuse. You should remember that, regardless of the frequency with which you file, all Chapter 13 plans must be filed in good faith.

Although you may be able to file repeatedly under the new bankruptcy law, it may not be possible to complete the bankruptcy and be discharged from your debts. Under the new law, a Chapter 13 debtor will be denied discharge if he or she received a discharge in a case filed under Chapter 7, 11, or 12 during the previous four years, or in a Chapter 13 case filed during the previous two years. The advantage of being able to refile under Chapter 13 (even if debtors are not permitted discharge) is that debtors are given the temporary protection of the automatic stay.

For example, imagine a debtor files for Chapter 13 bankruptcy two years after filing for Chapter 7. Under the law, the debtor cannot receive a discharge under Chapter 13 because the bankruptcies are too close together. But she would receive the benefit of an automatic stay, which would stop debt collectors from calling. She would also be able to spread out her existing debts over five years. Of course, if she still had debts remaining after five years, they would not be discharged and she would still be liable for them. However, the benefits of having a period of time—up to five years—to deal with secured debt, a time in which unsecured creditors must suspend their collection efforts, may outweigh not being able to get a discharge at the end of that period.

Under prior bankruptcy law, some debtors would file Chapter 13 cases immediately after Chapter 7 cases, or repeatedly file Chapter 13 cases without ever finishing payments under Chapter 13 plans. These debtors filed Chapter 13 so they could use the automatic stay to stave off foreclosure on a home or other asset. However, these kinds of tactics do not work so well under the 2005 law. The new law says that, in a debtor's second bankruptcy case within the span of a year, the automatic stay will end thirty days after the filing. In a debtor's third bankruptcy case within the span of a year, there will be no automatic stay at all, except as to unsecured creditors.

ADVANTAGES OF CHAPTER 7

There are several reasons that straight bankruptcy (i.e., bankruptcy filed under Chapter 7) may be preferable to Chapter 13. First, there are many debtors for whom the advantages of Chapter 13 do not matter: debtors with no nonexempt assets they particularly wish to keep, no debts excepted from discharge under Chapter 13, no prior discharge within the last eight years, and no cosigners on their consumer debt loans.

Second, the benefits of Chapter 13 may come at the price of committing the debtor's entire disposable income to creditors for three to five years. In Chapter 7, the debtor can keep post-petition earnings free and clear from discharged pre-bankruptcy debts.

Third, some debtors are not eligible for Chapter 13 bankruptcy, either because their income is not sufficiently regular to fund payments under a plan, or because the amount of their debt exceeds the limits discussed in chapter 19.

7 OR 13:
IS IT ALWAYS THE DEBTOR'S CHOICE?

When filing for bankruptcy, the choice between chapters is generally left to any eligible debtor. However, under the new bankruptcy law the trustee or any creditor can bring a motion in court to dismiss a Chapter 7 bankruptcy if the debtor's income is too high (that is, above the state median). In effect, this forces the debtor into Chapter 13 bankruptcy, if the debtor is to file bankruptcy at all.

Under the new law, a "means test" is used to determine whether a debtor's income is too high for a Chapter 7 case. If the debtor's current monthly income is above the state's median income for his or her type of family (e.g., four-person family, three-person family, and so on), then there is a presumption that the person should file bankruptcy under Chapter 13, not Chapter 7. The test is fairly complex and takes into account presumed income and a number of deductions. Under the means test, debtors must file a statement of their calculations. If a debtor's income is considered too high for Chapter 7, then creditors are notified within ten days of the filing of the petition, and can bring a motion to dismiss the bankruptcy petition.

Median income varies by state. In Illinois, for example, the median income in 2005 (adjusted for inflation) was approximately $41,000 for a one-person household, $53,000 for a two-person household, $62,000 for a three-person household, and $70,000 for a four-person household.

ⓘ CRAMMING DOWN UNDER THE NEW LAW

Cramming down is a practice allowed under the old bankruptcy law for some kinds of loans. Under the old law, if you owed $8,000 on your car but the car was worth only $5,000, the court could approve a "cram-down" of the loan to a secured claim of $5,000, with your monthly payments reduced to reflect the lower balance. Under the new law, cramming down is greatly limited—it is only available if you have bought or refinanced the car more than 2.5 years before filing for bankruptcy, and the loan can only be crammed down to the current retail value of the car, though this still might be less than the amount you have left to pay.

Neither the old law nor the new one allows the debtor to cram down a first mortgage loan on a home, though some courts may continue to allow cramming down of second and third mortgages loans if the home in question is worth less than the amount of the first mortgage loan.

If your income is under your state's median, your petition for bankruptcy still might be dismissed, although it is less likely. Courts also have the option of dismissing a Chapter 7 bankruptcy on grounds of **simple abuse,** though the new law does not clarify the precise meaning of this term.

Under the old law, courts had the power to dismiss cases on grounds of **substantial abuse.** Courts disagreed over the meaning of this term, and the issue came up relatively infrequently—perhaps because it could be raised only by the court itself or by a public officer known as the U.S. trustee, and could not be raised by creditors. Simple abuse would seem to be a lesser standard that can be raised by any party in interest, even creditors.

Another change is that the new law specifically provides for conversion of a bankruptcy case to Chapter 11 or 13, with the debtor's permission, as an alternative to dismissal.

( ) TALKING TO A LAWYER

Q. *I'm told that if I file for Chapter 7 but have a regular income, my case might get shifted to a Chapter 13 case. Is this true? If it is, what effect would that have on me?*

A. Under current bankruptcy laws, the court may dismiss a bankruptcy case either because the debtor has enough income to flunk the "income test," or because the debtor is otherwise abusing Chapter 7. It is not clear what facts will constitute "abuse" where the debtor's income is not so high as to flunk the means test.

If the case is dismissed due either to failure of the means test or some other abuse, the debtor may voluntarily convert the Chapter 7 case to a Chapter 13 case if he or she still wants to obtain relief under the bankruptcy laws.

—Answer by Marianne Culhane, Professor Creighton University School of Law, Omaha, Nebraska

A. Every individual debtor is subject to the Chapter 7 "means test," which determines eligibility for relief under Chapter 7. The means test is essentially a formula that takes into account monthly income and reasonable and necessary expenses and compares these factors to the median income in the state where you live. If you fall below the median income level in your state, you can file a Chapter 7 bankruptcy; if not, your case will be converted to Chapter 13. Be advised, though, that the formulas and numbers used in the means test can be complicated, and that the median income level varies from state to state. Your lawyer can advise you whether you qualify to file under the Chapter 7 means test. An advantage of the new law is that conversion to Chapter 13 is expressly stated as an alternative to dismissal of a Chapter 7 case.

—Answer by Judge David S. Kennedy, United States Bankruptcy Court, Western District of Tennessee

A. If your Chapter 7 bankruptcy is dismissed, and you choose not to convert it to Chapter 13, it will be as though the bankruptcy never occurred—so your debt will still be outstanding, and debt collection efforts can begin again.

—**Answer by David Greer, Williams Mullen Hofheimer Nusbaum, Norfolk, Virginia**

 **MEANS TESTING**

Thanks to the new bankruptcy law, the choice whether to file under Chapter 7 or Chapter 13 has been made easier for some debtors. As noted earlier, the new law establishes more stringent restrictions on the use of Chapter 7 by individual debtors whose incomes (based on actual income less set expenses, calculated under IRS workout guidelines) would fund significant payments to creditors if the debtors used Chapter 13 instead. The new legislation requires some Chapter 7 cases to be converted to Chapter 13 cases where a debtor's income is high (above the state's median) and his or her debts could be paid in significant part. The determination of whether a debtor meets these criteria is called **means testing**. Your lawyer should be able to tell you whether you qualify for Chapter 7.

GENERAL COMPARISON OF CHAPTER 7 AND CHAPTER 13 BANKRUPTCY

Chapter 7	Chapter 13
Straight Bankruptcy Liquidation	**Payment Plan for People with Regular Income**

Basic operation

Obtain mandatory credit counseling within 180 days before filing bankruptcy petition. File bankruptcy petition with court. Trustee appointed to administer bankruptcy. All nonexempt assets surrendered for liquidation and distribution. Debtor retains only exempt assets and those assets reaffirmed or redeemed and, if creditor agrees, collateral for loans. Money from liquidation is split among creditors, according to priority established by the Bankruptcy Code.

Obtain mandatory credit counseling within 180 days prior to bankruptcy. If a debt management plan is proposed, that should be filed as well. File bankruptcy petition and proposed payment plan with court. Payment plan provides payments over a period of three to five years. As a result of new law, more plans may be for five years. Payments are made from disposable income (i.e., whatever is left over after necessities [food, shelter, etc.] have been allowed for), while debtor retains assets. Individuals must complete "an instructional course concerning personal financial management" to assure their discharge.

Limitations

Debtor must pass the "means test" which determines eligibility for Chapter 7. Some people with income higher than state median income will not be eligible for Chapter 7.

For debtors owing less than $307,675 in unsecured debt and less than $922,975 in secured debt.

Percentage of consumer filings

71.5%. Of the 1,563,145 consumer bankruptcy filings in 2004, 1,117,766 were Chapter 7 filings.

28.4%. Of the 1,563,145 consumer bankruptcy filings in 2004, 444,428 were Chapter 13 filings.

Frequency

Discharge will be denied if a debtor got a prior Chapter 7 discharge within eight years, or a Chapter 11, 12 or 13 discharge within six years.

Discharge will be denied if a debtor got a prior Chapter 7, 11 or 12 discharge within four years, or a Chapter 13 discharge within two years.

Effect on debts

With exceptions noted in text (e.g., student loans, support obligations, taxes), most pre-petition debts are discharged (extinguished) upon conclusion of bankruptcy unless court denies the discharge. Personal liability to creditors ends when the court enters a discharge

All or a portion of debts paid off over a period of time under a specific plan. With exceptions noted in text (e.g., student loans, support obligations, taxes), most pre-petition debts discharged. Personal liability to creditors ends when the plan is completed and the court enters a

Chapter 7
Straight Bankruptcy Liquidation

Chapter 13
Payment Plan for People with Regular Income

order. Court may except one or more particular debts from the discharge, and creditors may retain liens on collateral, such as a home mortgage.

discharge order, but creditors may retain liens on collateral, such as a home mortgage.

Effect on home
Debtor may keep home under homestead exemption if there is little nonexempt equity, and if mortgage payments have been maintained. The mortgage holder may require the debtor to reaffirm the mortgage. Marital ownership law may also preserve the home. However, 2005 changes limit homestead exemption to $125,000 for homes acquired within 40 months of filing or if debtor committed in certain fraudulent acts.

Home may be preserved if plan is successfully completed and if there is not substantial nonexempt equity. The new bankruptcy law provides for homestead exemption of no more than $125,000 if home acquired 40 months before filing or if debtor engaged in certain fraudulent conduct.

Effect on car or truck
Vehicle might be taken by trustee or secured creditor (unless necessary for work) or arrangements are made to pay off lien by redemption or reaffirmation.

Vehicle will be preserved if plan is successfully completed and appropriate payments made. If not, it might be taken by creditors (unless arrangements are made to pay off lien).

Effect on nonexempt assets
All nonexempt assets may be required to be surrendered for distribution to creditors.

Debtor retains all assets if plan confirmed and successfully completed. If case is converted to Chapter 7, nonexempt assets must be surrendered for distribution to creditors.

Time to repay   Not applicable

Usually three years, sometimes up to five years. Under the new law, more will be for five years.

Payments
Most debts will be discharged, but some, such as taxes, student loans, and child support will have to be paid by debtor out of post-petition income.

All "disposable income" is available for payments; that is, whatever remains after necessities (food, shelter, etc.) are taken care of. New law changes Chapter 13 by providing that for debtors with above-median income, what is reasonable to pay will be determined in large part by IRS regulations.

Portion of debt repaid
Will depend on the value of nonexempt assets surrendered to pay off debts.

May allow for payment of less than the full amount of debts.

Chapter 7	Chapter 13
Straight Bankruptcy Liquidation	**Payment Plan for People with Regular Income**

Result at conclusion of bankruptcy

Bankruptcy court enters a discharge order, ending personal liability on all dischargeable pre-petition debts. Creditors may retain liens, such as a home mortgage, and foreclosure is still a possibility if the debt secured is not paid as agreed.

When all plan payments have been made, bankruptcy court enters a discharge order, ending personal liability on all dischargeable pre-petition debts. Holders of home mortgage may retain that lien, and foreclose if the mortgage debt is not paid as agreed.

Effect on credit

Record of bankruptcy remains on credit record for up to ten years from the date of filing.

Borrower must have made all payments in accordance with court-approved plan, after which court enters discharge order.

Record of bankruptcy filing may remain on your credit report for up to ten years from the date of filing, although some creditors will report a Chapter 13 bankruptcy for only seven years.

The World at Your Fingertips

A word of warning: when seeking legal information on the Internet, only consider information that reflects the changes imposed by the bankruptcy law passed in 2005. If you are seriously contemplating bankruptcy and you want to ensure that you receive accurate, up-to-date information, it may be worth talking to a bankruptcy lawyer.

• Good overall information on bankruptcy can be found on the American Bankruptcy Institute's website, which has particularly useful areas such as the Consumer's Corner, links to lists of lawyers who are certified bankruptcy specialists, and highlights of recent legislative developments; visit *www.abiworld.org/*.

• Filing-Bankruptcy.com features a section on the advantages and disadvantages of both Chapter 7 and Chapter 13. Visit *filing-bankruptcy-form.com/advantages-disadvantages.html*.

• Nolo.com provides information on when Chapter 13 is a better solution than Chapter 7. Visit *www.nolo.com*, click on

"Bankruptcy," then on "Chapter 7" to find the article, entitled "When Chapter 7 Bankruptcy is Better Than Chapter 13."

• FreeAdvice.com has a similar section, where it lists advantages and disadvantages of Chapter 7 and Chapter 13, at *bankruptcy-law.freeadvice.com/pros_cons.htm*.

• The law firm of Galler & Atkins in Atlanta, Georgia, has posted a chart on its website showing comparisons between Chapter 7 and Chapter 13. Visit *www.galleratkins.com/forms/compare.pdf*.

Remember This

• There may be several advantages to filing Chapter 13 instead of Chapter 7. The major advantage is that under Chapter 13 you will be able to retain and use all of your assets as long as you make the promised payments. Also, the discharge of debts is a bit broader under Chapter 13 than under Chapter 7.

• There may also be advantages to a Chapter 7 bankruptcy. For instance, Chapter 13 debtors may have to keep making payments for three to five years. In Chapter 7, a debtor can keep post-petition earnings free and clear from discharged pre-bankruptcy debts.

• Most debtors can choose whether to file for bankruptcy under Chapter 7 or Chapter 13. However, the new law passed in 2005 means that some bankruptcies will be eligible for discharge only in Chapter 13.

CHAPTER 21

Saving Your Home

What You Can Do to Protect Your Home Under Bankruptcy

Mr. and Mrs. Williams have accumulated substantial debts during their twenty years of marriage. Maintaining their standard of living while putting their three daughters through college has placed an even greater strain on their finances. When Mr. Williams loses his job, their financial situation becomes untenable. They have a beautiful home that they wish to keep at any cost, but they also know realistically that they must file bankruptcy to stop a foreclosure. What can they do to save their home?

What's the most important step you can take to preserve your home? First, under either Chapter 7 or Chapter 13, you will be able to keep your home only if you continue to make the required ongoing monthly payments on your mortgage. If you've fallen behind, under Chapter 7 you must make arrangements acceptable to your mortgage lender to catch up on any delinquent payments, and it's up to the mortgage company to decide whether to work with you. Under Chapter 13, you may be able to include any delinquent payments in your payment plan and pay them off over a specified period of time—say, three years—while maintaining ongoing monthly mortgage payments. To accomplish this, you must have sufficient cash flow to cover your regular payments to the Chapter 13 bankruptcy trustee as well as your regular ongoing mortgage payments. Bear in mind also, as discussed in previous chapters, that you must qualify income-wise in order to file Chapter 13 bankruptcy.

A sincere willingness to make monthly payments on your mortgage, however, will not ensure that you can keep your home. Though making such payments is necessary, it still may not be sufficient.

Another factor determining whether you'll keep your home is whether you own the property with your spouse. Let's say you have plenty of debt, but your spouse has little or none. Many states will completely block or significantly limit the ability of unsecured creditors to reach property that you own together with your nonfiling spouse. (This is not true, however, in community property states.) Much may depend on how (i.e., in what form of joint ownership) you hold the home. Talk to a lawyer in your state about whether your home could be protected.

CHAPTER 7

Even if you're willing to continue making the required monthly payments, you could still lose your home if you file for bankruptcy under Chapter 7.

With a Chapter 7 filing, if you have no equity in your home and you haven't made your payments (you are **in default**), the creditor can foreclose on your home (take it from you) during or after bankruptcy, even if your unsecured debts are discharged. The Chapter 7 discharge does not release the lien. Of course, a lender can also foreclose on your home in these circumstances if you do not file for bankruptcy; filing for bankruptcy will only delay the inevitable by a couple of months.

If you do have equity in your home, your *unsecured* creditors may also have an interest in your home, especially if it is worth more than the total of your mortgage debt and any applicable homestead exemption. In that case, the bankruptcy trustee may take possession of your home and sell it for the benefit of your unsecured creditors—in other words, it may become part of the assets collected for distribution by the trustee.

Whether the trustee will actually take your home will depend on two basic factors: how much equity you have in the home, and how much of the home's value is sheltered by exemption law from creditors.

The **homestead exemption** is the amount of your home's value that the law puts out of the reach of your unsecured creditors. In general, the lower your exemption and the greater the equity you have in your home, the stronger the chance that the trustee will take your home.

For example, assume that the market value of your home is $90,000, and you have a mortgage of $55,000. Your equity is the difference between those two figures, or $35,000. If your homestead exemption were $30,000 (as is the case in Colorado), your creditors could in theory seek to claim the $5,000 left over after your exemption is subtracted from your equity. As a practical matter, however, the trustee would probably not go to the expense and trouble of taking over your property and selling it for the benefit of unsecured creditors, especially since the costs of the sale would eat up the $5,000.

Of course, if the homestead exemption were a mere $5,000 (as is the case in Georgia and a number of other states), then the trustee could realize a great deal of money—in the above example, $30,000—through a sale of your home, which would make selling the home a more attractive option for the trustee.

The new bankruptcy law does not do away with state homestead exemptions, but it puts a lid on them in states with generous limits or no dollar limits at all. Under the new law, if you bought your home in the forty months before filing—specifically, within 1,216 days of filing—you can exempt no more than $125,000 of its value, unless you rolled over an interest from another house you owned in the same state. However, if you live in one of the many states in which the homestead exemption is less than $125,000, the lower state limit still applies.

In general, the greater the difference between the market value of your home and your mortgage debt, the more likely it is that the Chapter 7 trustee will find it worthwhile to take over your home and sell it for the benefit of creditors. Take the example of the house in Colorado given above, but now assume that its market value is $190,000, not $90,000. If the house is taken over by the trustee and sold for the benefit of the bankruptcy es-

( ) TALKING TO A LAWYER

Q. My lender has filed suit to foreclose on my home. Will bankruptcy stop that suit?

A. Yes. A bankruptcy may stop the foreclosure, at least temporarily, and assuming this is not your third bankruptcy case within a year. Upon the filing of a bankruptcy petition, an automatic stay ordinarily comes into effect. However, in Chapter 7 cases the automatic stay may just prolong the eventual foreclosure unless you and the holder of the mortgage can work out a satisfactory arrangement. When the discharge is granted, it is likely that the holder of the mortgage will again try to foreclose, assuming that it hasn't done so already.

In Chapter 13 cases, the debtor-homeowner might be able to cure the defaults on the mortgage under the plan and maintain ongoing payments. If so, the Chapter 13 debtor may be able to save the home from foreclosure. For this reason, Chapter 13 has been referred to as a "save the home" chapter. Chapter 13 offers broader and more effective ways of dealing with the possibility of foreclosure than does Chapter 7.

—Answer by Judge David S. Kennedy, United States Bankruptcy Court, Western District of Tennessee

A. Yes, bankruptcy can stop the foreclosure process in the short term. In order to retain your home in the long term, however, you need to be able to cure the arrears due to your mortgage company over a three- to five-year period—that is, make up in full all missed payments. In a Chapter 13 case, you must be able to make your payments to the Chapter 13 trustee each month—a portion of which will be used to repay the lender for your missed payments—*and* be able to continue making regular ongoing, mortgage payments. Bankruptcy may also be an effective way to buy some time in which to sell your home before foreclosure takes place, though the price you receive for your home may be reduced on account of the pending bankruptcy case. If you have equity in your home above and beyond your state exemptions and any costs of sale, a Chapter 7 trustee may be interested in selling your home for you—but, again, the price you fetch will likely be lower than it would be if you had not filed for bankruptcy.

—**Answer by Shayna M. Steinfeld, Steinfeld & Steinfeld, P.C., Atlanta, Georgia**

Q. What effect will bankruptcy have on my ability to get a mortgage in the future?

A. In my experience, future credit depends more on the phase of the moon than anything else. I have had several clients refinance houses out of Chapter 13 when they were current on their Chapter 13 payments.

Mortgage brokers have told me that it is possible to get a mortgage within two years of a Chapter 7 discharge. On the other hand, I have had other clients who found it incredibly difficult to obtain new credit under any circumstances.

—**Answer by Marc S. Stern, Law Offices of Marc S. Stern, Seattle, Washington**

A. The bankruptcy filing is a matter of public record. Most home mortgage lenders want to know why you had to file for bankruptcy. Was it due to a job loss, health issues, or a divorce? Do you now have a steady job? Are you now a good credit risk? It's a matter of you convincing the mortgage lender that you are a potentially good customer and credit risk. Watch out for unusually high interest rates or a lot of points.

—**Answer by Judge David S. Kennedy, United States Bankruptcy Court, Western District of Tennessee**

A. It is likely that the bankruptcy will not prevent you from getting a mortgage in the future, but it will greatly increase the cost of that mortgage once you get it (e.g., instead of a prime-plus-3-percent rate, you may be saddled with a prime-plus-8-percent rate). If you are proceeding in a Chapter 13 case, you may not incur debt during the bankruptcy process without court approval, including a mortgage.

—**Answer by Shayna M. Steinfeld, Steinfeld & Steinfeld, P.C., Atlanta, Georgia**

tate, the funds available for unsecured creditors would amount
to $105,000:

Selling Price	$190,000
Less: Mortgage Loan	$55,000
Value of Your Equity	$135,000
Less: Homestead Exemption	$30,000
Available for Unsecured Creditors	$105,000

Of course, determining equity is not a precise science. It depends on the selling price of your home—and how can you know
that before it is sold? In your bankruptcy filings, it may be in your
best interest to estimate the lowest possible sale price for your
home, thus making the sale of your home a less attractive option
for the trustee. For example, to determine your equity in the
home, you could deduct its sale costs, such as a typical realtor's
fee, which could seemingly knock 6 to 8 percent off its value. Or
you could determine the value of your home using foreclosure results (typically about 80 percent of retail value), which could
make your home seem to be worth about 20 percent less. Or you
might make reference to a tax-assessed value that is relatively
low. These are all useful strategies for making your estimated eq-

⚠ WHAT IF THE FORECLOSURE ISN'T ENOUGH?

A lender who recovers less from the sale of your house than the amount
that you owe will have an unsecured claim for the difference between
the two amounts. Thus, if your mortgage debt was $100,000 and the
sale of your house garnered only $90,000, you could be on the hook for
the additional $10,000, especially if you are not in bankruptcy. Depending
on what state you live in, the creditor could assert a claim for that amount
and try to recover it from your other assets. In some states, a confirmation action in state court is required to verify the foreclosing mortgage
company's entitlement to such a deficiency claim. In most states, there
is a limited right to a deficiency depending on the method of foreclosure.

▶ **KEEP THOSE PAYMENTS UP**

To avoid losing your home under Chapter 13, you must make your regular monthly payments to the Chapter 13 trustee *and* make all future monthly mortgage payments as they become due after the filing. If you've skipped some mortgage payments before you filed your Chapter 13 bankruptcy, you can put the delinquent mortgage payments under the Chapter 13 plan. If the loan was made after 1994, then you do not need to pay interest on the delinquency. In other words, you can spread the missed mortgage payments out and cure the default. However, to be sure of keeping your home, you must also make the *future* monthly payments on your home mortgage loan as they come due. If you don't, you may have to turn your home over to the lender.

uity in your home seem as low as possible, thus making it less likely that the home will be sold to satisfy creditors.

In a few states, such as Florida, there is no dollar limit on the homestead exemption, only a limit on the acreage that can be shielded from creditors. In Texas, unsecured creditors cannot seek payment from a homestead, so long as that homestead is not larger than one acre (in a city) or two hundred acres (anywhere else), *regardless of the value of the property*. These generous provisions remain under the new federal bankruptcy law, provided that you purchased your home more than forty months prior to filing for bankruptcy. However, a homestead owner must still make required monthly payments to the bank that is financing his home—even for a $2 million townhouse in downtown Dallas or a home in Palm Beach.

CHAPTER 13

To preserve your home under a Chapter 13 plan, you ordinarily must agree to continue your lender's lien on your home and to make the required ongoing monthly payments. You must also agree to pay any skipped payments (defaults) through your payment plan. Otherwise, you'll have to turn the property over to the lender.

It is possible that if housing values are greatly depressed, a lender might be willing to lower your monthly payments in order to gain some income and keep the house occupied. But don't count on it.

The World at Your Fingertips

• Legalhelpers.com features a Q & A section on bankruptcy law, including information on using Chapter 13 to save your home, at *www.legalhelpers.com/legal_helpers/chapter13.html*.

Remember This

• Under either Chapter 7 or Chapter 13, you will not be able to keep your home if you don't make the required monthly payments on your mortgage after the filing.

• Whether the trustee will actually take your home will depend upon two basic factors: how much equity is in the home and how much of the home's value is sheltered by law from creditors.

• Often, there is a homestead exemption with a dollar amount that is shielded from creditors, but don't assume that you will be able to keep your home simply because you file for bankruptcy.

• Remember that the new bankruptcy law caps the homestead exemption at $125,000 in all states for houses purchased up to forty months before filing, unless you rolled over an interest from another house you owned in the same state. Of course, if the state exemption is less than $125,000, the lower exemption applies.

• With your home on the line, you're well advised to discuss your situation with a bankruptcy lawyer.

CHAPTER 22

Where to Go for More Information

Throughout Part II of this book, we've given you a number of re-sources to help you find more information on a variety of topics associated with bankruptcy. This chapter provides even more re-sources for you to explore. Some may have been mentioned in previous chapters, but we still think they're the best places for you to start. This chapter also includes some reminders and tips you can use to go about getting additional information.

There is one caveat: Some of the information on these sites may not reflect all the changes effected by the bankruptcy law passed in 2005. To make sure you're getting advice based on the new law, talk to a lawyer who can give you up-to-date, ac-curate information about how the new bankruptcy law applies to you.

GO FOR BROKE: EIGHT WEBSITES TO GET YOU STARTED

While there's not exactly a dearth of bankruptcy- and debt-related sites on the Internet, finding good, credible sources can be somewhat challenging. Go for broke and check out the sources we've culled below. Some of these websites are housed within larger sites, but they do contain rather lengthy sections on topics associated with bankruptcy and debt. You're bound to find what you're looking for at one of these sites, or from a link featured on one of these sites. (Please note that they are not arranged in any order of preference.)

BankruptcyAction.com—www.bankruptcyaction.com—*An extensive site featuring information in a question-and-answer for-mat on a variety of topics associated with bankruptcy, such as: bankruptcy discharge, debt consolidation, secured credit cards, and rebuilding credit after bankruptcy. The site also includes a se-*

lection of audio clips (in the "Audio Answers" section), forms you can use with your bankruptcy lawyer, and more.

American Bankruptcy Institute—www.abiworld.org—Click on "Consumer Education Center" to access FAQs and a host of resources about bankruptcy. Topic areas include Chapter 7, Chapter 13, and filing for bankruptcy. Suggestions for further reading are also featured. The ABI's website also contains several publications explaining the ramifications of the new bankruptcy law. They are accessible at abiworld.net/bankbill/index.html.

Cornell's Legal Information Institute: Bankruptcy—www.law.cornell.edu/topics/bankruptcy.html—This LII site about bankruptcy law includes texts of federal and state statutes and federal and state judicial decisions. Be sure to visit the "Law About Commerce" section (featuring such subsections as "Debtor and "Creditor") to find other topics of interest.

I Hate Debt—www.ihatedebt.com—An extensive website run by Tom Allen, who also hosts the "I Hate Debt" radio show. This site contains information on everything from the history of debt to steps you can take to get out of debt, as well as a monthly newsletter for which you can sign up. Visit the "I Hate Debt Radio Show" section to listen to the live show, or check out past shows. Shows feature experts who cover a variety of topics, including debt negotiation, kids and money, dealing with creditor harassment, and more.

U.S. Bankruptcy Courts—www.uscourts.gov/bankruptcy-courts.html—This site of the Federal Judiciary features "Bankruptcy Basics," a downloadable seventy-two-page booklet that covers discharge in bankruptcy, liquidation, individual debt adjustment, terminology, and more. The site includes statistics and links to courts around the country.

DebtSteps.com—www.debtsteps.com—This site contains articles, tips, and resources on all things debt-related. It includes information about credit counseling, money management, bankruptcy facts, credit repair tips, and more.

Nolo.com—www.nolo.com—Click on "Debt & Bankruptcy" to access articles and information on a variety of topics, including *overspending, strategies for repaying debts, student loans, and credit repair. Financial calculator tools are also available.*

Commerce Clearing House—www.cch.com/bankruptcy/ Bankruptcy_04-21.pdf—*A very readable and up-to-date source of information.*

DON'T FORGET . . .

Check local venues for courses, lectures, seminars, and expert panels related to credit, debt, and bankruptcy. Start with your local library, bar association, area colleges, and senior citizens' centers to see what's in the works, or to suggest a topic for upcoming events. Local radio and TV stations also feature experts on money matters, so get with the programs. National radio stations and TV networks (e.g., CNN, CNBC) often provide salient programming, too. If you don't have cable, don't forget that many TV channels also have websites.

The Internet is also a great resource; countless message boards, user groups, mailing lists, and chat rooms exist in cyberspace—many of these could help you in your quest for knowledge and provide a "been there, done that" perspective from other users on issues that you're facing. Communicating with others who have been in your position is a great way of learning about other avenues to explore, and what pitfalls to avoid. Some websites may also provide an area where you can send in your questions and get answers. And many of the sites associated with debt and bankruptcy include online tools (e.g., forms, calculators) you can use for free.

That's about all for now. You owe it to yourself to begin checking out the resources we've provided.

We welcome your comments and suggestions for future editions of this book. Please visit us on the web at *www.abanet.org/publiced/*, or drop us a line via e-mail at: aba-pubed@abanet.org.

How and Where to Resolve
Credit Disputes

What if you believe that a credit grantor has treated you improperly? Resolving the problem involves a sequence of four possible steps, each one more aggressive than the other, though the first two steps are generally sufficient to solve most disputes.

1. Check to be sure that you have the correct information regarding your rights under the law and the credit grantor's obligations to you under the law. In addition to the information included in this book, this appendix provides information about other resources that you may wish to review.

2. Contact the creditor by phone. By talking to the creditor, you can get information about why the matter was handled in the way it was handled. Or you might just find that the creditor will take steps to satisfy you even if there hasn't been any violation of law. It's always a good idea to follow up by letter. Be sure to provide your name, address, account number, and a statement of your concern. If your initial contact is by telephone, get the name of the person with whom you talked. To compete effectively, most credit grantors wish to keep good customers by settling complaints fairly and quickly. Nonetheless, create a "paper trail" by keeping a written record or log of all of your contacts with the creditor. If you are not satisfied with the first response to your complaint or if you feel that the first person you talk to lacks authority to resolve your problem, ask to speak to a manager or write a letter to a senior executive, such as the creditor's president or a senior vice president.

3. If you are not satisfied with the resolution offered by the creditor, based on your study of your rights under the law, the next step is to contact any state or federal agency that reg-

ulates your creditor. It is best to write the appropriate agency and to supply a copy of the written record that you have maintained. By sending a copy of the letter to your creditor, you may focus attention on your complaint. While the regulatory agency may require some time to get to your problem, it will often be able to arrange a solution that will be satisfactory to you. Descriptions of the various regulatory agencies that might be involved, and their addresses, are included in this appendix.

4. If the regulatory agency fails to satisfy you, you can hire your own attorney to pursue the matter. However, if you do not win, you might be liable for your attorney's fees. In some cases this may be true even if you do win. Most attorneys will offer an initial consultation free of charge and will tell you if you appear to have a good case that is worth pursuing.

The remainder of this appendix provides resources that can be useful to you in step three of the resolution procedure detailed above. It tells you how to find the appropriate state or federal agency to contact if you want more information or want to file a complaint. If a financial institution has violated a law, the regulatory agency that oversees that category of institutions might be able to help you.

FEDERAL CONSUMER PROTECTION RESOURCES

To find an agency for a particular situation, access *www.firstgov. gov/Citizen/Topics/Consumer_Safety.shtml* for a comprehensive guide to federal agencies, ideas on how to file a complaint, etc.

The FTC

You should file complaints about consumer credit-reporting agencies or debt collection agencies with the Federal Trade Commission (FTC). The same goes for complaints about violations of the Truth in Lending Act and other federal laws involving credit issued by retail stores, department stores, and small loan and finance companies, and for credit-related complaints about oil companies, public utility companies, state credit unions, or travel-and-entertainment credit card companies. Mail your complaint to:

Federal Trade Commission
CRC-240
Washington, D.C. 20580
Tel: 1-877-FTC-HELP (382-4357) (toll-free)
www.ftc.gov

In addition, the FTC has an online consumer complaint form available at *rn.ftc.gov/pls/dod/wsolcq$.startup?Z_ORG_CODE= PU01,* and a special form for complaints of identity theft at *rn.ftc.gov/pls/dod/widtpubl$.startup?Z_ORG_CODE=PU03.*

Instead of contacting the FTC's national headquarters at the address shown above, you can also send your complaint to one of the FTC regional offices listed below:

1718 Peachtree St., NW
Room 1000
Atlanta, GA 30367

10 Causeway St.
Room 1184
Boston, MA 02222-1073

Suite 1437
55 East Monroe St.
Chicago, IL 60603

668 Euclid Ave.
Suite 520-A
Cleveland, OH 44114

100 N. Central Expressway
Suite 500
Dallas, TX 75201

1405 Curtis St.
Suite 2900
Denver, CO 80202-2393

11000 Wilshire Blvd.
Suite 13209
Los Angeles, CA 90024

150 William St.
Suite 1300
New York, NY 10038

901 Market St.
Suite 570
San Francisco, CA 94103

2806 Federal Building
915 Second Ave.
Seattle, WA 98174

Other Federal Agencies

Finding the appropriate agency for the creditor you're dealing with can be difficult. We provide some guidance below. For more, the FDIC's website has a good explanation of the different agencies and how to tell which one regulates the entity you're dealing with: *www.fdic.gov/consumers/consumer/rights/index.html*

Office of the Comptroller of the Currency

For issues relating to national banks—that is with the word "national" or N.A. in their name

Administrator of National Banks
Customer Assistance Group
1301 McKinney Street
Suite 3710
Houston, TX 77010
www.occ.treas.gov/mail1.htm
E-mail: consumer.complaint@occ.treas.gov

Federal Reserve

For issues relating to all non-national banks that say they are "Member Banks" or "Reserve Member Banks":

Board of Governors of the Federal Reserve System
Division of Consumer and Community Affairs
20th and C Streets, N.W., Stop 801
Washington, DC 20551
www.federalreserve.gov/pubs/complaints/

Federal Deposit Insurance Corporation

For issues relating to FDIC banks—i.e., banks whose deposits are insured but not regulated by either the Office of the Comptroller of the Currency or the Federal Reserve:

550 17th Street NW
Washington, DC 20429-9990
Tel: 202-736-0000
www.fdic.gov/about/contact/ask/regionaloffices.html#Washington

U.S. Department of Justice

For issues relating to civil-rights violations and fraud, especially on the Internet:

Civil Rights Division
Washington, DC 20530
Tel: 202-514-2000 (main number); 1-800-869-4499 (toll free)
www.usdoj.gov/crt/crt-home.html

U.S. Department of Housing and Urban Development

For issues relating to housing discrimination and predatory lending:

451 7th St. SW
Washington, DC 20410
Tel: 202-708-1112; 202-708-1455
www.hud.gov/

National Credit Union Administration

For issues relating to federal credit unions:

Office of Public and Congressional Affairs
1775 Duke St.
Alexandria, VA 22314
Tel: 703-518-6330
www.ncua.gov
E-mail: pacamail@ncua.gov

Office of Thrift Supervision

For issues relating to savings banks and savings-and-loans associations:

Consumer Affairs Office
1700 G St., NW
Washington, DC 20552
1-800-842-6929
www.ots.treas.gov
E-mail: consumer.complaint@ots.treas.gov

STATE CONSUMER PROTECTION RESOURCES

Alaska
Alaska Attorney General
Consumer Protection Unit
Office of the Attorney General
1031 West 4th Ave., Suite 200
Anchorage, AK 99501-5903
907-269-5100
Fax: 907-276-8554
www.law.state.ak.us/department/civil/
    consumer/cpindex.html

Arizona
Chief Counsel
Consumer Protection and
    Advocacy Section
Office of the Attorney General
1275 West Washington St.
Phoenix, AZ 85007
602-542-3702
602-542-5763 (consumer
    information and complaints)
Toll free in AZ: 1-800-352-8431
TDD: 602-542-5002
Fax: 602-542-4579
www.ag.state.az.us

Arkansas
Deputy Attorney General
Consumer Protection Division
Office of the Attorney General
323 Center St.
Suite 200
Little Rock, AR 72201
501-682-2007
Consumer Hotline: 501-682-2341
Crime Victims Hotline: 1-800-448-
    3014
Do-Not-Call Program: 501-682-
    1334
In-State Do-Not-Call Program: 1-
    877-866-8225
Toll free: 1-800-482-8982
TDD: 501-682-6073
Fax: 501-682-8118
E-mail: consumer@ag.state.ar.us
www.ag.state.ar.us

California
Director
California Department of
    Consumer Affairs

400 R St.
Suite 3000-1080
Sacramento, CA 95814
916-445-1254
916-445-4465
Correspondence and Complaint
    Review Unit: 916-445-2643
Toll free in CA: 1-800-952-5210
TDD/TTY: 916-322-1700 or 1-800-
    326-2297
www.dca.ca.gov

Colorado
Consumer Protection Division
Colorado Attorney General's Office
1525 Sherman St.
5th Floor
Denver, CO 80203-1760
303-866-5079
Toll free: 1-800-222-4444
Fax: 303-866-5443
www.ago.state.co.us/CONSPROT.
    stm

Connecticut
Department of Consumer
    Protection
165 Capitol Ave.
Hartford, CT 06106
860-713-6300
Toll free in CT: 1-800-842-2649
Fax: 860-713-7239
www.ct.gov/dcp/site/default.asp

Delaware
Director
Fraud and Consumer Protection
    Division
Office of the Attorney General
820 North French St.
5th Floor
Wilmington, DE 19801

302-577-8600
Toll free in DE: 1-800-220-5424
Fax: 302-577-6499
www.state.de.us/attgen/
E-mail:
    Attorney.General@State.DE.US

District of Columbia
Office of the Attorney General for
    the District of Columbia
Consumer & Trade Protection
    Section
Consumer Complaints
441 4th St., NW
Suite 450 North
Washington, DC 20001
202-442-9828
Fax: 202-727-6546
occ.dc.gov/occ/cwp/view,a,1223,Q,
    531282,occNav,|31688|.asp
E-mail:
    consumercomplaint.occ@dc.gov

Florida
Division of Consumer Services
Department of Agriculture and
    Consumer Services
407 South Calhoun St., Mayo
    Building
Tallahassee, FL 32399-0800
850-488-2221
800-435-7352
www.800helpfla.com/
www.800helpfla.com/ccform.html
    (complaint form)

Georgia
Administrator
Governor's Office of Consumer
    Affairs
2 Martin Luther King Jr. Dr.
Suite 356

Atlanta, GA 30334
404-656-3790
Toll free in GA (outside Atlanta
    area): 1-800-869-1123
Fax: 404-651-9018
www.georgia.gov/00/channel_title/0,
    2094,4802_5041,00.html

Hawaii
Office of Consumer Protection
235 S. Beretonia St., Suite 801
Leiopapa A Kamehameha Building
Honolulu, HI 96813
808-587-3222
www.state.hi.us/dcca/ocp

Idaho
Deputy Attorney General
Consumer Protection Unit
Idaho Attorney General's Office
650 West State St.
Boise, ID 83720-0010
208-334-2424
Toll free in ID: 1-800-432-3545
Fax: 208-334-2830
www2.state.id.us/ag/consumer/

Illinois
Office of the Attorney General
1001 East Main St.
Carbondale, IL 62901
618-529-6400
Toll free in IL: 1-800-243-0607
    (consumer hotline serving
    southern Illinois)
TDD: 618-529-0607
Fax: 618-529-6416
www.ag.state.il.us/consumers/
www.ag.state.il.us/consumers/
    conscomp.pdf (consumer
    complaint form)

Indiana
Chief Counsel and Director
Consumer Protection Division
Office of the Attorney General
Indiana Government Center South
402 West Washington St., 5th Floor
Indianapolis, IN 46204
317-232-6201
Consumer hotline (toll-free in IN):
    1-800-382-5516
Fax: 317-232-7979
www.in.gov/attorneygeneral/
    consumer/

Iowa
Assistant Attorney General
Consumer Protection Division
Office of the Attorney General
Director of Consumer Protection
    Division
1300 East Walnut St., 2nd Floor
Des Moines, IA 50319
515-281-5926
Fax: 515-281-6771
E-mail: consumer@ag.state.ia.us
www.state.ia.us/government/ag/
    consumer.html

Kansas
Deputy Attorney General
Consumer Protection Division
Office of the Attorney General
120 SW 10th
4th Floor
Topeka, KS 66612-1597
785-296-3751
Toll free in KS: 1-800-432-2310
TDD/TTY: 785-291-3767
Fax: 785-291-3699
E-mail: cprotect@ksag.org
www.accesskansas.org/ksag/Divisions/
    Consumer/main.htm

Kentucky
Director
Consumer Protection Division
Office of the Attorney General
1024 Capital Center Dr.
Frankfort, KY 40601
502-696-5389
Toll free in KY: 1-888-432-9257
Fax: 502-573-8317
E-mail:
    consumerprotection@law.state.
    ky.us
ag.ky.gov/cp/

Louisiana
Chief
Consumer Protection Section
Office of the Attorney General
301 Main St., Suite 1250
Baton Rouge, LA 70801
Toll free nationwide: 1-800-351-
    4889
Fax: 225-342-9637
*www.ag.state.la.us/Consumer
    Protection.aspx?index=5*

Maine
Director
Office of Consumer Credit
    Regulation
35 State House Station
Augusta, ME 04333-0035
207-624-8527
Toll free in ME: 1-800-332-8529
TDD/TTY: 207-624-8563
Fax: 207-582-7699
www.state.me.us/ag/index.php?r=clg

Maryland
Chief
Consumer Protection Division

Office of the Attorney General
200 Saint Paul Place
16th Floor
Baltimore, MD 21202-2021
Consumer complaint hotline: 410-
    528-8662
Consumer information: 410-576-
    6550
Health advocacy unit: 410-528-
    1840
TDD (MD only): 410-576-6372
Fax: 410-576-7040
E-mail: consumer@oag.state.md.us
www.oag.state.md.us/Consumer/

Massachusetts
Director
Executive Office of Consumer
    Affairs and Business
    Regulation
10 Park Plaza, Room 5170
Boston, MA 02116
General info: 617-973-8700
Consumer hotline: 617-973-8787
In MA: 1-888-283-3757
TDD/TTY: 617-973-8790
Fax: 617-973-8798
E-mail: consumer@state.ma.us
*www.ago.state.ma.us/sp.cfm?pageid=
    967*

Michigan
Consumer Protection Division
Office of the Attorney General
PO Box 30213
Lansing, MI 48909
517-373-1110
Complaint information: 517-373-
    1140
*www.michigan.gov/ag/0,1607,
    7-164-17334_17362–,00.html*

Minnesota
Manager
Consumer Services Division
Minnesota Attorney General's
    Office
1400 NCL Tower
445 Minnesota St.
St. Paul, MN 55101
612-296-3353
Toll free: 1-800-657-3787
Fax: 612-282-5801
E-mail: consumer.ag@state.mn.us
www.ag.state.mn.us/consumer/

Mississippi
Director
Consumer Protection Division of
    the Mississippi Attorney
    General's Office
PO Box 22947
Jackson, MS 39225-2947
601-359-4230
Toll free in MS: 1-800-281-4418
Fax: 601-359-4231
www.ago.state.ms.us/divisions/
    consumer/

Missouri
Deputy Chief Counsel
Consumer Protection and Trade
    Offense Division
PO Box 899
1530 Rax Court
Jefferson City, MO 65102
573-751-6887
573-751-3321
Toll free in MO: 1-800-392-8222
TDD/TTY toll free in MO: 1-800-
    729-8668
Fax: 573-751-7948
E-mail: attgenmail@moago.org

ago.missouri.gov/divisions/consumer
    protection.htm

Montana
Montana Consumer Protection
    Office
Department of Administration
1219 8th Ave.
PO Box 200151
Helena, MT 59620-0151
406-444-4500
Fax: 406-444-9680
www.state.mt.us/doa/consumer
    protection

Nebraska
Assistant Attorney General
Department of Justice
2115 State Capitol
PO Box 98920
Lincoln, NE 68509
402-471-2682
Toll free in NE: 1-800-727-6432
Fax: 402-471-0006
www.ago.state.ne.us/content/
    consumer.html

Nevada
Commissioner
Nevada Consumer Affairs
    Division
1850 East Sahara
Suite 101
Las Vegas, NV 89104
702-486-7355
Toll free: 1-800-326-5202
TDD: 702-486-7901
Fax: 702-486-7371
E-mail: ncad@fyiconsumer.org
ag.state.nv.us/actionbutton/bcp/bcp.
    htm

New Hampshire
Consumer Protection and Antitrust
    Bureau
New Hampshire Attorney General's
    Office
33 Capitol St.
Concord, NH 03301
603-271-3641
TDD toll free: 1-800-735-2964
Fax: 603-271-2110
www.doj.nh.gov/consumer/index.html

New Jersey
Department of Law and Public
    Safety
Division of Consumer Affairs
PO Box 45025
Newark, NJ 07101
973-504-6200
Toll free: 1-800-242-5846
E-mail:
    askconsumeraffairs@smtp.lps.st
    ate.nj.us
www.state.nj.us/lps/ca/ocp.htm

New Mexico
Director
Consumer Protection Division
Office of the Attorney General
PO Drawer 1508
407 Galisteo
Santa Fe, NM 87504-1508
505-827-6060
Toll free in NM: 1-800-678-1508
Fax: 505-827-6685
www.ago.state.nm.us/protectcons/
    protectons.htm

New York
Bureau Chief
Bureau of Consumer Frauds and
    Protection

Office of the Attorney General
State Capitol
Albany, NY 12224
518-474-5481
Toll free in NY: 1-800-771-7755
    (hotline)
Fax: 518-474-3618
www.consumer.state.ny.us/

North Carolina
Senior Deputy Attorney General
Consumer Protection Division
Office of the Attorney General
PO Box 629
Raleigh, NC 27602
919-716-6000
Fax: 919-716-6050
www.ncdoj.com/consumerprotection/
    cp_about.jsp

North Dakota
Director
Consumer Protection and Antitrust
    Division
Office of the Attorney General
600 East Boulevard Ave.
Department 125
Bismarck, ND 58505-0040
701-328-3404
Toll free in ND: 1-800-472-2600
TTY: 800-366-6888
Fax: 701-328-3535
E-mail: cpat@state.nd.us
www.ag.state.nd.us/CPAT/CPAT.htm

Ohio
Ohio Consumers' Counsel
77 South High St.
15th Floor
Columbus, OH 43266-0550
614-466-8574 (outside OH)

Toll free in OH: 1-877-PICK-OCC
(1-877-742-5622)
E-mail: occ@occ.state.oh.us
*www.ag.state.oh.us/consumer_
protection_enforcement/*

Oklahoma
Administrator
Department of Consumer Credit
4545 North Lincoln Blvd., #104
Oklahoma City, OK 73105
405-521-3653
Fax: 405-521-6740
*www.oag.state.ok.us/oagweb.nsf/
Consumer!OpenPage*

Oregon
Attorney in Charge
Financial Fraud/Consumer
Protection Section
Department of Justice
1162 Court St., NE
Salem, OR 97310
503-378-4732
Hotline (Salem only): 503-378-
4320
Hotline (Portland only): 503-229-
5576
Toll free in OR: 1-877-877-9392
TDD/TTY: 503-378-5939
Fax: 503-378-5017
*www.doj.state.or.us/FinFraud/
welcome3.htm*

Pennsylvania
Director
Bureau of Consumer Protection
Office of Attorney General
14th Floor, Strawberry Square
Harrisburg, PA 17120
717-787-9707

Toll free in PA: 1-800-441-2555
Fax: 717-787-1190
www.attorneygeneral.gov

Rhode Island
Director
Consumer Protection Unit
Department of the Attorney
General
150 South Main St.
Providence, RI 02903
401-274-4400
Senior Line: 1-888-621-1112
TDD: 401-453-0410
Fax: 401-222-5110
*www.riag.state.ri.us/civil/consumer.
php*

South Carolina
Administrator/Consumer Avocate
SC Department of Consumer
Affairs
3600 Forest Drive, Suite 300
PO Box 5757
Columbia, SC 29250
803-734-4200
Toll free in SC: 1-800-922-1594
Fax: 803-734-4286
E-mail: scdca@dca.state.sc.us
www.state.sc.us/consumer

South Dakota
Director of Consumer Affairs
Office of the Attorney General
500 East Capitol Ave.
Pierre, SD 57501-5070
605-773-4400
Toll free in SD: 1-800-300-1986
TDD: 605-773-6585
Fax: 605-773-7163
*www.state.sd.us/attorney/office/
divisions/consumer/default.asp*

Tennessee
Director
Division of Consumer Affairs
500 James Robertson Pkwy.
5th Floor
Nashville, TN 37243-0600
615-741-4737
Toll free in TN: 1-800-342-8385
Fax: 615-532-4994
www.state.tn.us/consumer/

Texas
Assistant Attorney General
Consumer Protection/Austin
    Regional Office
PO Box 12548
Austin, TX 78711-2548
512-463-2185
Fax: 512-463-8301
www.oag.state.tx.us
www.oag.state.tx.us/consumer/
    consumer.shtml

Utah
Director
Division of Consumer Protection
Department of Commerce
160 East 300 South
Box 146704
Salt Lake City, UT 84114-6704
801-530-6001
Fax: 801-530-6001
E-mail: commerce@br.state.ut.us
www.commerce.utah.gov/dcp/

Vermont
Consumer Assistance Program
104 Morrill Hall, UVM
Burlington, VT 05405
Chittenden County or out of state:
    802-656-3183
Toll free in VT: 1-800-549-2424

www.atg.state.vt.us/display.php?
    smod=8

Virginia
Senior Assistant Attorney General
    and Chief
Office of the Attorney General
Antitrust and Consumer Litigation
    Section
900 East Main St.
Richmond, VA 23219
804-786-2116
Toll free: 1-800-451-1525
Fax: 804-786-0122
E-mail: mail@oag.state.va.us
www.vdacs.virginia.gov/
    consumers/

Washington
Office of the Attorney General
103 East Holly St., Suite 308
Bellingham, WA 98225-4728
360-738-6185
www.atg.wa.gov/consumer/

West Virginia
Deputy Attorney General
Consumer Protection Division
Office of the Attorney General
812 Quarrier St., 6th Floor
PO Box 1789
Charleston, WV 25326-1789
304-558-8986
Toll free in WV: 1-800-368-8808
Fax: 304-558-0184
E-mail: consumer@wvnet.edu
www.wvs.state.wv.us/wvag/
    consumer/

Wisconsin
Regional Supervisor

Department of Agriculture
Trade and Consumer
Protection
Division of Trade and Consumer
Protection
200 North Jefferson St.
Suite 146A
Green Bay, WI 54301
920-448-5118
Fax: 920-448-5118
datcp.state.wi.us/core/
consumerinfo/

Wyoming
Assistant Attorney General
Office of the Attorney General
Consumer Protection Unit
123 State Capitol Building
Cheyenne, WY 82002
307-777-7874
Toll free in WY: 1-800-438-5799
Fax: 307-777-7956
E-mail: agwebmaster@state.wy.us
attorneygeneral.state.wy.us/consumer.
htm

INDEX

ABOUT THE AUTHOR

David L. Hudson, Jr. is an attorney and author residing in the Middle Tennessee area. He is a research attorney for the First Amendment Center at Vanderbilt University. He also teaches legal research and writing and constitutional law at Middle Tennessee State University in an adjunct position. He has authored or co-authored 10 books, including several on legal subjects. He writes regularly for the *ABA Journal* and the *ABA Journal E-Report*. He also is a First Amendment contributing editor for the ABA's *Preview of United States Supreme Court Cases*. He earned an A.B. from Duke University and a J.D. from Vanderbilt University Law School.